The Monster in the Garden

PENN STUDIES IN LANDSCAPE ARCHITECTURE

John Dixon Hunt, Series Editor

This series is dedicated to the study and promotion of a wide variety of approaches to landscape architecture, with special emphasis on connections between theory and practice. It includes monographs on key topics in history and theory, descriptions of projects by both established and rising designers, translations of major foreign-language texts, anthologies of theoretical and historical writings on classic issues, and critical writing by members of the profession of landscape architecture. The series was the recipient of the Award of Honor in Communications from the American Society of Landscape Architects, 2006.

The MONSTER *in the* GARDEN

The Grotesque and the Gigantic
in Renaissance Landscape Design

Luke Morgan

PENN

UNIVERSITY OF PENNSYLVANIA PRESS

PHILADELPHIA

Copyright © 2016 University of Pennsylvania Press

Published by
University of Pennsylvania Press
Philadelphia, Pennsylvania 19104-4112
www.upenn.edu/pennpress

Printed in the United States of America on acid-free paper
1   3   5   7   9   10   8   6   4   2

A catalogue record for this book is available from the
Library of Congress.
ISBN 978-0-8122-4755-8

For Hannah

Contents

Introduction: Reframing the Renaissance Garden   1

Chapter 1. The Legibility of Landscape: From Fascism to Foucault   17

Chapter 2. The Grotesque and the Monstrous   47

Chapter 3. A Monstruary: The Excessive,
the Deficient, and the Hybrid   82

Chapter 4. "Rare and Enormous Bones
of Huge Animals": The Colossal Mode   115

Chapter 5. "Pietra Morta, in Pietra Viva": The Sacro Bosco   135

Conclusion: Toward the Sublime   164

Notes   173

Bibliography   213

Index   233

Acknowledgments   245

Introduction

Reframing the Renaissance Garden

And after having remained at the entry some time, two
contrary emotions arose in me, fear and desire—fear of the
threatening dark grotto, desire to see whether there were any
marvelous thing within it.

— Leonardo da Vinci

In 1536, two female conjoined twins were dissected in the Orti Oricellari (Rucellai Gardens) in Florence. The humanist Benedetto Varchi, who was in attendance, gave a detailed account of the twins' anatomy in his lectures on the
generation of monsters (1548), before concluding that owing to "these & many
other similar Monsters & different ones, like those that you see in the loggia
of the Scala Hospital, we philosophically believe that there have been, & can
be monsters."[1]

It is significant that the site chosen for the dissection was a garden, albeit
one that was already well established as a learned academy and meeting place
of Florentine intellectuals.[2] Palla Rucellai's garden was a sophisticated example
of early sixteenth-century Florentine design, with many rare plants.[3] It also
contained several ancient statues from the Medici sculpture garden on the
Piazza di San Marco, which were auctioned off in 1494 after the expulsion of
Piero de' Medici.[4] Little remains today of the Oricellari besides the colossal
figure of Polyphemus, sculpted by Antonio Novelli, a pupil of Giambologna,
some decades after the dissection, and a seventeenth-century grotto.

In the late 1500s, the garden was purchased by Bianca Capello, the mis-
tress of Francesco I de' Medici, who put it to quite a different purpose. Clelio Malespini described one of the entertainments Capello contrived for the

grand duke and his friends in the garden. Assembling in the Oricellari after midnight, the group was met by a necromancer, whose appearance before them was accompanied by "infinite voices and laments, strange yowlings, gnashing of teeth, hands clapping, shaking of iron chains, cries, sighs, and infinite fireworks that exploded from all sides, issuing forth from many holes dug with marvelous artistry."[5] At a signal from this bizarre figure, a trapdoor in the ground, camouflaged with grass, suddenly opened to reveal a cavernous hole, into which the guests promptly fell. Awaiting them at the bottom were servants dressed up as devils, who were, however, soon expelled from the garden and replaced by beautiful girls wearing perfume, fine jewels, and little else.[6]

The Oricellari thus served successively as an academy, laboratory, and sideshow. Its design and classical imagery could impartially support any and all of these varied events and activities. The dissection of the conjoined twins must have been a bloody and, to at least some of those in attendance, queasy spectacle. Capello's later *festa* would likewise have inspired a frisson of pleasurable dread, enhanced by the dark garden with its unknown traps and fictive portals to another world.

Both the dissection and the festa temporarily transformed the Rucellai garden into another space. The mise-en-scène of Capello's elaborate practical joke was instrumental in provoking her guests' responses of fear followed by pleasure. Fear is not, however, a reaction usually associated with the experience of Renaissance gardens. More often than not gardens of the period are assumed to have been conceived as serene Arcadian refuges from reality—as if Francesco Petrarch's trecento dream of a day when it would be possible to walk back into the "pure radiance of the past" was finally realized in landscape design two centuries later.[7] Pleasure, serenity, and contemplation (*otium*) were all acknowledged desiderata of gardens during the Renaissance. In book 9 of his fifteenth-century treatise on architecture, for example, Leon Battista Alberti notes that they should be places of delight ("there should be gardens full of delightful plants") and pleasure ("there should also be truly festive space").[8] His comments imply the classical literary ideal of the *locus amoenus* ("pleasant place"), familiar from the works of Homer, Theocritus, Virgil, and numerous subsequent writers. Indeed, the idea of the locus amoenus became a standard convention in Renaissance evocations of real and imagined gardens.[9]

Yet despite its familiarity, this concept of the garden as an untrammeled reflection of paradise, or idealized place apart, is not as straightforward as might first appear. Why, if they were universally conceived as places of perfect amenity and pleasure, did some Renaissance gardens incorporate images of violence and suffering? Giambologna's colossal personification of the Apennines for the garden of the Villa Medici in Pratolino, for example, is depicted crushing the life out of a "monstrous head."[10] In the Sacro Bosco in Bomarzo, one giant viciously tears apart another, while nearby a dragon is mauled by a lion and a dog (figure 1). The jet of water that issues from the mouth of the struggling Antaeus in Bartolommeo Ammannati's sculptural group of Hercules and Antaeus for Niccolò Tribolo's fountain in the garden of the Villa Medici in Castello, can be interpreted as his last breath—a paradoxical motif—as he is squeezed to death.[11] Even the apparently harmless *giochi d'acqua* (water games) of the Renaissance garden were understood in military terms. As Anatole Tchikine has pointed out, the experience of being drenched by hidden jets of water was often likened to "a sudden attack of enemy soldiers emerging from secret hideouts" in sixteenth- and seventeenth-century texts.[12]

The theme of violence in the garden, which incorporates both the imagery (the struggling giants in the Sacro Bosco, for example) and the uses of historical landscape design (such as the Oricellari dissection), problematizes the traditional view that the development of Renaissance landscape design was motivated by a coherent and narrowly focused desire to reinstate the classical locus amoenus. Arguably, the concept of the garden as a locus amoenus is not adequate to the task of accounting for either the contradictory and seemingly incompatible motifs that appear in Renaissance landscape design or the highly varied historical functions of the garden. As Hervé Brunon has claimed, there are suggestions that the sixteenth-century garden was also (and simultaneously) conceived of as a "*topos* antagoniste."[13] Certainly, Capello's temporary transformation of the Oricellari at the end of the century would have produced an alternately hostile and pleasant space for the amusement of her guests, or, as Eugenio Battisti has put it, "after the Christian hell [came] an Islamic paradise."[14] Significantly, this antagonistic element—the landscape as unpleasant or frightening—is also present in the principal source of the imagery and iconography of Renaissance garden design: Ovid's *Metamorphoses*.

Ovid in the Garden Redux

John Dixon Hunt has observed: "It is doubtful whether any garden of the sixteenth and seventeenth centuries avoided some appeal, specific or general, to Ovid's poetic world."[15] His numerous examples include: the Alley of the

Figure 1. A Dragon Mauled by a Lion and a Dog. Sacro Bosco, Bomarzo. Photo: Luke Morgan.

Hundred Fountains in the garden of the Villa d'Este in Tivoli, which once depicted in relief stories from Ovid; the figures of Atlas and the centaur in the Water Theatre of the Villa Aldobrandini, in Frascati; Bernardo Buontalenti's Grotta Grande in the Boboli Gardens in Florence, which takes its narrative from the *Metamorphoses* (and provides Brunon's main example of the dramatic duality between pleasure and terror in Renaissance landscape design); and Giambologna's *Appennino*, which may have been based on illustrated editions of Ovid and which certainly recalls the passage in book 4 of the *Metamorphoses* where "Atlas was changed into a mountain as huge as the giant he had been."[16]

That Renaissance garden designers turned to the *Metamorphoses* for motifs and ideas is undeniable.[17] But this raises a further possibility that has received less attention: if Ovid's stories of transformation were so crucial to the statuary, grottoes, and other features of the early modern garden, then perhaps his characterization of landscape and the natural world in general also had some influence on Renaissance designers.

Ovid rarely mentions pleasure gardens or designed landscapes in the

Metamorphoses, though the story of Hermaphroditus makes use of a gardening metaphor. The prayers of Salamacis, in love with the beautiful youth, "found favour with the gods: for, as they lay together, their bodies were united and from being two persons they became one. As when a gardener grafts a branch on to a tree, and sees the two unite as they grow, and come to maturity together, so when their limbs meet in that clinging embrace the nymph and the boy were no longer two, but a single form possessed of a dual nature, which could not be called male or female, but seemed to be at once both and neither."[18]

Hermaphroditus's metamorphosis takes place in a peaceful, sylvan landscape, the main feature of which is a pool of water "like crystal," its edges "ringed with fresh turf and grass that was always green." There were "no marshy reeds around it, no barren sedge or sharp-spiked rushes."[19] This idyllic place is the setting for Salamacis's violent, sexually motivated attack: "she twined around him, like a serpent when it is being carried off into the air by the king of birds: for as it hangs from the eagle's beak, the snake coils round his head and talons and with its tail hampers his beating wings."[20] Despite the desperate attempts of Hermaphroditus to break free, Salamacis "was like the ivy encircling tall tree trunks, or the squid which holds fast the prey it has caught in the depths of the sea, by wrapping its tentacles round on every side."[21]

Ovid's poetic device, which depends on the ambiguity or contrast between a tranquil, idealized landscape and the frequently barbarous violence of the narrative, occurs again and again in the *Metamorphoses*. The companions of Cadmus, for example, in their search for fresh spring water, enter "an ancient forest which no axe had ever touched."[22] They discover a cave, resembling a garden grotto "overgrown with branches and osiers, forming a low arch with its rocky walls, rich in bubbling springs." Inside this cave, however, lurks a monstrous serpent, which attacks and slays them all with "its fangs, its constricting coils, and tainted poisonous breath" (figure 2).[23]

Serpents or dragons, not unlike the snake described by Ovid, appear in Renaissance gardens too: at Bomarzo, for example, but also at Pratolino and at Tivoli. An anonymous British visitor of 1610 described the d'Este dragon as belching water "being of so black a colour, that it resembleth an ugly smoke, fearful to behold" (figure 3).[24] This malevolent creature appeared in a garden which makes direct reference to Ovid's poem, and which has long been celebrated as a quintessential example of the Renaissance revival of the classical concept of the locus amoenus.

In the *Metamorphoses*, then, pleasant places provide the locale for acts of

Figure 2. Hendrik Goltzius, *The Dragon Devouring the Companions of Cadmus*, 1588. Courtesy of Special Collections, Baillieu Library, University of Melbourne.

terrifying violence and transformation. As the Ovid scholar Charles Paul Segal has written, in the poem there is a "disturbing conflict between art and nature, between the suspended, delicate beauty of sheltered woods and their virginal inhabitants on the one hand, and violent desire on the other."[25]

The Renaissance garden may have been designed to elicit *topophobic* responses as well as topophilic ones (both terror and delight), as in the *Metamorphoses*, despite the apparent counterintuitiveness of that proposition.[26] (It may not be easy to imagine being terrified by a garden, used as we are to the idea of the garden as a refuge or, again, "pleasant place.")[27] Leonardo da Vinci's "contrary emotions" at the entry to a garden grotto, for example, oscillated between "fear and desire." As complex cultural artifacts and works of art, gardens can accommodate a wide range of motifs and contradictory themes. Disharmony, conflict, and violence are certainly dramatized in more than one

Figure 3. Fountain of the Dragons. Villa d'Este, Tivoli. Photo: Luke Morgan.

sixteenth-century garden. These themes are also clearly present in the most important source of garden imagery in the Renaissance—Ovid's *Metamorphoses*. If for Ovid the Virgilian bond of "compassionate sympathy" between nature and its inhabitants can no longer be assumed, then perhaps there are hints of this too in the deliberately Ovidian landscapes designed during the Renaissance.[28]

An important premise of this book is that the troubling presence of the theme of violence, as well as what Brunon has called the "double négatif" of the locus amoenus in sixteenth-century landscape design—the *locus horridus*—indicate that there are some omissions in the literature of the early modern garden.[29] Foremost among these is the unexplained presence of what the Renaissance would have regarded as "monsters" in landscape design.

The Reality of Monsters

Varchi described the unfortunate conjoined twins, whose dissection in the Oricellari he witnessed, as "monsters." In the sixteenth century the term "monstrous" was synonymous with "abnormal." Conjoined twins, hybrid creatures, and physiological deficiencies or deviations were all, in the terms of the period, abnormal and therefore monstrous.

Many of the figures represented in Renaissance gardens are also monstrous in this sense. Previous writers have interpreted the harpies, invented hybrids, satyrs, and colossi of the late sixteenth-century landscape as expressions of artistic license (*fantasia*), the inventiveness and variety of nature, and as allusions to classical sources, such as, again, Ovid's *Metamorphoses*.[30] These figures, however, feature in other contemporary discourses besides those of art, literature, and mythology. In his *Des monstres et prodiges* (1573), for example, the French royal physician Ambroise Paré observed: "Many animal forms are likewise created in women's wombs (which are often found with fetuses and well-formed young), such as frogs, toads, snakes, lizards, and harpies."[31] For Paré, the harpy was a real phenomenon, not an exclusively mythical figure.

Paré's belief in the reality of monsters implies two further arguments of this book. First, although the imaginative world of Ovid and others was self-evidently evoked in early modern garden design and experience, so too was the "juridico-biological domain," as Michel Foucault called it, of the lawyers and the physicians.[32] Sixteenth-century medical, teratological, and legal texts thus provide new sources for the reconstruction of contemporary attitudes toward the representation of monstrosity (which frequently manifests as hybridity), in garden design.

Second, this book argues that in Renaissance treatises on painting and architecture the role of the "monstrous" in scientific discourse is performed by the concept of the "grotesque," which is a direct equivalent for it. From the painted *grotteschi* of villa and palace decoration to the "grotesque realism" of François Rabelais's chronicles of the giants Gargantua and Pantagruel, the status and legitimacy of the hybrid and scatological figures that proliferated in sixteenth-century visual and literary culture were energetically debated. These debates are also relevant to contemporary designed landscapes in which, it is argued, the grotesque and the "classical" cohabit.

The dramatic duality of the opposition between the locus amoenus and the locus horridus, and the juxtaposition of the grotesque mode and the classical mode, attest to the Renaissance garden's complexity and contradictoriness. In fact, the contradictions of sixteenth-century gardens are numerous. The famous Hell Mouth in the Sacro Bosco is simultaneously a terrifying anthropophagous cavern and an outdoor dining chamber. The so-called harpies of the Fontane delle Arpie in the Boboli Gardens are strange, hybrid creatures, fantastic artistic inventions which combine human and mythical features, but which resist firm identification. In a letter of 1541, the humanist Jacopo Bonfadio could not even decide what the garden was—a work of nature, a work of art, or a work of both, resulting in a "third nature" (*terza natura*) that, as he wrote, "I would not know how to name."[33]

On one level, the "monsters" of the Renaissance garden are signs of its contradictory character, which extends to its very identity. The intimate union of art and nature in the garden to the point where, in the best examples, the two could not be distinguished from one another rendered the garden difficult to inscribe within a binary system in which the things of the world were understood as one or the other, but not both at once. This also applies to the grotesque, which as Wendy Frith has suggested can "refer to the mixing of high and low, and thus to the collapsing of culturally constructed binary oppositions and hierarchies."[34]

Ovid's account of the fate of Hermaphroditus, which is often referred to in Renaissance treatises on medicine, abnormality, and monstrosity, suggests something similar. His metaphor for the union of male and female in a dual-sexed being is, perhaps not by chance, drawn from gardening. To describe the garden as a "third nature," as Bonfadio and, slightly later, the Milanese writer Bartolomeo Taegio do, is not so very different to Ovid's describing it as "a single form possessed of a dual nature, which could not be called male or female, but seemed to be at once both and neither."[35] (It is notable that, many centuries earlier, Pliny the Elder had used the Latin equivalent of *terza natura, tertia natura,* to describe hybrid—that is, "monstrous"—aquatic species, which seemed to him to be both animals and plants.)[36]

In early modern Europe, the figure of the hermaphrodite presented a challenge to binary habits of thought. Cases of the period make the legal necessity of determinate gender assignment especially clear. An example is provided by the 1601 case of Marie le Marcis, as reported by the French physician Jacques Duval in his treatise *On Hermaphrodites, Childbirth, and the Treatment That Is Required to Return Women to Health and to Raise Their Children Well* (1612).[37] According to Duval: "We had been told about a girl who, having been baptized, named, nourished, raised, and always clothed like the other girls of her lot, until the age of twenty, was finally recognized to be a man, and as such had carnal knowledge of a woman, many and different times, to whom he had become engaged by his word before witnesses, with a promise of future marriage."[38]

Marie le Marcis had been accused of "sexual misconduct" (tribadism, or same-sex intercourse)[39] for which she was sentenced to public humiliation and death. She was to be paraded naked before being hanged, strangled, and burned at the stake. Duval's intervention in the proceedings, his examination of Marcis and "discovery" of her male genitalia, meant that she could be securely designated male. The court consequently amended its judgment, stipulating that the hermaphrodite must live as a woman until the age of twenty-five but after that could begin to live openly as a man. Ten years later, Duval writes, Marie had indeed become Marin, with a full beard and an established profession as a men's tailor.

Marcis's "crime" was to be ambiguously gendered. The legal judgment confirms the social necessity of clear gender differentiations within the "juridico-biological domain" of a dimorphic system. Marcis was monstrous, even criminal, in the sense that she could not be classified according to the laws of nature or of society.[40] Duval's identification of Marcis as male enabled her gender to be fixed, thus saving her life.[41]

The garden, like the figure of the hermaphrodite, offers a challenge to binary habits of thought despite the long-standing tacit assumption that gardens are diametrically "other" to cities and the public sphere or that they are private refuges from the travails of everyday life. Although Bonfadio was mainly interested in the collaboration of art and nature, his perplexed claim that the garden as a third nature was somehow unnamable can be read more broadly as an implicit recognition of this difficulty of locating or "fixing" the garden within prevailing epistemological and discursive structures.

In their book *The Meaning of Gardens: Idea, Place, and Action* (1992), Mark Francis and Randolph T. Hester Jr. make a point similar to Bonfadio's but do not go quite as far. They suggest that in landscape design "apparent irreconcilables are clarified and mediated because the garden accepts paradox."[42] The latter point is clearly true, but their statement leaves open the question of how and why the garden goes about clarifying and mediating "irreconcilables." In addition, Francis and Hester give no indication of the sort of space that emerges from this process, unlike Bonfadio, who, despite being defeated by the problem, at least broaches it. Even the valuable foray into landscape history by the art historian James Elkins in which he states that it "may be that the next generation of scholarship will find the adjudication of various theories, and the investigation of conscious and unconscious ambiguities to be a profitable focus," stops short of addressing the challenging problem of the garden as a third nature.[43]

One influential theoretical account of gardens, as well as a seemingly incongruous variety of other spaces, from brothels to ships, that is sometimes mentioned in discussions of the ambiguities of designed landscapes is Foucault's essay "Des espaces autres" ("Of Other Spaces"). Foucault's brief remarks about what he calls "heterotopic" space have had a significant afterlife in a wide range of disciplines, but especially in architecture. Historians of landscape have occasionally referred to Foucault's claim that "the oldest example of these heterotopias that take the form of contradictory sites is the garden,"[44] but his argument has never been explored in detail for what it might reveal about Bonfadio's conundrum and, more generally, the ways in which the Renaissance garden might be said to incorporate polarities within its confines. In this book Foucault's comments provide a critical framework for a study of the significance of the monster in the garden. The concept of heterotopia implies, among other things, a more complex spatial model of the garden than that of the locus amoenus.

From the Grotesque to the Gigantic

In the theory and practice of Renaissance garden design, as in medicine, teratology, law, and art, the monstrous and the grotesque were far from neutral terms. Like monsters, *grotteschi* were sometimes criticized as "against nature" or derided as humorous but inconsequential *gestes*. At other times, however, the figure of the monster was regarded as a terrifying portent of impending catastrophe or sin.

Pejorative attitudes toward the abnormal or nonnormative body have had a long life. For example, when he visited the Sacro Bosco, which contains more "monsters" than any other garden of the Renaissance, the twentieth-century American literary critic Edmund Wilson described it as a discordant "patch of ugliness and horror."[45] His reaction recalls John Ruskin's famous denunciation of the grotesque: "The architecture raised at Venice during this period is among the worst and basest ever built by the hands of men, being especially distinguished by a spirit of brutal mockery and insolent jest, which, exhausting itself in deformed and monstrous sculpture, can sometimes be hardly otherwise defined than as the perpetuation in stone of the ribaldries of drunkenness."[46] Ruskin focuses his ensuing discussion of Venetian Renaissance architecture on the carved keystone of an arch on the western facade of Santa Maria Formosa (figure 4), which he describes as: "A head—huge, inhuman, and monstrous—leering in bestial degradation, too foul to be either pictured or described, or to be beheld for more than an instant."[47]

The monsters of the Sacro Bosco would almost certainly have appeared to Ruskin in a similarly negative light, as would many of the ornaments of the Renaissance garden. Wilson's and Ruskin's unstated criterion, against which, respectively, Pierfrancesco "Vicino" Orsini's sacred wood and Venetian architecture appear as "ugly," and even "monstrous," is a post-Enlightenment idea of the classical.

The Russian literary critic Mikhail Bakhtin has argued that all grotesque images are "ambivalent and contradictory; they are ugly, monstrous, hideous from the point of view of 'classic' aesthetics, that is, the aesthetics of the ready-made and the completed."[48] The "grotesque" realism of some of the key images of Renaissance landscape design suggests that the reification in modern scholarship of a generalizing and ultimately insipid idea of the garden as a simplistic ideality has had the effect of suppressing its multiple levels of reference and meaning. The colossal statuary of the garden provides an example.[49]

According to Bakhtin, "mountains and abysses" constitute "the relief of the grotesque body; or speaking in architectural terms, towers and subterranean passages."[50] Giambologna's *Appennino* in Pratolino is both a mountain and an abyss. Standing at approximately eleven meters tall, the figure is a colossal personification of the mountain range, but its interior contained a network of grottoes in which painted scenes of shepherds, mining, and metallurgy appeared, as well as two working fountains, one of which portrayed Thetis.[51] This is perhaps not quite as comprehensive as the "entire inhabited universe" that is located in the giant Pantagruel's mouth, but, as in Rabelais, one could still "descend into the stomach as into an underground mine."[52] Indeed, mining was represented in the belly of the *Appennino*.

There are well-known classical sources for Giambologna's giant, besides book 4 of the *Metamorphoses*, such as the figure of Atlas in Virgil's *Aeneid*, the architect Dinocrates's hubristic proposal to carve a colossal man out of Mt. Athos in honor of Alexander the Great, or Pliny the Elder's description of the Colossus of Rhodes.[53] The giants of the sixteenth-century garden are suggestive of what Charles Seymour Jr. has described as the "mystique of the colossus," which he claims was inspired "by humanistic admiration of the Antique."[54]

Figure 4. Grotesque Keystone. Santa Maria Formosa, Venice. Photo: Luke Morgan.

Another model for the colossi of Bomarzo and Pratolino may, however, have been provided by Francesco Colonna's description of the reclining giant in the courtyard of the "Egyptian Pyramid" that Poliphilo enters early in the *Hypnerotomachia Poliphili* (1499).[55]

> I was advancing carefully when I saw a vast and extraordinary colossus, whose soleless feet opened into hollow and empty shins. From there I went with trepidation to inspect the head. I guessed that the low groaning was the result of divine ingenuity, caused by the wind entering through the open feet. This colossus lay on its back, cast from metal with miraculous skill; it was of a middle-aged man, who held his head somewhat raised on a pillow. He seemed to be ill, with indications of sighing and groaning about his mouth, and his length was sixty paces. With the aid of his hair one could climb upon his chest, then reach his lamenting mouth by way of the dense, twisted hairs of his beard. The opening was completely empty; and so, urged on by curiosity, I proceeded without further consideration down the stairs that were in his throat, thence into his stomach, and so by intricate passageways, and in some terror, to all the other parts of his internal viscera. . . . And when I came to the heart, I could read about how sighs are generated from love, and could see the place where love gravely hurts it. All this moved me deeply, so that I uttered a loud sigh from the bottom of my heart, invoking Polia—and instantly heard the whole machine resonating, to my considerable fright.[56]

Colonna's giant is anguished, stricken down by lovesickness. Like the later *Appennino* and Hell Mouth, this despondent colossus is an open, permeable body that could be traversed and inhabited, but it is also one that simulates corporeality to an extraordinary extent. The giant body may be a marvel of "divine ingenuity," but it is very far from being an idealized or "completed" figure. It is, perhaps, all too human in its susceptibility to desire and in its physical malaise; that is, in its status as a material, or grotesque body.

In this book the colossi of the Renaissance garden are situated within two traditions: art history and folklore. In the latter, giants are envisaged as having colossal appetites and of being capable of ingesting vast amounts. This capacity to devour and envelope is connected to ancient fears about nature's destructive potential as well as being a distinctive feature of the grotesque. The disproportionate size of the giant expresses the disproportionate and frightening scale of nature itself in comparison with the human subject. The giant in the garden, as in popular traditions, implies the familiar reality of agrarian life: that nature could be both kind and cruel.

Like the monster, the giant contributes little to the concept of the garden as a locus amoenus. Indeed, the giant embodies nature's two opposed faces, the one amenable and creative and the other forbidding and destructive. More perhaps than any other figurative type, therefore, the giant expresses the dramatic duality between pleasure and fear that was a crucial feature of the experience of Renaissance garden design.[57]

In a more general sense, the obscurity or almost complete absence of classical models for landscape design in the sixteenth century should be regarded as liberating in effect.[58] With only the slightest hints to go on, designers and writers such as Colonna developed a garden type that was an authentic product of the Renaissance but involved little revival or "rebirth." There was no elaborate system of rules governing landscape design, as there was for architecture, for instance, which followed Vitruvius. If there had been, it is unlikely that there would ever have been a Sacro Bosco. The colossi of the Renaissance garden and Colonna's elegiac fabrications of the ancient world belong in the same category as the Orsini monsters: they are works of the imagination, informed by an antiquarian spirit, but essentially without precedent.

Each of the following chapters takes up one or more of these hypotheses. After a selective historiographical excursus, chapter 1 explores the feasibility of a history of the Renaissance garden in which reception and experience are emphasized over design and authorial intention. It then constructs a model of the garden as heterotopic space and considers the extent of the legibility of historical landscape design. Chapter 2 summarizes the meanings and cultural significance of the grotesque and the monstrous during the sixteenth century, with a particular focus on the antiquarian and artist Pirro Ligorio's writings about grotteschi and the physician Ambroise Paré's research into monsters. Chapter 3 presents a "monstruary" of the Renaissance garden. The contemporary attitudes toward the grotesque and the monstrous that are surveyed in the preceding chapter are brought to bear on three key examples of monstrosity in sixteenth-century landscape design: the "excessive" Goddess of Nature of the Villa d'Este, the "deficient" Hell Mouth in the Sacro Bosco, and the "hybrid" figure of the harpy, which is represented at several sites. Each belongs to a specific category of the monstrous in sixteenth-century thought. In Chapter

4, it is argued that the giant in the Renaissance garden is a dualistic figure, representative of both the locus amoenus and the locus horridus, as well as the classical and the grotesque. Chapter 5 extends these themes with reference to the Sacro Bosco, though it does not aim to provide a comprehensive interpretation of Orsini's creation. Instead, it draws attention to two understudied aspects of the Sacro Bosco: the idiosyncratic use of "living rock" for the statuary, and the presence of simulated ruins. Both again imply the grotesque. In addition, the chapter proposes that the deliberately ruined "Etruscan" temple suggests a further dimension of the Renaissance garden, characterized as a heterotopia: the "anachronism" of its motifs and structures, or the presence of plural temporalities within its confines.

This book began life as an attempt to answer two questions. First, why do monsters appear in sixteenth-century landscape design and, second, how would a sixteenth-century beholder have responded to the representation of monstrosity in gardens? In trying to answer these deceptively simple questions, I have frequently returned to Michael Baxandall's concept of a "period eye" in the art and experience of fifteenth-century Italy—in my mind's eye if not always in the body of the text.[59] Consequently, an implicit or, perhaps better (given the emphases of the book), *subterranean* theme throughout *The Monster in the Garden* is the specific modality or quality of the experience of these monsters, giants, and ruins. The book thus concludes with an account of "proto-sublime" experience in the Renaissance garden.

Chapter 1

The Legibility of Landscape

From Fascism to Foucault

An architectonic garden with the plants mortified by shears.
—Adolfo Callegari

There have been some significant shifts in the study of historical landscape design during the past forty years. A comparison of two important conferences on the Italian Renaissance garden reveals a number of changes in emphasis and approach: the first Dumbarton Oaks Colloquium on the History of Landscape Architecture (1971) and the thirty-second colloquium (2007). The proceedings of the 1971 meeting were edited by David R. Coffin and published as *The Italian Garden* (1972), while the proceedings of the 2007 meeting, edited by Mirka Beneš and Michael G. Lee, appeared as *Clio in the Italian Garden: Twenty-First-Century Studies in Historical Methods and Theoretical Perspectives* (2011).[1] The greater number of authors in the 2011 volume is itself noteworthy: nine as opposed to four. In a later contribution to the 1999 Dumbarton Oaks colloquium proceedings, which were published as *Perspectives on Garden Histories*, Coffin recalled the difficulty that he had encountered in finding even four contributors to *The Italian Garden*.[2] Lionello Puppi, in his essay on early modern villa gardens in the Veneto for the 1972 volume, also bemoans the "generally depressing state of historical and critical studies on the *'arte dei giardini.'*"[3]

Most of the participants in the 1971 colloquium were trained in art history, and applied the interpretative methods pioneered by such figures as Erwin Panofsky to the study of landscape design, in combination with extensive research campaigns in Italian archives. Elisabeth MacDougall's essay, for example, "*Ars Hortulorum*: Sixteenth-Century Garden Iconography and Literary Theory in Italy," acknowledges Panofsky's method in its title. As Coffin later noted, however, not all of the attendees were entirely in favor of this approach. In his role as respondent, Sir Geoffrey Jellicoe reminded the colloquium "that we should always remember that the essence of the Italian garden was its design," a point that was also insisted upon in the influential 1931 *Mostra del giardino italiano* in Florence (discussed in more detail below).[4]

This difference of emphasis in the study of the early modern Italian garden corresponds to broad changes in the discipline of art history.[5] The generation of the art historian Heinrich Wölfflin (1864–1945) was primarily interested in form and stylistic development, irrespective of symbolic or allegorical meaning as well as any historical and contextual factors that might have informed the work of art. In his discussion of the Villa Aldobrandini in Frascati, for example, Wölfflin wrote, "Even beyond the immediate surroundings of the villa, the entire garden was dominated by a tectonic spirit. This in itself was no novelty: in Renaissance gardens natural motifs—such as trees and water and rough ground—had all been stylised, and the different parts of the garden had been divided from each other and given a tectonic setting."[6] Wölfflin's analysis rarely deviates from this formalist analysis of design and tectonics. His only general reference to the larger sociocultural context is his comment that the purpose of the villa suburbana "was to allow a pleasant and harmonious existence untrammelled by the formalities of the town."[7]

Dissatisfied with formalism, subsequent historians interpreted works of art as symbolic, fundamentally meaningful cultural objects, rather than as autonomous manifestations of the abstract laws of artistic style. This approach, which entered the field (still probably not quite a "discipline") of garden and landscape history through the work of Coffin and his students has resulted in some works of lasting scholarly importance: Coffin's own studies of Roman Renaissance gardens and villas, MacDougall's comparative analyses of sixteenth-century gardens and literature, and Claudia Lazzaro's magisterial synthesis—*The Italian Renaissance Garden*—are all classic works.[8] Despite their differing objectives, however, the stylistic and the iconographical approaches both emphasized design and the intentions of architects and patrons over other considerations.[9]

Landscape history is no longer a subfield of art history, but its growing independence has not always worked in its favor. Unlike art history from the 1970s onward, the study of gardens and designed landscapes has generally been impervious, even resistant, to broader developments in the humanities and social sciences. It is telling, for example, that although Roland Barthes's polemic about the "death of the author" in literature, along with Michel Foucault's reformulation of authorship as a function of discourse are now well known (perhaps even clichéd), we have never had a comparable account of the landscape designer.[10]

Indeed, critical theory has made few inroads in landscape history, despite the theoretically sophisticated work of individual historians such as Louis Marin, who draws on Jacques Lacan and Barthes in his study of Versailles as a representation of Louis XIV.[11] There are, of course, many other possibilities: the spatial theories of Henri Lefebvre and Michel de Certeau, for instance, would seem to lend themselves to landscape history.[12] De Certeau's concept of walking as the spatial equivalent of a speech-act might, for example, provide one theoretical basis for a reception history of the garden.

As Mirka Beneš put it in her 1999 historiographical survey of the field, "One can fantasize at present . . . about a Lacanian or Foucauldian interpretation of Italian gardens. . . . Or, what about a rigorous critique of Italian Renaissance gardens in terms of social distinction, modeled after Bourdieu's *La Distinction*."[13] It is, unfortunately, still necessary to fantasize (though the philosophical firmament may have changed). This book is, among other things, a response to Beneš's observation. It proposes that Foucault's concept of "heterotopic" space and Mikhail Bakhtin's work on "grotesque realism" provide a basis for a reframing of the Renaissance garden in which greater importance is attributed to experience and reception. Before exploring this hypothesis, however, it is necessary to examine a watershed in the early development of landscape history—one that has exerted an extraordinary influence outside its ideological context down to the present.

The *Mostra del giardino italiano* and Its Legacy

Since the 1930s, the Italian garden has frequently been defined as an architectonic, geometric, and morphologically stable spatial formation—a manifestation of the triumph of art over nature—the principles of which were established during the Renaissance. In his classic study of the Villa d'Este in Tivoli (1960), for example, Coffin stated: "Italian sixteenth century gardens were simply to decorate architecture. In the tradition of ancient Roman gardening, all the elements of nature—water, stone, and verdure—were meant to reveal man's dominance."[14]

Coffin's claim recalls the views of Ugo Ojetti, the architect, writer, and president of the organizing committee of the vast *Mostra del giardino italiano*, installed in the Palazzo Vecchio in Florence in 1931.[15] In his preface to the catalogue accompanying the exhibition, Ojetti wrote that the defining characteristic of the "Italian garden" was "the continuous and orderly and visible dominion of man over nature" through design.[16] Nature was "made obedient and domesticated"[17] to the extent that, as Adolfo Callegari put it in his catalogue entry on Venetian gardens, which he describes as "architectonic," the plants were "humiliated by shears."[18]

Ojetti was a frequent collaborator of the Fascist journalist Luigi Dami, whose book *Il giardino italiano* had been published a few years earlier (1924), and he was clearly influenced by Dami's account of the development of Italian landscape design. Dami writes approvingly of nature submitting "to the tyranny of art" in the Renaissance garden.[19] According to him, the sixteenth-century garden

> is the outcome of a keen mind and of a deliberate will. In it nothing is casual, nothing uncertain or temporary. Everything is definite, decided, well balanced, closely connected with the rest with no wavering or weakness of any sort. It is made for man, arranged for him so that he may live and be at ease in it; and in fact, man in such a garden is king; in the Italian garden there is no room for romantic sentimentality. . . . Here instead, nature is composed of a certain number of soulless things, each one of which can be catalogued, numbered, indicated in exact terms, of which man can dispose as he likes best . . . we choose them and surround ourselves with them, ordering them to be not as their natural instinct would suggest, but as our will commands. . . . The builder of our garden looks upon nature as rough material to be moulded according to his fancies.[20]

Dami and Ojetti's chief bête noire was the English landscape garden or what Ojetti called the "Romantic" garden ("giardino romantico all'inglese").[21] In Dami's opinion, "A garden arranged to the 'imitation of nature' was a mere delusion, or at most a sentimental aspiration."[22] Ojetti believed that the classical *tempietti*, which from the late eighteenth century were erected in the faux ("finto") "romantic forests" of the new gardens, constituted a "lament for the lost architecture."[23] Both Dami and Ojetti lament the loss or obscuration of the "Italian garden," by which they meant the garden type that emerged in sixteenth-century Italy (in the environs of Florence and Rome). By the eighteenth century, the principles of Renaissance landscape design had been superseded by the English style in a Europe-wide phenomenon.

The explicit purpose of the *Mostra del giardino italiano* was, as Ojetti wrote, "to restore to honor an art that is singularly ours, which after having conquered the world was obscured by other styles or hidden under foreign names."[24] The exhibition thus had a nationalistic purpose not unlike the contemporary German celebration of the sixteenth-century painters Lucas Cranach the Elder, Hans Holbein, and, more problematically given his cosmopolitanism (and, indeed, Italophilia), Albrecht Dürer. Both cases imply a political appropriation of the concept of style in the visual arts as an expression of unified and coherent nationality. They also testify to what Walter Benjamin called the "aestheticized politics" of Fascism.[25]

For Ojetti the Italian garden was a "garden of intelligence," which echoes Dami's claim that the sixteenth-century "garden is the outcome of a keen mind and of a deliberate will."[26] Their emphasis on the penetrating mind and will of the designer has several implications. First, it establishes a dualistic relation between the *intellectual* Italian garden and the *emotional* and, by implication, irrational English or "Romantic" garden. Mind is pitted against emotion; reason against sentiment. It is no coincidence that Ojetti believed that the time was right for a revival of the Italian garden owing to the recent "return of reason in architecture" (by which he must mean the modern movement).[27] Ojetti's emphasis on the rationality of Renaissance landscape design has become a definitive one in subsequent scholarship. Cristina Acidini Luchinat, for example, wrote in 1996 that by definition a garden required order and rationality.[28] She argues that this is a basic principle throughout Italy, irrespective of regional differences. For her the Italian garden is demonstrably a "garden of reason," as Mussolini-era architects and writers insisted; an idea that she states was consolidated in subsequent twentieth-century scholarship.

Second, Ojetti and Dami characterize nature as mere raw material, inchoate, mute, and "soulless," as Dami put it. In their account, the application of the mind and will of the designer or "garden builder" has a transformative effect on the elemental latency and formlessness of nature. The designer's interventions on this malleable territory are necessarily decisive, even violent. In a striking discussion of the use of chiaroscuro lighting effects in Renaissance gardens, for example, which recalls Giorgio de Chirico's uncanny and dramatically lit cityscapes, Dami writes: "Here too there are no soft transitions, blandishments or complexities, but firm and resolute blows. . . . I might call it almost a game in black and white, carried out along violent lines. Shadows are rigid, compact and deep as in a public square in August, and even when they cut the air, they seem to cut planes across a geometrical body."[29]

This uncompromising language of "blows" and "cuts" is, finally, inescapably gendered. Claudia Lazzaro has drawn attention to the efforts of Italian writers of the 1930s to identify the garden as male. A review of Ojetti's *Mostra* in the Fascist newspaper *Il Popolo d'Italia*, for example, noted that the gardens selected for excursions in association with the exhibition all still possessed "the original and male structure of our architecture."[30] Gherardo Bosio in another review, this time for *Domus*, described the Italian garden as "subjugated" to the villa but, nonetheless, unmistakably "male" in character.[31] Arguably, therefore, Dami and Ojetti's oppositional logic—the Italian garden versus the English or Romantic garden, mind versus emotion, and art versus nature—reduces to a single binary: male versus female.

Lazzaro and D. Medina Lasansky have convincingly demonstrated how this rhetoric corresponds to that of Italian Fascist politics.[32] Under Il Duce, who was himself regularly promoted as an athletic and strong masculine ideal, Italy was to be virile and male again, no longer weak and vulnerable to foreign influence. The *Mostra del giardino italiano* actively promoted this ideology in its rejection of the English and Romantic garden types, which had so perniciously inveigled their way across the peninsula and in the violent metaphors and images of male control and domination that Italian garden writers of the period favored.

The *Mostra* was installed in fifty-three rooms of the Palazzo Vecchio, the most important of which was the Salone dei Cinquecento (or Sala Grande). In this room, ten *teatrini* or scale models of historical Italian garden "types" were exhibited. These ranged from a "giardino dei romani" (Roman garden), which was based on Pompeian wall paintings, to a "giardino romantico" complete with a *tempietto*. Each model was designed to illustrate and corroborate Ojetti's arguments.[33]

According to the catalogue, the architect Enrico Lusini's model (figure 5) of a "giardino fiorentino del Cinquecento" (Florentine garden of the sixteenth century) was inspired by a number of sources: Niccolò Tribolo's landscape design for the Villa Medici in Castello, Giorgio Vasari's detailed description of the same garden in his *Lives of the Artists*, the lunettes by Giusto Utens depicting Castello (figure 6), and the Boboli Gardens in 1599 (as well as some details taken from the designs of Bartolommeo Ammannati).[34] Lusini's model purported, in other words, to be based on extant images and descriptions of Castello, and thus provides an opportunity to compare representations of the garden from the Renaissance with those of the 1930s.

Figure 5. Enrico Lusini, Model of a "Giardino fiorentino del Cinquecento."
From *Mostra del giardino italiano*, 1931. Courtesy of Alinari Archives/Brogi
Archive, Florence.

Lusini's model is clearly based on Utens's painting, but the differences
are revealing. The cypresses at the centre of the garden have become much
larger and architectonic in appearance. Not unlike the later French development of the *palissade*, they almost have the solid density of walls. To each side,
the geometry of the compartments has become emphatic. In fact, as Lazzaro
points out, in Lusini's model nature is banished to the peripheries, entirely
superseded by a superimposed abstract pattern.[35] The variety and contrast of
Tribolo's original design—important principles of the Renaissance garden that
are partially preserved in the Utens lunette—have been eliminated in favor
of a perfectly symmetrical ground plan.[36] The precisely clipped, or perhaps
"humiliated," box hedges in the foreground likewise have few equivalents in
Renaissance landscape design.

Lusini also contributed to the restoration of historical gardens.[37] It may
not be surprising, therefore, that his "giardino fiorentino del Cinquecento"

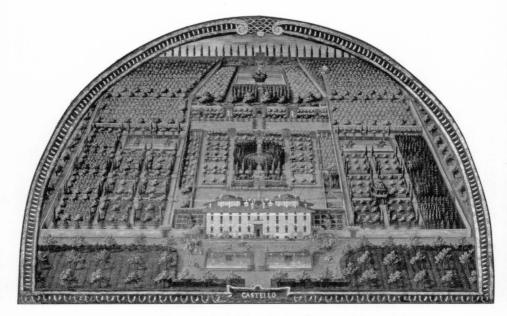

Figure 6. Giusto Utens, *Villa Medici di Castello*, 1599. Museo di Firenze
Com'era. Courtesy of Raffaello Bencini/Alinari Archives, Florence.

more closely resembles the garden of the Villa Farnese in Caprarola restored
in the 1940s (figure 7) than it does any sixteenth-century garden. The rigorous
geometry of the Villa Farnese restoration, like that of Lusini's model, is the
product of a much later cultural moment—a retrospective revision of the Renaissance garden motivated by contemporary ideas about design and national
identity rather than by a close study of the historical evidence.[38]

Renaissance sources reveal a rather different attitude toward the significance of geometrical design and the relations between art and nature in the
garden. Leon Battista Alberti believed that "it is obvious from all that is fashioned, produced, or created under her influence, that Nature delights primarily in the circle."[39] For this reason he argued that the "circles, semicircles, and
other geometric shapes that are favored in the plans of buildings can be modeled out of laurel, citrus, and juniper when their branches are bent back and
intertwined."[40] A few years later Francesco di Giorgio Martini recommended
in his *Trattato di architettura, ingegneria e arte militare* (after 1482) that whole
gardens be designed as geometrical figures (circles, squares, and triangles).[41]

Alberti's brief comments have often been interpreted as implying that the

Figure 7. Villa Farnese, Caprarola, restored 1940s. Photo: Luke Morgan.

geometry of the Italian Renaissance garden provides evidence of the period's belief in the preeminence of the individual human subject in an increasingly secular world. Nature thus submits to and is *improved* by art in the Renaissance garden. This is precisely the view advanced by Italian writers of the 1930s.

Rudolf Wittkower's critique of the assumption that Renaissance architects were more interested in aesthetic and formal issues than they were in the sacred function of ecclesiastical buildings is relevant here. Leon Battista Alberti's advocacy of centrally planned churches, for example, seemed to an earlier generation of scholars to imply a lack of interest in the practicalities of liturgy and worship (centralized planning makes the placement of the altar problematic, for example). Yet, as Wittkower argued, "in such centralized plans the geometrical pattern will appear absolute, immutable, static and entirely lucid. Without that organic geometrical equilibrium where all the parts are harmonically related like the members of a body, divinity cannot reveal itself."[42]

Wittkower's hypothesis has implications beyond architectural history. Although the imagery of Renaissance landscape design is almost exclusively profane (Ovidian), contemporary ideas about nature as God's Creation and of God himself as a "Deus Geometer" may well have informed the layout of sixteenth- and early seventeenth-century gardens, as they did contemporary architecture. It follows that an insufficiently acknowledged objective of Renaissance landscape design was to reveal the divine order, that is to say, the inherent geometrical order, of the natural world, not to "improve" or supersede nature through the imposition of an artificial geometrical scheme. This is the sense in which Alberti's statement that "Nature delights primarily in the circle" should be understood. God's Creation is, indeed must be, inherently rational and constructed on geometrical principles. Landscape design of the period thus sought to reveal nature's concealed order rather than impose a new, artificial geometrical regime.[43] In short, nature was conceived as anything but "soulless," as Dami anachronistically thought.

The notion that the geometry of the sixteenth-century landscape was imposed rather than revealed is an example of the strong tendency to interpret historical gardens in terms of sets of polarities or as Manichean "battles of seeming oppositions."[44] The most important of these oppositions is that of art and nature, the early modern contest between which is usually considered to have been won by art. As Coffin put it: "All the elements of nature—water, stone, and verdure—were meant to reveal man's dominance." Certainly, the concept of *paragone* (rivalry) was as important in landscape design as it was in other fields, and some evidence can be found in support of the idea that the garden was occasionally conceptualized during the period as a triumph of art over nature. The Florentine sculptor Baccio Bandinelli, for example, claimed that "the things one builds must be the guide and superior to those one plants," when he was asked to design a fountain for the Boboli Gardens in 1551.[45]

Bandinelli's opinion is not, however, representative. (It is no coincidence that Bandinelli is the only sixteenth-century source cited by Ojetti in the *Mostra del giardino italiano* catalogue.) Other artists expressed exactly the opposite view. Lorenzo Lotto, for example, in his design for an intarsia panel cover for the choir of Santa Maria Maggiore in Bergamo, depicted David being flogged by Absalom. David's neck is tied to the figure of Nature, personified as the many-breasted goddess Artemis. The meaning is clear: Lotto depicts the subjugation of men and women to nature.[46]

In some Renaissance writings on landscape and gardens, the relationship between art and nature was conceived as a collaborative one. Claudio Tolomei, for example, described a garden grotto near the Trevi Fountain in Rome as follows: "Mingling [*mescolando*] art with nature, one does not know how to discern whether it is a work of the former or the latter; on the contrary, now it seems to be a natural artifice, then an artificial nature."[47] Jacopo Bonfadio made the same point in a letter of 1541, when he wrote that in garden design the mutual (and benign) interaction of art and nature produces more extraordinary effects than either could achieve on its own.[48]

Neither the geometry of the Renaissance garden nor the sixteenth-century concept of the garden as a third nature legitimize the triumphalist rhetoric of Dami and Ojetti. The modern view of the Renaissance garden as a representation of the domination of nature by art finds little justification in the historical sources. The Fascist project was, of course, closely linked to political convictions about national identity, strength and vitality, which help to explain (if not justify) the willful historiographical misrepresentation of the Renaissance garden by Italian designers and writers of the 1920s and 1930s. What is more surprising is that such a blatant fabrication could survive intact and unnoticed in the subsequent work of postwar landscape historians.

A Reception History of the Italian Renaissance Garden

Ojetti's characterization of the Italian garden as a "garden of reason" in which nature was manipulated, dominated, and ultimately humiliated is a reductive one that overtly privileges design over experience and use. The reception history of Renaissance landscape design indicates that for contemporary visitors the garden was both more complex and less anodyne.

Two descriptions of gardens suggest the range of possible responses to landscape design during the Renaissance. They might be thought of as opposing poles or extremes, between which other early modern responses can be plotted. The first is the fictional landscape of Francesco Colonna's *Hypnerotomachia Poliphili* (1499), and the second is Giorgio Vasari's detailed discussion of the garden of the Villa Medici in Castello in his "Life" of Niccolò Tribolo (1568).[49]

The *Hypnerotomachia* consists of two books. The protagonist Poliphilo narrates the first himself, while the second is told from the point of view of Polia—Poliphilo's beloved—the pursuit of whom is the premise for Colonna's antiquarian fantasy. The conceit upon which the narrative hinges is the literary one of a dream within a dream. Poliphilo's descriptions of gardens, buildings, works of art, and a host of beautiful nymphs are therefore twice removed: Poliphilo dreams that he is dreaming them.

At the beginning of the first book, Poliphilo falls asleep and immediately succumbs to a nightmare. He finds himself in a dark wood (figure 8), where he becomes "incapacitated by terror"—an important Renaissance literary image of the landscape as antagonistic or frightening.[50] He soon manages to escape the wood, however, and discovers a stream. Lying down on the bank, he allows "a sweet lassitude" to overcome him and he falls asleep again.[51] The reader is now inside the second dream (or the dream within the dream). As one of the prefaces to the first Venetian edition of the book puts it, here Poliphilo encounters "pyramids, obelisks, huge ruins of buildings . . . a great horse, an enormous elephant, a colossus, a magnificent portal . . . a fright, the five senses represented in five nymphs, a remarkable bath, fountains, the palace of the queen who is Freewill, and an excellent royal feast . . . [a] variety of gems or precious stones . . . a game of chess in a ballet with music in triple time; three gardens, one of glass, one of silk and one a labyrinth, which is human life; a peristyle of brick in whose centre the Trinity was expressed in hieroglyphic figures, that is, in the sacred engraving of the Egyptians."[52]

In his descriptions of the "priceless and superhuman novelties" that he encounters, Poliphilo discusses the "voluptuous" effects of the architecture, the "unspeakable splendour," and the "superabundance" of the realm of his dream.[53] His "ardent desires" are directed equally toward the nymph Polia and the architectural and artistic works of antiquity, inducing in his "furnace of a heart" an "insatiable appetite" and "sweet inflammation," not to mention "amorous and lofty imaginings."[54] Much of what Poliphilo comes across is so aesthetically overwhelming or profound, in fact, that it exceeds his capacity to describe it. Such works belong, he says, to the category of "divine arcana" and "deep mystagogy."[55]

Poliphilo's sensual rapture becomes overwhelming, almost to the point of intolerability, when he encounters the Fountain of Venus on the garden island of Cythera:

> This incredibly delicious and pleasant place with its unbelievable
> decoration of spring greenery, the birds chattering in the pure air
> and flying twittering through the new foliage: all this gave the
> utmost delight to the external senses; and as I listened to the lovely
> nymphs singing melodies together with their unusual instruments,
> and watched their sacred actions and modest movements, I felt
> ardently impelled to the height of bliss. Moreover, as I carefully and
> curiously examined the building that displayed such nobility of

Figure 8. The Dark Wood. Woodcut from Francesco Colonna, *Hypnero-tomachia Poliphili* (Venice, 1499). Courtesy of Special Collections, Baillieu Library, University of Melbourne.

design and such elegant arrangement, and breathed avidly such fragrance as I had never known before, by immortal Jupiter! I truly did not know which of my senses I should fix firmly on to my intended object, distracted as I was by so many different pleasures, by such excessive gratification, and by such voluptuousness.[56]

This account of garden response might be compared with the one that Lusini supposedly relied upon for his 1931 model of a "giardino fiorentino del Cinquecento": Vasari's description of the garden of the Villa Medici in Castello. Unlike Colonna, whose protagonist delights in the sounds of birds and music, the olfactory pleasures of the garden, and the elegance of the architectural design ("my hungry eyes" as Poliphilo puts it), Vasari was exclusively concerned with the aesthetic or visual elements of the garden. Vasari writes: "In the middle of the garden are high and thick cypresses, laurels and myrtles growing wild, and forming a labyrinth surrounded by a hedge two and a half *braccia* high, so regular that it looks as if it had been produced by the brush."[57] Vasari's comparison of Tribolo's design to painting is high praise, but it clearly privileges the visual medium and ignores the crucial sensual dimensions of garden experience that so inflame Poliphilo ("I truly did not know which of my senses I should fix firmly on my intended object").

Vasari's exclusive emphasis on design, which reduces gardens to images, has exerted the greatest influence on landscape history. There is, however, substantial evidence from the period that the primacy of vision was never absolute (despite modern claims that the ocularcentric scopic regimes of modernity originate in the Renaissance).[58] The designer of the Medici garden in Castello, Tribolo, is known to have favored the sense of touch over vision for example. As he stated in response to Benedetto Varchi's famous questionnaire on the paragone: "Sculpture is . . . [the art] of using one's hands to show what is true. . . . [I]f a blind man . . . happened to come upon a marble or wood or clay figure, he would claim that it was the figure of a [living person, but] . . . had it been a painting, he would have encountered nothing at all . . . [because] sculpture is the real thing, and painting is a lie."[59] Tribolo is reiterating a common topos in early modern aesthetic debates about the relative merits of painting and sculpture, but it is not without interest that as a sculptor and garden designer, he emphasizes the greater truthfulness of touch.[60]

Whereas Vasari's responses are to a real place, Poliphilo's are fictional, but this does not mean that they are without precedent, despite his penchant for unusual images (on the shores of Cythera, Colonna writes, there is "abundant evidence of the fragrant coitus of monstrous whales").[61] Poliphilo's descriptions of fountains and running water, for example, recall other historical sources.

Early in his exploration of the landscape of the *Hypnerotomachia*, Poliphilo is faced with a choice between three routes, indicated by three inscribed portals. Typically, he decides to follow the nymph Thelemia (Desire) despite the advice of her counterpart Logistica (Reason), who cautions him that "things perceived give more enjoyment to the intellect than to the senses alone."[62] Ignoring this advice in favor of the sensual, Poliphilo enters "a voluptuous place, its grounds clad with green herbs and flowers; a place of abundant solace and ease, running with clear, gushing springs and loud with the noise of meandering brooks. It was a delicious, well-watered place, with open meadows and the cool, almost cold shade of the leafy trees."[63]

Colonna emphasizes the sound of running water, describing the garden as "voluptuous" and "delicious," that is, in nonvisual terms. In fact, the water features of early modern gardens were *usually* described in terms other than the visual or architectural. The words used during the period are revealing and often onomatopoeic. Common ones include *mormorio* (murmur), *gorgoli* (gurgling), *gemitii* (trickling), *spruzzamenti* (sprays), *bollori* (bubbles), *tremoli* (ripples), *grondaie* (dripping), *spume* (foam), and *zampilli* (jets).[64] There clearly existed a highly sophisticated lexicon of terms for the description of the varied sounds of moving water in the garden that was capable of subtle distinctions.

The vocabulary of fountain design was comparatively impoverished. In his essay "Of Gardens" (1625), for example, Francis Bacon writes simply: "Fountains I intend to be of two natures: the one that sprinkleth or spouteth water; the other a fair receipt of water, of some thirty or forty foot square, but without fish, or slime, or mud."[65] Fountain design is therefore of two fundamental types—spouts and cascades—but is always subservient to the properties of water. Bacon has nothing more to say on the subject.

In a letter of 26 July 1543 to Giambattista Grimaldi, Tolomei wrote that contemporary fountains appealed not only to "seeing" but also to "hearing, bathing and tasting."[66] The same is self-evidently true of gardens, if not more so. The visual appearance of landscape design remains important, but the experience of Renaissance gardens was surely not *exclusively* visual. Historical evidence, such as the terms that the period developed for distinguishing between subtle differences in the aural effects of water, underlines the point. The neglect of these dimensions of the garden suggests that modern landscape history has followed Vasari in tending to privilege visual and architectonic elements over other forms of experience.

The possibility of a more inclusive reception history of the garden has started to receive attention within the discipline.[67] The work of John Dixon Hunt and Michel Conan on, respectively, the "afterlife" and the "social reception" of gardens has begun to shift the emphasis from designers and patrons to the responses of the historical audience for landscape art.[68] Yet even Conan has written: "It is not altogether obvious how social reception should be defined, and whatever the definition, the methods for garden reception study have to be invented."[69] It is indeed easy to endorse the claim that more attention should be paid to the reception of designed landscapes, but it is much harder to see how exactly this might be accomplished in a way that makes a tangible contribution to our understanding of the sociocultural significance of historical gardens.

Conan identifies four potential approaches or methods: (i) the reconstruction of the point of view of the historical visitor; (ii) the study of the reinterpretation and adaptive reuse of inherited cultural forms; (iii) the analysis of historical representations of gardens; and (iv) the study of reception as cultural judgment, the individual's response necessarily expressing views that are shared within his or her culture at large.[70] Landscape historians have, arguably, always practiced the second and third methods. Historical representations of gardens provide one of the discipline's most important resources.[71]

Although it is unmentioned by Conan, D. R. Edward Wright's essay "Some Medici Gardens of the Florentine Renaissance: An Essay in Post-Aesthetic Interpretation" (1996) is an early, exemplary study of the first and fourth approaches. Wright draws attention to the historical emphasis on aesthetic intentionality in garden history and the concomitant neglect of the social dimensions of use and response. The purpose of his essay is, he writes,

> to re-study a group of well-known sixteenth-century gardens from
> the perspective of the user rather than the designer, examining
> conventions of utilisation and functional requirements in relation
> to physical infrastructure, with the aim of establishing protocols of
> interpretation that are not misleadingly skewed toward the discur-
> sive categories of formal/visual analysis. It is hoped that such an
> approach will result in an expanded discourse that will open the
> way to alternative, non-stylistic models of historical comparison
> and typological categorization. . . . This is not intended so much to
> replace visual/aesthetic readings as to integrate them into a different
> discourse where that seems appropriate.[72]

On the basis of this hypothesis, Wright proceeds to reinterpret the Medici gardens in Castello, Pratolino, and those of the Palazzo Pitti (the Boboli Gardens), from the perspective of sixteenth-century ideas about agriculture, health, and the beneficial medical effects of excursions to gardens. The result is an original account of three major early modern gardens. Wright demonstrates that, in contrast to the arguments of Ojetti and later writers, "in Renaissance treatises this visual enjoyment of *giardini* is always treated as a secondary consequence of the ordered patterns resulting from agricultural necessity and consider-ations of use."[73] The positive medical effects of visits to gardens are shown to be central to the understanding of them during the period. Wright's argument thus depends on the reconstruction of a specific historical point of view, which he accomplishes through a detailed study of contemporary agricultural and medical literature.

Conan's "horizon of perception" is not dissimilar to Michael Baxandall's art historical account of the "period eye."[74] If, as Baxandall argued, our understanding of Renaissance works of art necessitates the reconstruction of the conditions of spectatorship (or with *how* people thought as well as *what* they thought), which were formed by a host of extraneous activities, practices, and experiences—from barrel gauging to dancing—then a reception history of the Renaissance garden should similarly attempt to incorporate the potential interpretative equipment and experience of the historical beholder. The imaginative world of Ovid and others was self-evidently evoked in early modern garden design and experience, but so too, arguably, were other discourses such as the "juridico-biological domain," as Foucault called it, of the lawyers and the physicians.[75]

Most Renaissance gardens contained examples of what the period would have defined as "monsters"—harpies, sphinxes, dragons, giants, and invented hybrids. The significance of their presence cannot be determined through recourse to familiar interpretative frameworks, such as the idea that the Renaissance garden was a self-conscious revival of the locus amoenus or the many subsequent redactions of Ojetti's "garden of reason." Indeed, the view that the exclusive objective of Renaissance designers was to reinstate the locus amoenus of classical antiquity is as reductive as Ojetti's characterization of the Italian garden as a triumph of rationality in which nature is manipulated, dominated, and humiliated. Both assumptions drastically simplify a historical form that could patently accommodate contradiction and diversity.[76] The demonstrable capacity of landscape design to provoke radically divergent responses, not all of which may have been pleasurable (as in Capello's temporary transformation of the Oricellari into what Hervé Brunon has called a "*topos* antagoniste"), combined with the largely unremarked violence of some of its most familiar motifs, and the disturbing presence of monsters, suggests that the Renaissance garden was a more contradictory cultural artifact than has been acknowledged.

An important premise of this book is that a reception history of the Renaissance garden must take into account a wide range of discourses or *mentalités* besides literary and art historical traditions. It seeks to reconstruct one of these "mental conceptions" in some detail through focusing on the theme of monstrosity and its equivalent in art and aesthetics—the grotesque. Medical and legal texts of the period, for example, provide important evidence of what and how people thought about monsters, abnormality, and difference.

The monster has multiple meanings in early modern European culture, but it is rarely a benign presence. This has implications for our understanding of the historical garden as an idyllic, untroubled locus amoenus. A handful of other historians have begun to work toward a similar conclusion in recent years. Brunon's important argument about the duality of the Renaissance garden was mentioned in the Introduction. Eugenio Battisti's highly original book *L'antirinascimento* (1962), which unaccountably remains untranslated into English, is a major precedent for Brunon's observations (and for those of the present book). Writing against the grain of contemporary scholarship, Battisti emphasized the survival and persistence of irrational, "anticlassical," occult and superstitious attitudes in the Renaissance. Gardens and their ornaments provided one of his main examples.

More recently, Zakiya Hanafi has suggested (without elaborating in detail), that the Renaissance garden functioned "as a liminal space, where transgression was licit and worldly values were turned upside down."[77] Citing Battisti, she states: "The monstrous statues of Bomarzo, Pratolino and Castello were fitting accoutrements for this dreamlike pilgrimage, this 'initiatory process, from Inferno to Eden' so often planned and staged in late Renaissance and Baroque gardens."[78] Marcello Fagiolo and Maria Luisa Madonna have likewise argued that the meaning of the garden of the Villa d'Este in Tivoli is associated with Typhon, "this monster, whose countless voices sometimes resemble the gods and sometimes wild animals or the forces of nature, [and who] embodies the elemental power of disorder."[79] Another example is provided by Anne Bélanger's hypothesis that the monstrous figures of the Sacro Bosco in Bomarzo imply a concept of the garden as potentially frightening and of nature as arbitrary and amoral, even cruel.[80] The implication of her argument, like Brunon's, is that Renaissance gardens are places of pleasure *and* peril, order *and* confusion.[81]

These points suggest that the monsters of Renaissance landscape design were not eccentric outliers or idiosyncratic addenda to the garden's main themes but were integral to its definition and meaning. What is needed, therefore, is a theoretical framework in which they can be seen as part of a larger unity that is capable of accommodating duality, contradiction, and paradox. The rest of this chapter is dedicated to exploring one possible model for a reframing of the Renaissance garden along these lines—Foucault's concept of heterotopic space.

A Framing Concept: The Garden as Heterotopic Space

Although Foucault's best-known articulation of his theory of heterotopic space appears in "Of Other Spaces" ("Des espaces autres"), which was originally delivered as a lecture in 1967 and only published shortly before his death as an article, he first introduces the idea in 1966 in one of his earliest books—*The Order of Things*—and again (also in 1966), in a radio broadcast. In the book, Foucault compares heterotopias with utopias, as he does in the later, more influential lecture and article, but he restricts his comments to language:

> *Heterotopias* are disturbing, probably because they secretly undermine language, because they make it impossible to name this *and* that, because they shatter or tangle common names, because they destroy "syntax" in advance, and not only the syntax with which we construct sentences but also that less apparent syntax which causes words and things (next to and also opposite one another) to "hold together." This is why utopias permit fables and discourse: they run with the very grain of language and are part of the fundamental dimension of the *fabula*; heterotopias (such as those to be found so often in Borges) desiccate speech, stop words in their tracks, contest the very possibility of grammar at its source; they dissolve our myths and sterilize the lyricism of our sentences.[82]

Jorge Luis Borges's famous classification of animals, which he claims to derive from a Chinese encyclopedia entitled *Celestial Emporium of Benevolent Knowledge*, is thus heterotopic rather than utopic because, as Foucault states, it disturbs and threatens with collapse "our age-old distinction between the Same and the Other."[83] This has, in Foucault's analysis, a destabilizing and destructive effect on our accustomed ways of thinking about and organizing the world. If animals can be defined and categorized on the basis of whether they belong to the emperor, are drawn with a fine brush, or have just broken a water pitcher, to name three of Borges's distinctions, then the whole logic and stability of categories in general becomes questionable, especially given the key category in this taxonomy of animals: those which are "included in the present classification." From this perspective, the rational or "scientific" basis of our own methods of categorization and differentiation may begin to appear just as arbitrary.

Foucault's second discussion of heterotopias—in the radio broadcast "Ut-opie et littérature"—proposes a science of heterotopias, which would be dedicated to the study of "absolutely other spaces." At this stage in his thinking, heterotopias are clearly dramatically at odds with ordinary or everyday spaces, a distinction that is softened in the 1967 lecture. Foucault gives an interesting example that does not appear again. According to him, children's games produce a different space, which simultaneously mirrors and contests the child's surroundings. He mentions tents and dens in gardens as well as games played under the covers of beds.[84]

In "Of Other Spaces" Foucault deals more explicitly with architecture and architectural space than he does in *The Order of Things*. He retains very little from his initial, brief formulation of the concept in that book, except perhaps a Borgesian taste for ostensibly incongruous taxonomies. His examples of heterotopic space include: boarding schools, military service, what he calls "honeymoon trips," rest homes, psychiatric hospitals, prisons, cemeteries, theaters, cinemas, gardens, museums, libraries, fairgrounds, "Polynesian villages," hammams, Scandinavian saunas, Brazilian bedrooms, American motel rooms, colonies, brothels, and ships.

For Foucault utopias are "sites with no real place," whereas heterotopias are "real places."[85] They are, in a sense, dissonant microcosms (Foucault's term is "counter-sites"), which represent the real sites of their culture but which simultaneously contest and invert them. Their functions are reducible to two: first, there is the heterotopia that serves to create an illusion. Second, there is the "heterotopia of compensation," which aims to perfect poorly constructed real spaces. Brothels serve as an example of the former, whereas Puritan colonies in America and Jesuit ones in South America provide examples of the latter.

Foucault suggests that a systematic description of these diverse "other spaces," which he now dubs "heterotopology," would begin with five principles. The last three are important for the garden. The third principle is that the heterotopia "is capable of juxtaposing in a single real place several spaces, several sites that are in themselves incompatible."[86] His examples include theaters and cinemas. The garden, however, is the oldest form of these contradictory sites. Foucault writes:

> We must not forget that in the Orient the garden, an astonishing creation that is now a thousand years old, had very deep and seemingly superimposed meanings. The traditional garden of the Persians was a sacred space that was supposed to bring together inside its

rectangle four parts representing the four parts of the world, with a
space still more sacred than the others that were like an umbilicus,
the navel of the world at its centre (the basin and water fountain
were there); and all the vegetation of the garden was supposed
to come together in this space, in this sort of microcosm. As for
carpets, they were originally reproductions of gardens (the garden is
a rug onto which the whole world comes to enact its symbolic perfection, and the rug is a sort of garden that can move across space).
The garden has been a sort of happy, universalizing heterotopia
since the beginnings of antiquity (our modern zoological gardens
spring from this source).[87]

Cemeteries, museums, and libraries exemplify the fourth principle:
namely, that heterotopias are linked to heterochronies, or "slices in time."[88]
Foucault has in mind the collecting or archival impulse, which he regards as
the unceasing effort to accumulate time in a single place that is itself outside
time, and which he considers an essentially modern phenomenon.

The fifth and last principle concerns access. Foucault states that heterotopias are closed but penetrable after certain gestures or rites. They are, in
other words, only semipublic. Prisons and saunas or bathhouses function
in this way, but so do motel rooms. These are, in Jean Starobinski's phrase,
spaces that will "always remain sealed off yet at the same time [are] perilously
exposed."[89]

Foucault himself never developed these ideas any further. He could, in
fact, be said to have abandoned them immediately after he delivered his lecture in 1967. His concept of heterotopia is not, in other words, central to
his work as a whole, though it obviously reflects his lifelong interests in social institutions as well as in regimes of spatiality, power, and exclusion. For
the geographer Edward Soja, Foucault's concept is "frustratingly incomplete,
inconsistent, incoherent."[90] These difficulties have not, however, prevented a
large number of writers in, especially, architectural history and theory, from
adopting the idea (it is worth noting that the lecture "Des espaces autres" was
originally delivered to a group of architects).

Oddly perhaps, heterotopia loses its original critical, antagonistic, and
oppositional force in the course of its travels within architectural theory—as
the basis of formalist accounts of modernist and contemporary architectures,
as a way of explicating incongruity and self-reflexivity in the work of historical
practitioners, as a means of thinking about architecture at the beginning of

modernity as a discourse, and as a legitimating concept employed to promote a group of new contemporary practices as, ironically, unified.[91] Or, to be more precise, although lip service is paid to the idea that heterotopic space is unsettling, discordant, and critical, in the application of the concept to a wide range of structures, spaces, and practices, this assumption is almost never adequately substantiated.

Benjamin Genocchio has suggested that the problem with many of the subsequent uses of Foucault's concept is that the "heterotopia is invariably reified as a handy marker for a variety of centreless structures or an elastic postmodern plurality. Not only do such appropriations avoid questions concerning the coherency of Foucault's argument but, in so doing, they lose the disruptive, transient, contradictory and transformative implications of what remains a far more fluid idea."[92] As Genocchio states, Foucault himself was aware of the fundamental difficulty that "even to imagine another order/system is to extend our participation in the present one."[93]

The problem boils down to the inescapability of binary structures and systems of thought. To name a heterotopia is to situate it in opposition to some other spatial formation on the basis of a concept of difference. That, in turn, is to eliminate its critical, contestory potential. It becomes "other" to the sociospatial norm, anesthetized, and safely dispatched to the margins. Yet for Foucault heterotopia is a real place, or at least an *idea* about real places in which binaries confront one another, are impossibly juxtaposed or distributed in incommensurable relations of propinquity. The "incoherence" of his theoretical formulation may thus reflect, however intuitively, the inexpressibility of heterotopic space—"the stark impossibility of thinking *that*," as Foucault writes about Borges's taxonomy of animals—but that does not mean it does not exist or that the concept has no critical value.[94] Incidentally, this acknowledgment of the difficulty of the concept of heterotopia also has something in common with Bonfadio's definition of the garden as a third nature, which he "would not know how to name."

A Heterotopology of the Garden?

Renaissance gardens may seem more utopic than heterotopic. Certainly, they are not usually described as critical or antagonistic spaces (although it is worth recalling Edmund Wilson's horrified reaction to the Sacro Bosco at Bomarzo and Brunon's concept of the garden as a "*topos* antagoniste"). Foucault,

however, thought that the garden was probably the oldest form of heterotopic space. The influence of his concept in studies of the built environment,
whether misconstrued or not, and the fact that the garden serves as one of his
key examples suggest that there may be something useful to be salvaged from
his work for landscape history.

What could it mean to describe a Renaissance garden as heterotopic,
without lapsing into a simplistic characterization of it as formally pluralistic,
which it certainly sometimes is, or as absolutely distinct from, or opposed in
some sense to other spaces, or, even more weakly, as merely "ambiguous"? An
ephemeral garden of the late sixteenth century offers as good a starting point
as any for an attempt at an answer.

The elaborate festivities mounted in celebration of the wedding of Grand
Duke Ferdinand de' Medici to Christina of Lorraine in 1589 included the tri-
umphal entry of Christina into Florence and a three-week-long series of fetes
and *intermezzi*. This was followed by a *sbarra* (tournament) and a *naumachia*
(sea battle), both of which took place in the courtyard of the Palazzo Pitti. The
diarist Pavoni records the entry into the courtyard of one of the participants
in the sbarra, Don Virginio de' Medici, who arrived on a pageant car dressed
as a knight. According to Pavoni, Don Virginio was followed by

> [a] garden which, while it entered the grounds began extend-
> ing itself around and about, which made, with its beautiful and
> unexpected view all the surrounding people marvel, nor could they
> see by what it was transported, appearing as though it moved by
> enchantment: and in this garden was seen woven, and by a masterly
> hand made, different kinds of fancies, like ships, small galleys, tow-
> ers, castles, men on horseback, pyramids, groves, an Elephant, and
> other animal quadrupeds, and it was all made of greenery; inside of
> which were heard different sorts of birds, which with the diversity
> of their singing made a harmony sweet and soft.[95]

Several of the conditions of heterotopic space are present in this remarkable, mobile garden. It contained representations of boats, as well as being
itself a kind of ship, which Foucault argues is the heterotopia par excellence:
"The boat is a floating piece of space, a place without a place, that exists by
itself, that is closed in on itself and at the same time is given over to the infinity of the sea."[96]

Unanchored, literally placeless, but remaining nonetheless a place, this garden also constitutes a succinct meditation on Bonfadio's definition of the garden as a third nature. As Pavoni writes, it was ornamented with representations of people, animals, and other structures "made of greenery," by which he must mean topiary work. The artifice of the garden's ornaments and its concealed machinery, which caused the audience to "marvel," was thus the result of the ingenuity of late sixteenth-century Florentine engineering but also of nature, the collaborative partner of art in Renaissance landscape design.

Part *veduta* and part menagerie, this "floating piece of space" is suggestive not only of Renaissance exploration (an elephant and pyramids appear, for instance) but of the archival impulse, which Foucault argues is characteristic of the heterotopia and which also appears in gardens of the period. The urge to collect everything in one timeless place was assisted by contemporary sea voyages or the ship, which, Foucault adds, sails "from port to port, from tack to tack, from brothel to brothel . . . as far as the colonies in search of the most precious treasures they conceal in their gardens."[97] The float was also, of course, part garden and part theater, two of the environments that Foucault identifies as capable of juxtaposing incompatible spaces.

Like the temporary garden described by Pavoni, most actual Renaissance gardens represent or make some kind of reference to other landscapes or spaces. These range from the local, such as rivers and mountain ranges, to the distant.[98] In the garden of the Villa Medici in Castello, for example, there are sculptures representing the city of Florence, the Arno and Mugnone rivers, and the Apennines. All of these natural features are personified and "miniaturized," as it were, so as to allow their juxtaposition within the restricted space of the garden.

One of the best known of these representations is the so-called Rometta at the end of the principal latitudinal axis of the garden of the Villa d'Este in Tivoli (figure 9). This axis, or pathway, is known as the Alley of the Hundred Fountains, and is punctuated at regular intervals by grotesque heads and boats, as well as eagles, obelisks, d'Este fleurs-de-lis, and scenes from Ovid's *Metamorphoses*. At the other end of the alley is the Fountain of Tivoli (now known as the Oval Fountain), the main feature of which is a colossal statue of the Tiburtine Sibyl, representing Tivoli itself above a waterfall. The Rometta, a representation of the ancient city, is likewise dominated by a large female personification of Rome. Tivoli and Rome thus interact across the axis, implying, perhaps, Tivoli's contribution to Rome's prosperity (in the form of building materials and water). As Claudia Lazzaro suggests, "the polarities of country and city, nature and art on the extreme sides of the garden also reflect Ippolito

FONTANA,E PROSPETTO DI ROMA ANTICA CON L' ISOLA TIBERINA DAL LATO SINISTRO DEL VIALONE DELLE FONTANELLE

Figure 9. G. F. Venturini, Rometta, Villa d'Este, Tivoli, 1691. Engraving from G. B. Falda, *Le fontane di Roma*. Courtesy of Dumbarton Oaks, Research Library and Collection, Washington, D.C.

d'Este's own life, lived between the ecclesiastical center of power in Rome and his retreat in Tivoli."[99]

There is also, however, a less hierarchical relationship between the two represented places. The d'Este garden eliminates distance and civic stature, bringing the spa town and the metropolis together in a single space and making them equivalent to one another in scale and importance. Polarities, as Lazzaro calls them, are perhaps mediated, but to what effect? The Rometta is in fact a highly idealized representation of Rome, which emphasizes the city's ancient monuments and *castelli* or water termini. It might be thought of as "compensating" in Foucault's sense for the imperfect reality of late sixteenth-century Rome. It is also, intriguingly, a miniature, toy-like representation or model of the city, which is seen as if from a distance. *Urbs* and *orbis* are here inverted. The Rometta temporarily transforms landscape into cityscape, but this transformation has the quality of a game. Indeed, the effect is not unlike that of the inventive play of children, which Foucault referred to in his radio broadcast of 1966 and which is one of the clearest examples that he gives of heterotopic space. As he suggests, in building an alternative space within the space of the home, children temporarily produce somewhere different: the space of the game simultaneously reflects and contests the surrounding spatial environment. [100]

Many Renaissance gardens contained seemingly incompatible elements and allusions: from the miscellaneous "Aztec," Etruscan, classical, literary, and personal references in the Sacro Bosco to the juxtaposition of a colossal classical mode (the figure of Oceanus at the center of the Isolotto), with grotesque and genre or "low-life" figures in the Boboli and the menagerie of animals that appear in the grotto at Castello (in one of the niches, for example, a unicorn is depicted alongside an elephant, bulls, a goat, and a lion; figure 10). A particularly striking example appears at Soriano nel Cimino near Bomarzo, where a wall fountain depicts the hybrid goat-woman Amalthea, nurse of the infant Zeus, adjacent to the Old Testament figure of Moses (see figures 42 and 43).

Incongruity or apparent incompatibility does not, however, necessarily imply the heterotopic. In his critique of Georges Teyssot's understanding of Foucault's concept, Daniel Defert argues: "The incongruity of the contents is what defines the architecture as a heterotopia [in Teyssot's analysis]—not the qualitative or symbolic play of opposition-contestation with respect to existing spaces that the heterotopia institutes through its function, its form, and its ruptures." [101] To extend Defert's distinction to the garden: the heterotopic play of opposition and contestation is, arguably, *not* found in the Grotto of the Animals at Castello, which certainly appears as an incongruous zoological collection, combining the mythical with the mundane (and irrespective of habitat or hostility), but which does not significantly disrupt or oppose categories of Renaissance knowledge and differentiation.

In contrast, playful opposition is fundamental to the Hell Mouth in the Sacro Bosco. It is both a terrifying image of a monstrous head and an outdoor dining room. Upon entry, Orsini's guests were figuratively devoured, but the purpose of the room nullifies or inverts the initial meaning, quite literally. In other words, a different space is produced that simultaneously contests and mirrors the surrounding space of the Sacro Bosco. [102]

It is worth recalling here Foucault's original formulation of the concept of heterotopia. In *The Order of Things*, he had argued with reference to Borges's fictive Chinese encyclopedia that heterotopias undermine language and that they "desiccate speech, stop words in their tracks, contest the very possibility of grammar at its source." He was thus initially concerned with the space of language rather than built space or designed landscapes. His concept of a

Figure 10. Grotto of the Animals. Villa Medici, Castello. Photo: Luke
Morgan.

linguistic structure always on the brink of collapse, self-denial, or atomiza-
tion through a kind of double movement of statement and opposing statement, which, however, never becomes authentically dialectical in the synthetic
Hegelian sense, may have an analogue in one of the most fundamental design
concepts of the Renaissance garden: namely, its adherence to a principle of
"*topoi*, not narrative," which might now be extended with reference to another, much later, fictional garden.[103]

The Legibility of Landscape

When the eponymous protagonists of Gustave Flaubert's *Bouvard and
Pécuchet* (1881) suddenly become enamored of landscape design and decide to
remodel their own garden, they are bewildered by the "infinity of styles" that

are available to them.[104] After much deliberation and research, they decide to install an incongruous group of symbolic structures, including an "Etruscan tomb" with an inscription, recalling the tomb of Nicolas Poussin's *Et in Arcadia Ego* (c. 1639), a "Rialto," a "Chinese pagoda," a mount, and various topiary works in the shape of peacocks, stags, pyramids, and armchairs. Despite their "improvements," however, when Bouvard and Pécuchet proudly unveil the garden for the first time at dinner, their guests fail to respond as they should; that is, according to the categories of response prescribed in Boitard's *The Architect of the Garden*.[105] These categories include the Melancholy or Romantic, the Exotic and the Pensive, the Mysterious and the Fantastic.

What is important here is not so much the failure of Bouvard and Pécuchet's scheme as the idea that certain elements within a garden are capable of evoking predetermined responses and that these elements will cohere on the model of a linguistic statement or narrative. They assume that a "Melancholy or Romantic" frame of mind, for instance, can be engineered through the inclusion of ruins; that moss and tombs will always connote "the Mysterious"; and so on. Although these elements may indeed produce meanings, or sentiments (though not, frustratingly, for Bouvard and Pécuchet's guests), it does not necessarily follow that they will resolve into a stable and coherent message or statement.

Bouvard and Pécuchet's garden may epitomize the condition of *all* gardens and designed landscapes, including Renaissance ones, albeit in extremis. Henri Lefebvre has suggested that "both natural and urban spaces are, if anything, 'over-inscribed': everything therein resembles a rough draft, jumbled and self-contradictory."[106] This condition is complicated still further by the immersive, synesthetic, and multisensual experience of the garden.[107] The implication of Lefebvre's argument is that authorial control (or *authority*), over the spatial message, is nearly impossible to assert and maintain, but it is also suggestive of Foucault's point that heterotopias undermine and contest language at its source. It is indicative that despite their extremely literal and programmatic approach to landscape design and its affects, for instance, Bouvard and Pécuchet are ultimately unable to predetermine and direct their audience's responses. The "grammar" and "syntax" of landscape design simply will not settle into a coherent order.

James Elkins has proposed that "gardens, more than paintings or sculptures, are often intentionally vague or ambiguous in reference."[108] The descriptions of Tribolo's design for the Villa Medici in Castello by Vasari (1568) and Michel de Montaigne (1581) illustrate Elkins's point. Vasari gives a lengthy account of the symbolism of Tribolo's garden, which he states was dedicated to extolling "the greatness of the Medici house."[109] Montaigne, however, mentions nothing of the kind, emphasizing instead the fountains and giochi d'acqua, and noting the garden's "curiosities" and "amusements," but not the apparent political or propagandistic purpose of its imagery.[110] The point is not that Montaigne missed something important but rather that the inherent openness of the garden precludes the possibility of interpretative closure or definitiveness, and that this openness disrupts "syntax," loosening the bonds that permit words and things to "hold together," as Foucault put it.

There are numerous other historical cases of the inherent "polysemy" of landscape design.[111] The various contemporary descriptions of and itineraries for Louis XIV's garden at Versailles, including his own, reveal that there was no single, standardized route through it, in which the garden revealed its meaning(s).[112] Malcolm Kelsall, writing about the eighteenth-century garden at Stourhead, doubts whether "even the clearest allusions constitute a program," and even denies altogether the presence of a detailed Virgilian narrative, which he suggests "modern scholarship has invented."[113] In the twentieth century, Bernard Tschumi claimed that his design for the Parc de la Villette in Paris was intended to move "towards interpretative infinity, for the effect of refusing fixity is not insignificance, but semantic plurality."[114] Similarly, Hunt has argued that Ian Hamilton Finlay's use of fragments and quotations in his landscape designs "make exceptionally clear the refusal of any narrative or extended exposition of ideas."[115]

These examples raise an important question: Is it actually possible to make a coherent "reading" of a space? In Lefebvre's opinion, the answer is: "Yes and no. Yes, inasmuch as it is possible to envisage a 'reader' who deciphers or decodes and a 'speaker' who expresses himself by translating his progression into a discourse. But no, in that social space can in no way be compared to a blank page upon which a specific message has been inscribed (by whom?)."[116] The Medici garden in Castello again provides an example. Vasari's lengthy account of the meaning of Tribolo's design comprises a step-by-step description of his own passage through the garden but, as the alternate description of Montaigne indicates, Vasari's translation of his "progression into discourse" is not the only one possible, nor even necessarily the best one possible. In short, Vasari's interpretation is not authorized by the presence of a specific, stable, and universally "readable" message that Tribolo somehow inscribed in the garden.

Another way to think about this condition would be to put it in Foucault's terms. If the Hell Mouth in Bomarzo "desiccates speech," then this may be an instance of the garden's potential to confront its visitors with much more than ambiguity, incongruity, or even a generalized openness and freedom of interpretation. The Sacro Bosco, in particular, might be characterized as heterotopic in the sense that it continuously denies or calls into question its own "utterances," which results in a form of lexical and syntactic incommensurability or instability. Its notorious resistance to interpretation would then become a consequence of its internal denial and critique of its own propositions.

Most important here, however, is that if the garden is both a site and a counter-site, a microcosm with "very deep and seemingly superimposed meanings," or a mirror—another of Foucault's examples of heterotopia—then the presence of monsters becomes more explicable. Monsters are the antithesis of the normal. Consequently, they could not be allowed to occupy ordinary social space, as the case of the hermaphrodite Marie le Marcis amply demonstrates. They had to be legislated against, institutionalized, banished (in reality or in the imagination) to the margins, suppressed or repressed, and even punished. Their early modern domain was the carnival, the theater, the collection of curiosities, the freak show, the courtroom, the dissecting table, the prison, and the garden.

As contradictory spaces, gardens are capable of accommodating difference and juxtaposing polarities. Political power, for example, is a common theme of urban space and one that is sometimes present in garden design (such as in the Medici garden in Castello, according to Vasari), but the theme of monstrosity is more rarely encountered in the public spaces of Italian cities and towns. Monsters can, however, be admitted to gardens, which as heterotopic spaces simultaneously affirm and contest norms rather than "reconciling" difference. The garden functions as a kind of distorting or critical mirror, bringing together disparate and even opposed concepts, figures, and formations and revealing the limitations, omissions, and repressions of normative thinking in the process. It is, for this reason, a uniquely privileged site in early modern European culture. The next chapter examines some of the ways in which monsters were conceptualized and received in early modern Europe, with particular reference to their representation in gardens.

Chapter 2

The Grotesque and the Monstrous

Grotesques, like monsters, populate the margins of representation and of knowledge.

—Philippe Morel

Il Sodoma's decorative scheme for the cloister of the abbey at Monte Oliveto in Siena (1505–1508), includes a lesene frescoed with motifs derived from classical grotteschi and medieval marginalia. The sinuous tendrils and arabesques of the plant-like forms, familiar from the recently excavated Domus Aurea in Rome, support images of the "marvels of the east."[1] These were the monstrous races, which, from Pliny the Elder onward, were thought to inhabit the distant regions of the world. Sodoma has depicted a Cynocephalus (dog-head), a monocular Cyclops, an acephalous Blemmyae whose face appears in his chest, an Abarimon, whose feet, according to Megasthenes and Pliny, turn backward, a noseless representative of the Sciritae, an Anthopophagus (man-eater), whose open mouth nearly completely obscures his face, an example of the Pandae with unnaturally long ears stretching down to its elbows, and a horned man (figure 11).[2] Sodoma's composition is synthetic. It provides an early example of the popularity and rapid proliferation of the new style of ornament known as "grotesque" in sixteenth-century Italy; but it is also suggestive of the longevity and continuing interest of the period in monsters.[3] Sodoma's figures were earlier depicted in medieval miniatures and sculpture, such as, for example, those in the churches of the order of Cluny.[4] From Pliny to Augustine and into the Renaissance, monstrous and marvelous creatures—both anthropoid and bestial—held a powerful sway over people's imaginations. If, on the one hand, the sixteenth-century *trattatisti* from Cesare Cesariano to Gian Paolo Lomazzo

Figure 11. Il Sodoma, *Grotteschi* and the "Marvels of the East," 1505–1508. Fresco from the cloister of the Abbey of Monte Oliveto, Siena. Photo: Luke Morgan.

dedicated many pages to debating the legitimacy of the grotesque in art, on the other, physicians, natural historians, and teratologists attempted to categorize and explain monstrous births, hybrid creatures, and legendary beasts. This chapter proposes that the two themes come together in Renaissance garden design, as they do in Sodoma's decorations for the abbey at Monte Oliveto.

Like a "Sick Man's Dreams": From Grotteschi to Grotesque Realism

The rediscovery of grotesque ornament in the Renaissance, and the subsequent debates over its merits, were inspired by two principal sources, one visual and the other textual. Around 1480, the ornamental paintings of what was later identified as the Domus Aurea were rediscovered.[5] This vast structure, which had been built over in antiquity, seemed to the Renaissance to be underground—a network of caves or grottoes. For this reason, as Benvenuto Cellini wrote, the painted decorations of the vault and the walls were described as grotteschi in reference to their location in what were misinterpreted as grotte, or grottoes.[6] The grotesque in the visual arts, therefore, derives from a misnomer, but one that is, nonetheless, logical. The strange, hybridized, biomorphic forms of the Roman paintings seemed appropriate to their hidden underground site. Their mysterious character was enhanced by the shadowy caves that they had until recently been concealed in.[7]

The fortuitous origin of the word "grotesque," if not precisely in the garden, then at least in the idea of the subterranean, or of the grotto, makes it unsurprising that the new ornamental system was soon utilized in garden decoration (such as the Grotto of the Animals in the garden of the Villa Medici in Castello, among many others). There is an obvious relationship between the garden grotto and grotteschi. Moreover, just as the artificial grotto in the Renaissance garden was often utilized as an outdoor dining room (see, for example, Giovanni Guerra's drawing of a meal accompanied by music inside the Hell Mouth in the Sacro Bosco; figure 12), the early explorers of the Domus Aurea had themselves lowered into the underground chambers, taking with them apples, ham, and wine.[8] In his discussion of grotteschi, the designer of the Villa d'Este gardens in Tivoli, Pirro Ligorio, likewise writes at length of an underground banquet organized by the Roman emperor Domitian.[9] Clearly, the rooms of the subterranean palace and the interiors of garden grottoes were regarded as equally convivial places for meals. As is suggested below, eating and consumption are also important themes of the garden in general.

Figure 12. Giovanni Guerra, Drawing of the Hell Mouth, 1604. Sacro Bosco, Bomarzo. Courtesy of Albertina, Vienna.

The decorations of the Domus Aurea have another corollary in landscape design. Metamorphosis is the central theme of ancient Roman grotteschi. Most sixteenth-century gardens also drew on or referred to Ovid's *Metamorphoses*. Ovid's stories of transformation thus constitute a poetic analogue of the metamorphic motifs of Nero's palace. Change and metamorphosis are intrinsic to the garden as an artistic medium. Unlike most art forms of the Renaissance, the garden's natural or organic materials were subject to seasonal changes and the life cycle. The principle of metamorphosis, leading to hybrid forms, is therefore a defining feature of both grotteschi and the garden.[10]

The second source of Renaissance ideas about the grotesque was provided by two classical treatises: Vitruvius's *De architectura* (c. 25 B.C.E.) and Horace's *Ars poetica* (c. 19 B.C.E.). In chapter 5 of book 7 of his work on architecture, Vitruvius provides a concise history of mural painting. He states that the ancients correctly observed the principle that a "painting is an image of that which exists or can exist." According to Vitruvius, however, this rule was no longer followed. Contemporary artists instead demonstrated a "depraved taste":

> For monsters are now painted in frescoes rather than reliable images of definite things. Reeds are set up in place of columns, as pediments, little scrolls, striped with curly leaves and volutes; candelabra hold up the figures of aediculae, and above the pediments of these, several tender shoots, sprouting in coils from roots, have little statues nestled in them for no reason, or shoots split in half, some holding little statues with human heads, some with the heads of beasts.
>
> Now these things do not exist nor can they exist nor have they ever existed. . . . How, pray tell, can a reed really sustain a roof, or a candelabrum the decorations of a pediment, or an acanthus shoot, so soft and slender, loft a tiny statue perched upon it, or can flowers be produced from roots and shoots on the one hand and figurines on the other? . . . Minds beclouded by feeble standards of judgment are unable to recognize what exists in accordance with authority and the principles of correctness.[11]

Vitruvius's condemnation of the composite figures of painting is unequivocal. For him, these "monsters" were unacceptable for the simple reason that they had no basis in reality. They were blatantly erroneous from the point of view of naturalism and logic.

Horace too denounced the grotesque imagery of his period, but in more ironic terms. If Vitruvius's tone is one of moral outrage, Horace's is more amused, though no less critical. In the first lines of *Ars poetica*, Horace suggests that laughter is the only possible response to a painting of a composite figure with a human head, horse's neck, feathers, an assortment of limbs, and a fish's tail. For him, such images resembled a "sick man's dreams" (*aegri somnia*).[12] Horace introduces that element of the grotesque that becomes fully developed in François Rabelais—humor and (in Rabelais, scatological) wit—something that is distinctly lacking in Vitruvius's appraisal.[13] As Victor Hugo observed much later: "The grotesque is everywhere: on the one hand it creates the formless and the terrifying, on the other hand the comic, the buffoon-like."[14]

The discoveries in the excavated Domus Aurea must have immediately recalled the criticisms of Vitruvius and Horace. Indeed, some sixteenth-century writers endorsed the views of their ancient predecessors, while others argued in favor of grotteschi.[15] The former group (of "Vitruvians") included two of the earliest translators of *De architectura*, Cesare Cesariano (1521) and Daniele Barbaro (1556), both of whom dutifully condemned the grotesque as being against nature.

Others wrote in support of grotteschi. Anton Francesco Doni (1549), for example, attempted to reconcile the *capricci* and *bizzarrie* of the painters with the laws of nature.[16] His argument, which has something in common with contemporaneous attempts to explicate "monsters" and abnormal births, was that nature itself produced strange and outlandish forms. This, he claimed, justified the *fantasia* of artists, who, he suggests, are entitled to produce what he calls "chimeras."[17] Sebastiano Serlio, in his *Cinque libri d'architettura* (Venice, 1540) went further, emphasizing the complete freedom of the artist from nature.

Giorgio Vasari, however, was more cautious, even ambivalent, about the merits of the grotesque. He defined grotteschi as a "species of very licentious and ridiculous painting" (*una spezie di pitture licenziose e ridicole molto*) that was nonetheless governed by certain rules.[18] Michelangelo's opinion of the grotesque (or at least the opinion attributed to him by Francisco da Hollanda in 1548) suggests a similar attitude:

> But if, in order to observe what is proper to a time and place (*por guardar o decoro melhor ao lugar e ao tempo*), he [the painter] change (*mudar*) the parts of limbs (as in grotesque work [*obra gruttesca*], which would otherwise be without grace and most false) and convert a griffin or a deer downward into a dolphin or upward into any shape he may choose, putting wings in the place of arms, and cutting away the arms if wings are better, this converted limb, of lion or horse or bird, will be most perfect according to its kind (*perfeitissimo como d'aquelle tal genero que elle é*); and this may seem false but can really only be called well invented or monstrous (*bem inventado e monstruouso*). And sometimes it is more in accordance with reason to paint a monstrosity (for the variation and relaxation of the senses and in respect of mortal eyes, that sometimes desire to see that which they never see and think cannot exist) rather than the accustomed figure (admirable though it be) of men and animals; and from this follows the insatiable human desire (*desejo humano*), which sometimes more abhors a building with its columns, windows and doors, than another feigned and false *alla grottesca* (*fingido de falso grutesco*), that has columns made of creatures growing out of

stalks of flowers, with architraves and cornices of branches or myrtle and doorways of reeds and other things, that seem impossible and irrational (*impossibeis e fora de razão*); yet it may be very great, if done by one who understands (*se é feito de quem o entende*).[19]

Toward the end of the century, Lomazzo reiterated the position of Michelangelo/Hollanda, arguing that grotesques were acceptable within the constraints imposed by nature and decorum.[20]

The sixteenth-century debates about the grotesque, the metamorphic and the composite were not confined to painting. Alina Payne has pointed out that for "a Renaissance architect Vitruvius' *De architectura* both vindicated mixtures and offered the link to the monsters of classical literature."[21] The "monsters [which] are now painted in frescoes rather than reliable images of definite things" were, in Vitruvius's view, an example of "bad" mixtures (*mescolanze*). ("Assemblage" may convey the sense of *mescolanza* in Renaissance architectural theory more effectively than "mixture.") In contrast, the invention of the Corinthian capital was, for Vitruvius, a story about the "good" mescolanza that resulted from the sculptor Callimachus's chance encounter with a young girl's tomb marker.[22] Vitruvius relates how a basket containing the girl's possessions and covered with a roof tile was placed on her grave, underneath which was an acanthus root. As time passed the leaves and tendrils of the plant curled over the edges of the tile, creating coils at the edges. Callimachus was inspired by this composition—a mixture of disparate elements and materials—to invent the Corinthian capital (figure 13). In Payne's summary, "To the Corinthian as good *mescolanza* Vitruvius opposes the irrational of the Pompeian grotesque, the failed *mescolanza*, the monster."[23]

The Renaissance garden was also an assemblage (of, in fact, the exact components of the tomb marker that inspired Callimachus to invent the Corinthian capital). It too was a mixture of the organic and the inorganic. It was also, as several sixteenth-century writers argued, the outcome of a collaboration between nature and art. In his description of a grotto near the Trevi Fountain in Rome, for example, Claudio Tolomei uses the word *mescolando* ("mixing" or "mingling"). Tolomei writes: "Mingling art with nature, one does not know how to discern whether it is a work of the former or the latter; on the contrary, now it seems to be a natural artifice, then an artificial nature."[24] This idea is also familiar from accounts of gardens, from Jacopo Bonfadio's statement that in those of the region of Lake Garda "nature incorporated with art is made an artificer, and the connatural of art; and from both of them is made a third nature, which I would

Figure 13. The Invention of the Corinthian Capital. Engraving from Roland
Fréart de Chambray, *A Parallel of Antient Architecture with the Modern* (Lon-
don: Printed by T.W., 1723). Courtesy of the Victoria and Albert Museum,
London.

not know how to name,"[25] to the Milanese Bartolomeo Taegio's similar reflection: "Here are without end the ingenious grafts that show with great wonder to
the world the industry of a wise gardener, who by incorporating art with nature
brings forth from both a third nature, which causes the fruits to be more flavor-
ful here than elsewhere."[26] In short, the concept of mescolanza is as applicable to
garden design as it is to architecture. In both cases, hybridized forms, composite
structures, and combinations of materials are implied. These are also, of course,
defining features of the grotesque.

   One of the lengthiest late sixteenth-century accounts of the grotesque is
by the designer of the garden of the Villa d'Este in Tivoli, Pirro Ligorio. His

article on grotteschi, which was intended as an encyclopedia entry and is several pages long, offers a unique opportunity to compare theory with practice.[27] It suggests the relevance of the scholarly discourse on grotteschi to the imagery of contemporary gardens.

Pirro believed that grotteschi were meaningful and not mere decoration.[28] In his view, "the grotesque pictures of the pagans are not without meaning and are contrived with some fine philosophical skill and depicted poetically, because, as we have been able to see, in these same ancient paintings are subjects of consonance and conformity. They parallel one another like a palinode of answers and harmonies. . . . Wherefore, hieroglyphic letters have been used to signify in small principles various events such as mundane governments, those of the greatest powers, and imperial deeds and commands."[29] For Pirro, grotteschi were like hieroglyphs—an arcane symbolic language, which could only be understood by the initiated. According to him, the figure of the crane, for example, signified "pride of feminine beauty," the stork stood for piety, the dove meant purity, and the swan indicated the century, as did the raven, the stag, and the elephant.[30] David R. Coffin has pointed out that Pirro conflates two contemporary interests here: the recently rediscovered grotteschi and the ancient Egyptian hieroglyphic script.[31] In Pirro's account, the grotesque images in the Domus Aurea and elsewhere were "speaking pictures" or emblems.[32]

The cross-axial Alley of the Hundred Fountains, which links the Rometta to the Oval Fountain in the garden of the Villa d'Este (figure 14), indicates the relevance of Pirro's ideas about the grotesque to landscape design. The middle channel of water was originally decorated with stucco reliefs depicting scenes from Ovid's *Metamorphoses* (most of which are no longer extant). Ovid's poem was—to reiterate—the principal source of the Renaissance garden's imagery and iconography, but the presence of these stories of transformation has additional significance in Tivoli. Pirro quite deliberately relates them to grotteschi in his article. The last few pages of his text consist of a comprehensive (and alphabetical) enumeration of the ancient legends of metamorphosis, of men and women who turn into animals, vegetables, and the elements.[33] The stories have an obvious relevance to grotteschi, the main subject of which is metamorphosis and hybridization, but they are also common in gardens. Pirro mentions, for example, the legends of Polyphemus (represented in the Orti Oricellari and at the Villa Aldobrandini in Frascati), Galatea (depicted in a grotto at the Villa Medici in Pratolino), Diana (to whom a grotto at the Villa d'Este was dedicated), Pegasus (who appears in the Sacro Bosco in Bomarzo, the Villa Medici in Pratolino, and the Villa d'Este), Neptune (statues of whom

ALTRA VEDVTA PRINCIPALE IN PROFILO DEL VIALONE GRANDE DETTO DELLE FONTANELLE NEL GIARDINO ESTENSE IN TIVOLI

Figure 14. Venturini, Engraving of the Alley of the Hundred Fountains, 1691, Villa d'Este, Tivoli. From G. B. Falda, *Le fontane di Roma*. Courtesy of Dumbarton Oaks, Research Library and Collection, Washington, D.C.

appear in many gardens), the Muses (who were portrayed on a mount signifying Parnassus in Pratolino and at the Villa Medici in Rome) and Vertumnus (whose presence is frequently signified by the motif of ivy-clad columns, such as those of the Fountain of Proserpina at the Villa d'Este).

Although in gardens the moment of metamorphosis is not always depicted, these subjects cannot, in general, be dissociated from the idea of change or transformation, which is a fundamental condition of the garden. The flowing water of the Alley of the Hundred Fountains, which streams from tier to tier, underlines this principle. The grotesque is also literally present in Pirro's concept for the alley. Grotesque heads are embedded in the retaining wall of the alley, all spewing water from their mouths (figure 15).

Grotesque heads are omnipresent in sixteenth-century Italian gardens. They take several forms and are deployed in a variety of ways. In the garden of the Palazzo Farnese in Caprarola, for example, several arches are adorned with grotesque anthropomorphic keystones. Similar keystones appear in gardens

Figure 15. Grotesque Head, Alley of the Hundred Fountains. Villa d'Este, Tivoli. Photo: Luke Morgan.

throughout Italy, including a notable group representing the head of Bacchus flanked by the heads of two satyrs within the courtyard adjoining the Giardino Giusti in Verona.[34]

Indeed, the Giardino Giusti is entirely under the sign of the grotesque head. At the top of the hillside, facing the parterres, statuary and fountains is a colossal, ferocious-looking mask, derived from the Hell Mouth in the Sacro Bosco (figure 16). Unlike its source, however, the Giusti head cannot be entered but, instead, supports a balustraded viewing platform that is reached by following the winding paths leading up the hillside. It is perhaps best understood as a gigantic grotesque head or a dramatically enlarged keystone (not unlike the one at Santa Maria Formosa, nearby in Venice, that so horrified Ruskin), which has been detached from its architectural context and made to preside over the garden. Indeed, the anthropomorphic grotto entrance at the Villa Aldobrandini in Frascati, the fireplaces at the Villa della Torre in Fumane di Valpolicella, and the colossal "masks" at Bomarzo are all related to the grotesque keystone.[35]

Figure 16. Grotesque Head. Giardino Giusti, Verona. Photo: Luke Morgan.

Grotesque heads and masks spewing water also adorn fountains, water steps, and water chains in Renaissance gardens.[36] In these examples, water activates the image, representing a range of bodily fluids, from vomit to sweat and tears. When Montaigne saw Bartolomeo Ammannati's personification of the Apennines at the Villa Medici in Castello, for example (figure 17), the figure appeared to him as a "very hoary old man seated on his rear with his arms crossed, from all over whose beard, forehead, and hair water flows incessantly, drop by drop, representing sweat, and tears."[37] This representation of bodily fluids in sixteenth-century garden design suggests another important dimension of the grotesque, one that is exemplified by the Hell Mouth in the Sacro Bosco.

The Hell Mouth is an ambiguous, hybrid structure. Ostensibly, it represents the entrance to the underworld, but it is also a grotto, an outdoor dining room, and an anthropomorphic building carved out of the local rock. The idea that a building has a facade, or face (*faccia* or *facciata*), probably originates with Leon Battista Alberti and had become widely accepted by the end of the fifteenth century. Both Vasari and Vincenzo Scamozzi compare the main door and windows of a building's facade to, respectively, the mouth and eyes of a face.[38] Other writers had already developed this anthropomorphic metaphor further. Antonio Averlino Filarete believed that "the building is truly a living man. You will see it must eat in order to live, exactly as it is with man. It sickens or dies or sometimes is cured of its sickness by a good doctor . . . it needs to be nourished and governed and through lack it sickens and dies like man."[39]

The Hell Mouth is, in this context, an extremely literal version of the metaphor. Its mouth is the door, and its eyes are the windows. As Claudia Lazzaro has pointed out, in his late sixteenth-century treatise on agriculture Giovanni Saminiati explicitly recommended that grottoes should be ornamented with frightening masks and be equipped with interior dining tables.[40] The Hell Mouth may have inspired Saminiati's suggestion, or vice versa: the grotto and the treatise are contemporary with one another.

What does not seem to have been noticed, however, is that the motif of the Hell Mouth is remarkably consistent with the imagery and themes of Rabelais's novel *Pantagruel* (1532), a copy of which Pierfrancesco "Vicino" Orsini owned.[41] Indeed, Mikhail Bakhtin has suggested that the image of the gaping mouth is the real "hero" of Rabelais's comic chronicle.[42] The giant Pantagruel's name means "all-thirsting," and the notable events of his childhood are mostly associated with eating, drinking, and swallowing. In his infancy, for example,

Figure 17. Bartolomeo Ammannati, *Appennino*. Villa Medici, Castello.
Photo: Luke Morgan.

Pantagruel required the milk of four thousand six hundred cows, often devouring the cows themselves as well. He effortlessly consumed live bears as if they were chickens and eventually had to be chained to his cradle so as to prevent him from eating everything in sight. As Bakhtin writes: "All of these feats are related to sucking, devouring, swallowing, tearing to pieces. We see the gaping mouth, the protruding tongue, the teeth, the gullet, the udder, and the stomach."[43]

For Bakhtin, this emphasis on the orifices and interior imperatives of the body is a distinctive feature of what he calls "grotesque realism." He argues that "the most important of all human features for the grotesque is the mouth. . . . The grotesque face is actually reduced to the gaping mouth; the other features are only a frame encasing this wide-open bodily abyss."[44] For this reason, eating and drinking are highly significant manifestations of the "open unfinished nature" of the grotesque body.[45] In the act of consumption, "the body transgresses . . . its own limits: it swallows, devours, rends the world apart, is enriched and grows at the world's expense."[46]

The Hell Mouth at Bomarzo is both a mouth framing an abyss and a place to eat. It invites the participation of the visitor, who would have supplied the missing dimensions of consumption (food and drink)—while simultaneously serving as the object of consumption—and of sound (conversation, laughter, music). The "horrid face," as an inscription in the garden describes it, appears as perpetually ready and waiting to devour anyone who ventures inside, leading to a symbolic death in the maw of the monster. Paradoxically, however, one of the main reasons for entering the grotesque mouth was to eat, drink, and listen to music (as depicted in Giovanni Guerra's 1604 drawing; see figure 12). It is at once, therefore, a bodily grave and an unusual dining chamber.

The Hell Mouth is also deliberately witty. The erudite *détournement* of Dante inscribed upon the lips of the Hell Mouth, "Lasciate ogni pensiero voi ch'entrate" ("Abandon all thought, you who enter here"), is an appropriation of the famous line from *Inferno*, "Lasciate ogni speranza voi ch'entrate" ("Abandon all hope, you who enter here"). Humor is, as Victor Hugo observed, an integral element in the grotesque, but it also had an established place in Renaissance garden design. As early as the fifteenth century, Alberti had approved of the presence of "ridiculous" or comic statues in gardens "provided they have nothing in them obscene."[47] Despite Alberti's caveat about obscenity, in gardens of the following century the humor verges on the scatological in an authentically Rabelaisian manner. At the lowest end of the central axis of the Villa Medici at Pratolino, for example, was a figure of a laundress and a urinating boy by Valerio Cioli, which may have been based on a woodcut from the *Hypnerotomachia Poliphili* (1499). According to contemporary accounts, the boy was designed to continuously soil the washerwoman's laundry.

The representation of bodily functions in the Hell Mouth and Cioli's Laundress group—on ingestion and micturition, respectively—suggests that the two sculptures are exemplary images of the "devouring and generating lower stratum," or of the *material body*.[48] The imagery of both, like their functions, is in the end prosaic. In his discussion of *Pantagruel*, for instance, Bakhtin argues that the gaping mouth is "the open gate leading downward into the bodily underworld . . . [and] . . . is related to the image of swallowing, this most ancient symbol of death and destruction. At the same time, a series of banquet images are also linked to the mouth (to the teeth and the gullet)."[49] Chthonic death and banqueting are the chief themes of the Hell Mouth.

The emphasis of the Hell Mouth on the lower bodily stratum, on eating or devouring, testifies to its grotesque character. The eating here is not just figurative but participatory. Not only is the bodily relation and exchange between the beholder (or occupant) and the building made uncannily explicit in the Hell Mouth, through its literal if colossal anthropomorphism, its function as a dining chamber is instantiated by its imagery. One is consumed immediately prior to participating in an act of consumption oneself in a vertiginous *mise en abyme* of ingestion. The grotesque body is, fundamentally, "a body in the act of *becoming*. It is never finished, never completed."[50] The Hell Mouth exemplifies this idea. It appears as if frozen in the moment of swallowing and devouring, and thus of change.[51] This also relates it to the metamorphic motifs of the garden in general.[52]

The imagery of the material body derives from old popular traditions associated with festivals and celebrations. As anthropologists and historians have shown, in early modern Europe such rituals or carnivals functioned as brief moments of respite from the restrictions of class, gender, and place in which, for a day or two, the established order was turned upside down under the auspices of mock kings, princes, and bishops of misrule. In his study of Rabelais's "grotesque realism," Bakhtin went further and claimed that carnival was not a historically specific social phenomenon restricted to early modern festival culture but constituted a transhistorical discursive mode. Writing in which distinct forms of literary discourse ("high" and "low," for example) are deliberately brought into conflict with one another is, in Bakhtin's terms, "carnivalesque." The Hell Mouth, which is at once terrifying and comic in Hugo's sense, clearly fulfills this criterion.

Subsequent writers have pointed out that the mocking, subversive, and critical activities of carnival were generally tolerated by ruling elites.[53] As carefully controlled and temporary inversions of the usual order of things, they served to consolidate and reinforce class and gender stratification in hierarchical societies. It has been argued that Bakhtin overestimated the critical agency of the carnivalesque, partly as a result of his own circumstances as a philosopher and literary critic in the Soviet Union with scholarly interests in Western culture.[54]

That criticism, however, does not invalidate Bakhtin's fundamental insight: that the functions and imagery of the lower stratum, the prosaic necessities, processes, and desires of the body, form the substance of a neglected literary and artistic tradition of "grotesque realism." Filarete's original suggestion that buildings are no different to bodies in their susceptibility to sickness, and the grotesque Hell Mouth, both foreground the imperfect, material body. To reiterate: this is a mundane body that needs feeding and tending, that is in a constant state of change, and that may "sicken and die like a man."

In summary, the sixteenth-century debates about grotteschi in art and mescolanza in architecture, along with the Rabelaisian theme of grotesque realism, all informed the design and experience of contemporary gardens. One of the main reasons for the neglect of the grotesque as a landscape theme is straightforward. If, as Bakhtin has argued, all grotesque images are "ambivalent and contradictory; they are ugly, monstrous, hideous from the point of view of 'classic' aesthetics, that is, the aesthetics of the ready-made and the completed," then the grotesque can have no place in a model of the garden that reifies a simplistic idea of classical revival.[55] It certainly could not be accommodated to the triumphalist model of the Italian garden promoted by Ugo Ogetti and his collaborators on the *Mostra del giardino italiano* and subsequently enshrined in the postwar historiography of landscape history.[56]

The neglect of the grotesque in studies of the Renaissance garden is not an isolated phenomenon or a peculiarity of studies in the history of designed landscapes. Frances S. Connelly has argued that art history too has been opposed to the grotesque from its inception: "The neoclassical foundations of art history and aesthetics, with their emphasis on ideated beauty and rational inquiry, set up an intrinsic hostility toward the grotesque."[57] Ruskin's appalled comments on the "leering," "bestial," and "monstrous" keystone of Santa Maria Formosa in Venice again provide an example.

The ideological investments of the early art historians and the impact of contemporary events on long-standing disciplinary assumptions are, today, well known.[58] One consequence of the troubled backdrop against which the formation of the modern discipline of art history took place in the twentieth century was the suppression of those aspects of Renaissance visual culture that did not conform to a notion of classical revival predicated upon idealism and rationality. The sixteenth-century interest in grotteschi has certainly suffered this fate. David Summers has pointed out that "*grotteschi* have always been difficult to reconcile with notions of neoclassicism, but if *grotteschi*, their provenance notwithstanding, might be excluded as 'unclassical,' they might also suggest that the revival of the art of antiquity was more than the recovery of monumental sculpture and the study of proportion."[59]

From this perspective, the Renaissance garden can be seen to have fallen victim to the same premise as painting, sculpture, and architecture, imposed retrospectively on the basis of a kind of heroic utopianism in the face of twentieth-century totalitarian politics and their consequences. Garden design, like art, was conceived as an ideal, apolitical, and untrammeled medium of rational expression (though it could just as easily be pressed into service as an archetype of the chauvinistic "rationalism" of Italian Fascism). The sepulchral and unruly forces of the grotesque, like those of contemporary politics, could have no place in this idealized model of the garden. As Peter Gay has observed: "[Aby] Warburg's celebrated formula that Athens must be recovered over and over again from the hands of Alexandria was more than an art historian's prescription for the understanding of the Renaissance, with its painful struggles with alchemy and astrology; it was a philosopher's prescription for life in a world threatened by unreason."[60] The modern lack of attention to the presence of the grotesque in early modern garden design, in favor of an almost exclusive emphasis on the garden as a locus amoenus, Arcadian realm, or idealized place apart, may be a consequence of equally wishful thinking; of a desire, or legitimate need, to represent the Renaissance as a superior cultural moment in a dystopian present.

This is not to say, of course, that the revival of classical culture is irrelevant to the Renaissance garden. Indeed, gardens were the most important sites for the renewed interest in monumental sculpture, or the classical "colossal mode" in the sixteenth century (as is argued in chapter 4). The brief hints about gardens offered by ancient writers such as Pliny the Elder likewise had an important influence on Renaissance ideas about landscape design despite their cryptic character. Rather, the "classic" coexisted with the grotesque in the Renaissance garden. Instead of being antithetical to classical art, as Alessandra Zamperini has claimed, the grotesque is arguably contingent on the classic, impossible without its "other."[61] Connelly makes this point succinctly: "The grotesque is a boundary creature and does not exist except in relation to a boundary, convention or expectation."[62]

Figure 18. Giambologna, Fountain of Venus, installed 1592. Grotta Grande,
Boboli Gardens, Florence. Photo: Luke Morgan.

Giambologna's Fountain of Venus (installed in 1592) in the third room of the Grotta Grande in the Boboli Gardens in Florence provides an example (figure 18). A marble figure of Venus at her bath, depicted in a sinuous *contrapposto*, stands on a mound of rock (*spugna*) and shells, which is installed within a square marble basin. At each corner of the basin a faun is depicted leering lecherously at the nude Venus from below. In contrast to the elevated classicizing figure at the apex of the fountain, the fauns symbolize base desire. The jets of water issuing from their open mouths might be read as saliva or even ejaculate, alluding to "the generation of water in the depths of the earth, through the sexual metaphor of excited male responding to sensuous female."[63] As has been suggested, bodily fluids are commonly represented in grotesque realism, as are the sexual organs and functions of the body. Giambologna's fountain group contrasts the austere, contained, or, as Bakhtin would say, "completed" elegance of Venus, who appears oblivious to the lust that she incites, and the ogling fauns with their distorted facial features, open mouths, and half-formed bodies (Giambologna's fountain recalls other, similarly voyeuristic subjects, such as Susannah at Her Bath).

In one sense, the Fountain of Venus inverts Signorelli's fresco of Empedocles in the Brizio Chapel of the Duomo in Orvieto (figure 19). In the painting, the classical philosopher of the elements leans illusionistically out of his frame, a kind of porthole, to gaze with astonishment—he holds his hand up in surprise—at the grotesque beasts depicted cavorting around him. In the Grotta Grande, the relationship between classic and grotesque is reversed: the beasts now gaze, albeit with lust rather than wonder, at a figure that epitomizes the millennial conventions of neoclassical art.

The interrelationship between classic and grotesque in the garden is thus made clear by Giambologna's fountain. Venus signifies water, while the fauns are symbols of the earth.[64] Together they make up an image of generation rather than procreation, but one that nonetheless relies metaphorically on the language of sexuality.[65] This metaphor, which is typical of grottoes and gardens, implies the interdependence of the two modes. Their relationship is complementary rather than antithetical.

The concept of the grotesque that has been developed in this chapter—as an integral dimension of Renaissance neoclassicism or the necessary shadow of the classical, in the absence of which neither has any definition—also applies to the monstrous. Notably, in his discussion of grotteschi, Cellini rejected the term "grotesque" altogether, preferring "monster."[66] Indeed, the writings of the *trattatisti* on the grotesque in art have a significant amount in common

Figure 19. Signorelli, Detail of Empedocles, 1499–1452. Brizio Chapel, Duomo, Orvieto. Photo: Luke Morgan.

with those of the sixteenth-century teratologists, natural historians, and physicians on "monstrous" births and bodies. If for Cesariano and Barbaro the grotesque was an unnatural deviation from the (classical) norm, for many writers in the fields of medicine and law the figure of the monster was similarly against nature. Yet monsters, like the grotesque, were frequently represented in sixteenth-century gardens—the early modern artistic medium most directly concerned with nature.

On Monsters and Marvels: From Portent to Mutant

An inscription in the Sacro Bosco proclaims that there is no need to travel the world to witness marvelous things:

> VOI CHE PEL MONDO GITE ERRANDO
> VAGHI DI VEDER MARAVIGLIE ALTE ET
> STUPENDE, VENITE QUA, DOVE SON
> FACCIE HORRENDE, ELEFANTE, LEONI,
> ORSI, ORCHI ET DRAGHI

> You who have traveled the world
> longing to see great and
> stupendous marvels, come here, where there are
> horrendous faces, elephants, lions,
> bears, orcs and dragons.[67]

"Stupendous" and "horrendous" creatures appear, rather, right here at Bomarzo. This claim reflects the broad shift that Lorraine Daston and Katherine Park have identified as occurring during the fifteenth and sixteenth centuries. They argue that prior to the Renaissance, monsters and the monstrous races (such as those depicted by Sodoma at Monte Oliveto) were generally thought to inhabit the distant margins of the world—far-flung places, which could, due to their obscurity, be freely imagined. By the late fifteenth century, however, these prodigies increasingly began to migrate toward the European centers, and in large numbers.[68]

For example, although Cornelius Gemma included a conventional list of monstrous races—"men completely wild in appearance and way of life: Fauns, Satyrs, Androgynes, Ichthyophages, Hippopodes, Sciopodes, Himantipodes,

Cyclops"—in his *De natura divinis characterismis* (1575), unlike earlier writers, he stated that "it is not necessary to go to the New World to find beings of this sort; most of them and others still more hideous can still be found here and there among us, now that the rules of justice are trampled underfoot, all humanity flouted, and all religion torn to bits."[69]

Gemma considered the monster to be a sign of divine wrath—a consequence of the schism in the church. For him, monstrosity was both portentous and "hideous." His view, though a common sixteenth-century one, was not, however, universal. As Daston and Park argue, several contradictory attitudes coexisted in early modern Europe.[70] Monsters were simultaneously regarded as terrifying portents, enjoyable *lusus naturae* (jests of nature), and, in a characteristic development of the period, the result of natural causes, that is to say, mutant medical specimens that could be explicated through empirical observation and dissection, such as the one performed on the conjoined twins in the Orti Oricellari in Florence in 1536.[71]

The Renaissance was also an era of exploration. Just as previously unknown plants began to make their way into European botanical collections, so too were new creatures discovered in distant places and represented. Yet even these first-hand encounters did not significantly undermine the period's belief in the existence of both monstrous races and strange beasts. Or rather, imaginative representations of monsters now competed with depictions of actual animals, the two categories sometimes intermingling.[72]

Albrecht Dürer's "half-invented" Rhinoceros—a compelling artistic projection based on hearsay rather than fact—is an example, but there are others, including some from fountain and garden design.[73] Gianlorenzo Bernini's anthropomorphic *tatù* or armadillo (not a crocodile, as is sometimes thought), of the Fontana dei Quattro Fiumi in Piazza Navona in Rome, is one of the most prominent (figure 20). According to Filippo Baldinucci, this creature was simply "a terrible monster" ("uno spaventevole mostro").[74] In contrast, the natural historian Michelangelo Lualdi gave detailed information about Bernini's creature and its characteristics.[75] First he provided its correct name (its species) and location. Next he suggested (approximately) the creature's genus, associating it with the tortoise of Europe because of its similar protective armor. Then he commented on the defensive function of the creature's armor.

Baldinucci's armadillo is thus a prodigy—terrifying and monstrous—whereas Lualdi's is a curious natural specimen. Both readings, the one essentially teratological and the other derived from natural history, were acceptable as late as the seventeenth century. Given the frequency with which these

Figure 20. Gianlorenzo Bernini, Detail: Armadillo, Fontana dei Quattro Fiumi, 1645–1651. Piazza Navona, Rome. Photo: Luke Morgan.

attitudes appear in the literature of the period it would be surprising if they did
not influence the representation of the monstrous in contemporary gardens.

In medieval and early Renaissance teratology, monsters generally appear
as omens or portents, signs of immanent misfortune. The infamous monster
of Ravenna provides a good example (figure 21). The Florentine apothecary
and diarist Luca Landucci wrote in March 1512: "We heard that a monster
had been born at Ravenna, of which a drawing was sent here; it had a horn on
its head, straight up like a sword, and instead of arms it had two wings like a
bat's, and at the height of the breasts it had a *fio* [Y-shaped mark] on one side
and a cross on the other, and lower down at the waist, two serpents, and it was
hermaphrodite, and on the right knee it had an eye, and its left foot was like
an eagle's."[76] Two weeks later, Ravenna was sacked by papal troops. Landucci
commented: "It was evident what evil the monster had meant for them! It
seems as if some great misfortune always befalls the city where such things
are born; the same thing happened at Volterra, which was sacked a short time
after a similar monster had been born there."[77]

Figure 21. The Monster of Ravenna. From Jakub Ruf, *De conceptu et genera-tione hominis, et iis quae circa haec potissimum consyderantur libri sex*, 1445, fol. 51. Courtesy of Wellcome Library, London.

Toward the end of the sixteenth century, however, there were increasing at-tempts to account for monsters within medical and pseudoscientific categories. Ambroise Paré's *Des monstres et prodiges* (*On Monsters and Marvels*), which was first published in the same year that Orsini wrote to Giovanni Drouet about the "new designs" (*dissegni nuovi*) that he had devised for his Sacro Bosco (1573), exemplifies early modern attitudes toward monsters more completely than any other work.[78] It is also a synthetic study that draws extensively on the previous and contempo-rary literature of monsters from Aristotle and Pliny to Pierre Boaistuau.[79]

For Paré, monsters were simultaneously religious and political portents, scientific specimens, and evidence of the creative play of nature. Although he discusses the natural and biological causes of the generation of monsters, he also writes about mythological beasts, such as harpies and marine monsters, drawing no firm distinction between the natural and the supernatural. Jean Céard has nonetheless argued that Paré's treatise is the most sustained sixteenth-century attempt to "naturalize" monsters.[80] In Paré's work, the monster becomes a sign of nature's copiousness and variety, albeit not without a lingering sense of its portentousness. Paré's efforts to systematically categorize the "types" of monstrosity provide a useful starting point from which to investigate the monstrous figures of the garden.

Paré begins his book with a long discussion of the "causes of monsters," focusing on the "human reasons" in the absence of any adequate explanation for the existence of "persons [who] are made with only one eye in the middle of the forehead or the navel, or a horn on the head, or the liver upside down" and those who "are born having griffin's feet, like birds, and certain monsters which are engendered in the sea."[81]

The first "cause" is the "glory of God." Monsters are, in this context, astonishing creations that demonstrate and magnify the artistry of God's works: marvels, in other words. A girl with two heads, who was born in Verona in 1475, for example, is described by Paré as a "new spectacle of Nature."[82] Later in the treatise, Paré elaborates on this point: "God is not tied nor subject to following the order He has established in Nature."[83] The revelation of the (divine) order of nature—nature as model—was an important objective of Renaissance designers that is expressed in the geometry of their gardens. Paré's comments suggest that the comparatively "irrational" spectacle of the monster was just as compelling a demonstration of God's glory as the Euclidean logic of landscape design. Logical consistency was not necessarily expected of divinity.

Monsters, however, could also signify God's wrath. According to Paré, nature especially abhors hybrid creatures, which result from the brutish and disorderly copulations of men and women. He warns, for example, that "women sullied by menstrual blood will conceive monsters."[84] The Monster of Ravenna provides an example, which, like Landucci before him, Paré discusses as a "proof" of God's anger at the warmongering of Pope Julius II.[85] Paré notes that an earlier example of the monster as a portent or sign of some "forthcoming misfortune," from Verona, was provided by a colt that was foaled in 1254, which had a man's face and horse's body.[86]

Paré's next causes are "too great a quantity of seed" and, conversely, not enough. In the first case, the subject may have two heads or even two bodies joined to one another. Hermaphrodites are likewise the result of a "superabundance of matter."[87] The consequence of too little seed may be, in contrast, the lack of a hand, limb, or head.[88] These two monstrous types, the first representative of excess and the second of lack, are fundamental to Paré's thought, and examples of both recur throughout his treatise.

The imagination is also sometimes responsible for the generation of monsters. Paré cites a range of sources, including Aristotle and Moses, in corroboration and discusses a case reported by Damascene of a "furry girl" whose hirsute appearance was the result of the mother having gazed "too intensely" at a painting of John the Baptist during intercourse.[89] This example provides further evidence of both the operation of *decoro* in early modern visual culture and the agency of certain kinds of image. The stealthy return of the nude in European art occurred first within the confines of the bedroom, a site to which, like the private garden, there was limited access. The belief that the attributes of a figure in a painting—the hair of the Baptist's shirt, for example—could be transferred directly to an unborn child via the mother's gaze is suggestive of the complexity of the exchange between the work of art and the beholder that the Renaissance attributed to the act of looking. In Paré's example, there is no firm boundary between representation and physiological effect. There are, in other words, real (monstrous, in this case) consequences to gazing "too intensely."

Next, Paré moves on to more recognizably empirical causes of the generation of monsters. He states that "the narrowness or the smallness of the womb," what he calls the "indecent posture of the mother," which includes being seated or having one's legs crossed for too long, binding the belly too tightly, as well as blows and falls can all lead to deformed offspring. Hereditary diseases and other illnesses can cause dwarfism, gouty children, and even big bellies or unusually large buttocks. Essentially, Paré is of the view that imperfect parents will tend to pass on their defects to their children.[90]

Corruption and putrefaction also produce monsters. Paré gives an example from Boaistuau of a poisonous snake that grew in the body of a dead man.[91] The "mixture or mingling of seed" is yet another cause. Here Paré returns to his discussion of hybrid creatures, which he now says are the consequence of sodomy, atheism, and bestiality, all of these practices being "unnatural."[92] The cohabitation of different species of animal likewise engenders composites "because Nature always strives to recreate its likeness."[93] Paré cites Coelius Rhodiginus, who reports that "a shepherd named Cratain in Sybaris having exercised his brutal desire with one of his goats, the goat, some time afterward, kidded a kid which had a head of human form and similar to the shepherd but the rest of the body resembled the goat."[94] The creature must have seemed a satyr.[95] This monster and others, such as the centaur-like creature that Paré states was born near Verona in 1254, clearly inhabited two distinct discursive realms—the "scientific" and the mythological—not unlike Bernini's armadillo.

Paré devotes the next few pages to "wicked spital beggars" and their various tricks and deceptions. His examples include "a woman beggar who pretended to have a canker on her breast," a man who went about as a leper despite his good health, and, most disturbingly perhaps, "a hedge-whore beggar-woman pretending to be sick with Saint Fiacre's disease, and a long thick gut made by trickery came out of her bum."[96]

The final cause, which Paré again spends several pages on, is demonic magic and sorcery. Devils, witches, and sorcerers are all responsible for the generation of monsters and various maladies, but Paré exhibits some skepticism about the extent of the influence of black magic. He accepts some stories but rejects others and often gives natural reasons instead of supernatural ones for common medical conditions. The sensation of oppression, for example, popularly believed to be caused by incubi was actually caused by indigestion, according to Paré.[97]

The rest of the treatise is concerned with a consideration of monsters by habitat—marine, flying, terrestrial, and celestial monsters are all discussed in turn. It is in this last part of *On Monsters and Marvels* that Paré deals at greater length with legendary monsters and mythical beasts, such as Tritons, Sirens, hippogryphs, whales (which he acknowledges is to stretch the word "monster"),[98] and their counterparts in the air and on the land. He is more credulous here than in the earlier pages, where he is generally concerned to discover the natural reasons or causes for monstrous births. Or, to be fair, he clearly feels obliged to mention several legendary monsters, which he has not himself witnessed and whose causes he cannot determine. This is, again, suggestive of the persistence of several traditions of the monster—popular and proto-scientific. Even Paré found himself unable to omit the strange and exotic beasts that had populated earlier works from antiquity onward. His comments on marine monsters are representative: "It must not be doubted that just as one sees several monstrous animals of diverse shapes on the earth, so also are there many strange sorts of them in the sea, some of which are men from the waist up, called Tritons, others [are] women, called Sirens, [or, Mermaids], who are [both] covered with scales, as Pliny describes them (Pliny, 9th Book of his *Natural History*), without, nonetheless, the reasons which we have brought to bear before, regarding the fusing and mixing of seed, being able to apply in the birth of such monsters."[99]

Several broad categories of monster emerge from this summary. For Paré, as for earlier writers, the monster remains a portent or omen. This sense has actually always been implicit in the word "monster," which derives from the Latin words *monere* (to warn), *monstrum* (that which is worthy of warning), and *monstrare* (to point to that which is worthy of warning).[100] But monsters can also be marvels or natural wonders, signs of the infinite creativity and variety of nature and thus of the "glory of God." The artistic interest of Paré's period in the grotesque and the hybrid is related to this concept of the monster as evidence of God's status as the supreme Creator. Paré's chief contribution was to begin the systematic identification and categorization of natural or physiological causes for the appearance of "monstrosity" or abnormality and deformity in human beings. This did not, however, prevent him from condoning and perpetuating earlier traditions of the monster.

The concept of the monster as a natural wonder or marvel, rather than as a dread omen, is especially relevant to the early modern garden. An important subject of Renaissance landscape design was nature itself, which was conceived as both medium and collaborator. The conceptual links between the garden, the *Wunderkammer*, the library, and other collections and categorizations of natural phenomena are well known. A key criterion for inclusion in, especially, the Wunderkammer, or cabinet of curiosities, was the perceived *meraviglia* (marvelousness) of an object. Renaissance collections often contained strange, hybridized specimens of nature's ludic propensity—the lusus naturae that demonstrated a ceaseless capacity for invention. Paré notes, for instance, that there is little explanation for the "effigies of men and other animals," which sometimes appear in rocks and plants, besides the assumption that "Nature is disporting herself in her creations." Later, in his discussion of "Marine Monsters" he writes: "There are found in the sea such strange and diverse sorts of shells that one can say that Nature, chambermaid of the great God, disports herself in the manufacture of them."[101] Nature is also seen to "disport herself" in the *giochi* and *scherzi*, the paradoxical inversions (the *water*-breathing dragons of the Villa d'Este, for instance) and the illusionistic tricks (such as trompe l'oeil extensions of allées), of the early modern garden.[102] These motifs and devices all contribute to the omnipresent thematic emphasis in historical landscape design on the variety, *copia*, and inventiveness of nature itself.

The Sacro Bosco provides the key example of the relationship between the Renaissance garden and Renaissance ideas about hybridity and monsters. It is, literally, a park of monsters (Parco dei Mostri, as it is now called). But monsters of various kinds appear in other gardens of the period too. In the Boboli Gardens in Florence, for example, four fountains around the Isolotto (by the school of Giambologna but, because of their deterioration, replaced circa 1778 with marble copies of the *pietra serena* originals by Innocenzo Spinazzi and others), depict hybrid creatures with human heads and torsos, short, wing-like appendages, scaly bipartite tails, and snakes, which writhe in their hair (figure 22). They lean into *tazze* in the form of large shells and are shown astride toothy, voracious-looking fish.

These fountains are known as the Fontane delle arpie, but they are almost certainly not harpies. They are male, for a start, but they also lack talons and proper wings. It is more likely that they are invented hybrids with no specific referent, virtuosic demonstrations of the fantasia of the artist.[103] In sixteenth-century Italian art theory, there are numerous accounts of composite or hybrid figures of this kind, nearly all of which recall the opening lines of Horace's *Ars poetica* and accordingly belong not only to the debates about the legitimacy of grotteschi but also to the period's general concern with elevating the status of the visual arts: *ut pictura poesis* (as is painting, so is poetry), as Horace famously wrote.[104]

As early as 1504, Pomponio Gaurico noted with cautious approval in his *De sculptura*: "Even though the human figure is their fundamental object, sculptors are nonetheless moved to compose such figures as satyrs, hydras, chimeras and monsters, such as have never been seen anywhere."[105] Michelangelo's conviction that sometimes it was appropriate to "change the parts of limbs" might also be recalled here.[106] Although it is unrelated, Michelangelo's approval of the substitution of arms with wings in certain circumstances could almost be an appraisal of the so-called harpies in the Boboli.

Michelangelo equates the idea of invention with the monstrous, as if they were interchangeable terms: "This may seem false but can really only be called well invented or monstrous." So too does Varchi when he explains the different meanings of the term *mostro* in his *Lezione una della generazione de' mostri* (1548). According to him, "the description *mostri dell'animo* applied to those who surpassed all others in their works of hand or mind."[107] For Michelangelo, whom Varchi describes as himself a "monster of nature" (*mostro della*

Figure 22. School of Giambologna, one of the four Fountains of the Harpies. Isolotto, Boboli Gardens, Florence. Photo: Luke Morgan.

natura), such manifestations of poetic license require the "proper" time and place, which implies that the artist's decision to depict a "monstrosity" rather than an "accustomed figure" should be dictated by a consciousness of what is appropriate in each situation.[108]

Gardens may have been the *most* appropriate places for the display of invention, fantasia, and the monstrous during the Renaissance. The acceptability of the pagan, sometimes wanton, and often disturbing imagery of Ovid's *Metamorphoses* is indicative of the garden's uniqueness. This point is underlined by the fact that Pope Paul IV's decision to consign the *Metamorphoses* to the *Index of Prohibited Books* in 1559 had no perceivable impact on landscape design. Gardens seem to have been immune to the newly austere atmosphere of Counter-Reformatory Italy, which saw the Council of Trent denounce nudity in art and the consequent notorious addition of loincloths to the nudes of Michelangelo's *Last Judgment* in the Sistine Chapel by "Il Braghettone" ("the breeches maker"), Daniele da Volterra. The censorship of the fresco was begun in 1565, at approximately the same date that Gillis van den Vliete's nude and spectacularly pagan Fountain of Nature was being erected in the garden of the Villa d'Este nearby in the Roman spa town of Tivoli.[109]

The early modern aesthetic doctrine of decorum (*decoro*) helps to explain, to some extent, the lack of effect of contemporary strictures on the garden. According to Pirro, for example, "lascivious things should be used or placed in locations which were not always seen, since they are not worthy of being permitted in every location."[110] His comment does not imply that lascivious things are always unworthy or indecorous but implies rather that they are unworthy in certain situations. Coffin has suggested that Pirro had in mind the passage in Ludovico Dolce's dialogue in which Aretino claims that Giulio Romano's explicit engravings of sexual intercourse are not actually lacking in decorum because they were never intended for squares or churches.[111] Context, in other words, was everything.

A private garden would have been the ideal site for "lascivious" things. If, as was argued in chapter 1, Poliphilo's responses to the gardens of Cythera provide an alternative model for a reception history concerned with the entire sensorium rather than the exclusively visual, then the ardency of his aesthetic rapture, which is provoked by buildings and landscapes as much as nymphs, may be suggestive of the lascivious potential of the Renaissance garden. The *Hypnerotomachia* is, as Alberto Perez-Gomez has suggested, an "erotic epiphany of architecture," and the inflamed Poliphilo is a connoisseur or lover in the etymological sense of "amateur" whose responses to the "voluptuousness" of the gardens he encounters are entirely appropriate in a way that they would not have been in another environment.[112] Arguably, gardens offered a greater degree of freedom, social as well as artistic, than most other sites of the period.

The freedoms of the garden were not, however, infinite. Gardens, like all works of art, reflect contemporary attitudes and sociocultural conventions of thought. Although gardens may have been ideal locales for the display of grotesque, monstrous, fantastic, and even lascivious things, they were nonetheless inescapably constrained by contemporary mentalités. The category of monstrosity, for example, has always been culturally produced rather than naturally given. It requires a normative standard against which the "monster" can be defined and from which it is perceived as deviating. On the first page of his treatise on monsters Paré writes: "Monsters are things that appear outside the course of Nature (and are usually signs of some forthcoming misfortune), such as a child who is born with one arm, another who will have two heads, and additional members over and above the ordinary. Marvels are things which happen that are completely against Nature as when a woman will give birth to a serpent, or to a dog, or some other thing that is totally against Nature."[113] For Paré, the standard was simply natural law, but this notion is, like every other historical conceptualization of nature, a product of its era. "Nature," as Raymond Williams has pointed out, is probably the most complex word in the language.[114]

Monstrosity should therefore be thought of as a discourse that is generated by its multiple contexts in just the same way that normality and "the natural" are discourses. This acknowledgment has had the effect, in recent scholarship, of reorienting the field away from individual monsters to the social and cultural processes that produce the category of monstrosity in the first place.[115] Extending the work of his teacher Georges Canguilhem, Michel Foucault thus sees the monster primarily in terms of the challenge that it presents to law:

> The frame of reference of the human monster is, of course, law.
> The notion of the monster is essentially a legal notion, in a broad
> sense, of course, since what defines the monster is the fact that its
> existence and form is not only a violation of the laws of society but
> also a violation of the laws of nature. The field in which the monster
> appears can thus be called a "juridico-biological" domain. However,
> the monster emerges within this space as both an extreme and an
> extremely rare phenomenon. The monster is the limit, both the

point at which law is overturned and the exception that is found
only in extreme cases. The monster combines the impossible and
the forbidden.[116]

It follows that the monsters of the Renaissance garden, if they are to be understood, need to be situated within the contemporary discourses of not only law
but also teratology and medicine. They are, among other things, artifacts of a
belief system, or "episteme" as Foucault called it, which can be reconstructed
from the corpus of Renaissance treatises and other writings.[117]

Paré's treatise, like Varchi's detailed account of the conjoined twins who
were dissected in the Orti Oricellari, provides valuable evidence of contemporary attitudes toward abnormality, deformity, monstrosity, and difference.
Varchi's conclusions are not dissimilar to those of the trattatisti with regard to
the grotesque. The two discourses, of aesthetics and medical science, clearly
shade into one another despite the fact that one concerns what is appropriate
in art while the other is focused on what is normal in human physiology.

In both, nature and the natural are implicitly normative. Like monsters,
grotteschi were for writers on one side of the debate "against nature" and
thus inadmissible. For others, however, the monstrous and the grotesque were
evidence of the creative play of nature, the "chambermaid," as Paré writes, of
the "great God." Yet, as has been argued, the grotesque is a boundary creature.
Its existence and manifestation is dependent on what can be called (however inadequately), the "classical." In aesthetics, the concept of the classical
has a similar function to that of nature in teratology and medicine. Both are
norms, however implicit, against which, respectively, the grotesque and the
monstrous can be identified and defined.

The Renaissance garden exceeds classical aesthetics. The material body, for
example, its permeability and capacity for extension—the mundane corporeality of the *living* body rather than the static, complete, and reified body, the
body expunged of its functions—is an important theme of sixteenth-century
landscape design.[118] Grotesque realism cannot, in other words, be restrained
by the rules of decorum and rationality. Gardens are perhaps better equipped
to express the duality (or interdependence) between the classical and the grotesque than any other early modern artistic medium.

In landscape history the monstrous figures of the garden have most often
been interpreted as expressions of artistic license (fantasia), as depictions of
the inventiveness and variety of nature, and as allusions to classical texts such
as Ovid's *Metamorphoses*.[119] Additional sources have been identified in Italian

Renaissance literature—Ludovico Ariosto's *Orlando furioso* and Torquato Tasso's *Gerusalemme liberata*, for example.[120] These explanations are persuasive, but arguably not definitive. Many of the sixteenth-century garden's "monsters" feature in other early modern discourses besides those of art, literature, and mythology. Teratological and medical texts also engage with actual and legendary examples of physiological abnormality, from conjoined twins to harpies. In these treatises, the category of "monstrosity," which, to reiterate, is always culturally produced rather than naturally given, frequently has particular symbolic and social meanings. It is likely that these meanings also adhered to the monsters of the garden.

Chapter 3

A Monstruary

The Excessive, the Deficient, and the Hybrid

If the imprecations of beggars and demons as well as the potentially malign influence of the maternal imagination are omitted from Ambroise Paré's survey of monsters, three main categories are left.[1] The first category is the excessive, which includes the doubled and the supernumerary. According to Paré, "too great a quantity of seed" will result in progeny with an excess of body parts. The conjoined twins described by Benedetto Varchi, giants, and hermaphrodites such as Marie le Marcis, provide examples. Paré's second category is the deficient or incomplete. Too little "seed," Paré writes, can cause deficiency.[2] Dwarfs, such as the famous Medici court dwarf Morgante (ironically named after Luigi Pulci's fictional giant), who was depicted by Bronzino and Valerio Cioli, and people with missing body parts belong to this category.[3] The third main type of monster is the hybrid. Paré claims that hybrid creatures are the consequence of bestiality and interspecies copulation. As a result they are literal signs of sin.[4]

Paré's typological distinctions reflect those of other writers of the later sixteenth and early seventeenth centuries. In *The Sicke Woman's Private Looking-Glasse* (1636), for example, the Englishman John Sadler writes that in the generation of monsters "the matter may bee in fault two wayes, by defect or by excesse. By defect when as the child hath but one legge or one arme. By excesse, when it hath three hands, or two heads."[5] The frontispiece of the second edition of the Italian physician Fortunio Liceti's *De monstrorum natura* (1634) also implies that there are three principal types of monstrous body: bodies with too many parts, those with too few parts, and human-animal hybrids.[6] Similarly, in *De conceptu et generatione hominis* (1554),[7] the classic work of synthesis prior to Paré's, the Zurich surgeon Jakob Rüff discusses the inadequate seed that caused a child to be born with only one arm and the excess of seed that resulted in children with two heads or three legs.[8] He also discusses intercourse between species, which generates hybrid creatures.[9]

Many of the figures of Renaissance garden design correspond to Paré's categories.[10] The Fountain of Nature at the Villa d'Este in Tivoli, which was based on cult images of Diana of Ephesus, provides an example of Paré's excessive type. The classicist Gérard Seiterle, among others, has argued that in ancient representations of the Ephesian Diana, the breasts were more likely to be bull's testicles, which would have made the goddess a composite figure, combining male and female attributes (*doubly* monstrous in Paré's terms—both excessive and hybrid).[11] The Renaissance misinterpreted the protuberances as breasts, but the figure remains a powerful or "superabundant," to recall Poliphilo, image of fertility.[12] It is also, clearly, a figure of excess.

Deficient or incomplete figures likewise feature prominently in the repertoire of Renaissance garden design. Disembodied heads, for example, appear in the Sacro Bosco in Bomarzo, the Villa Aldobrandini in Frascati, the Giardino Giusti in Verona, the Villa della Torre in Fumane di Valpolicella, and elsewhere. The grotesque keystones (*mascheroni*), capitals, and other motifs of most gardens of the period belong to this category.

After the grotesque ornament, the hybrid is probably the most common type: harpies, sphinxes, sirens, and other fantastic composites can be found in nearly all important sixteenth-century gardens. Yet in Paré's opinion, mixed or hybrid creatures are especially abhorred by nature and by God, which makes their presence of particular interest.

This chapter focuses on significant examples of Paré's three main categories of monster in the Renaissance garden. It has two objectives: first, to survey the existing literature on each type and, second, to suggest other discursive contexts for a reconstruction of their conditions of spectatorship or contemporary reception.[13] What are some of the implications of reconceptualizing these familiar figures of the garden as "monsters"?

Excess: The Fountain of Nature, or Bodily Fluids

> Monsters involve all kinds of doubling of the human form, a duplication of the body or some of its parts. The major terata recognized throughout history are largely monsters of excess, with two or more

heads, bodies, or limbs, or with duplicated sexual organs. One might ponder why the excess of bodily parts is more discomforting than a shortage or diminution of limbs or organs.

—Elizabeth Grosz[14]

The Flemish artist Gillis van den Vliete sculpted the d'Este Fountain of Nature (figure 23) in 1568.[15] It was originally installed in the central niche of the Fountain of the Organ (also known as the Fountain of the Deluge).[16] According to a contemporary French description of the gardens, statues of Apollo and Diana were planned for the side niches.[17] In 1611, however, the Fountain of Nature was moved to its current position in the lower, northwest part of the garden. In its place, a *tempietto* was erected to protect the organ mechanism, which had been devised by Lucha Clericho (Luc LeClerc) and Claude Venard.[18] David R. Coffin suggests that the extant statues of Apollo and Orpheus were placed in the niches at the same time.[19]

The Fountain of Nature is based on the second-century Farnese Artemis (restored by Giuseppe Valadier in the nineteenth century and now in the Museo Nazionale in Naples) and reflects the antiquarian interests of the designer of the d'Este gardens, Pirro Ligorio.[20] The fountain figure has a similar tower on her head, although, unlike the Farnese version, it is castellated. The tower secures a rigid mandorla-like veil that frames the goddess's head and two small griffins, which sit on her shoulders. Eight rather than two griffins adorn the Farnese Artemis. The d'Este figure wears a pectoral around her neck, closely modeled on the Farnese statue; both works are decorated with a relief scene depicting winged figures and zodiacal symbols. A garland of helichrysum and a necklace with acorn pendants, enclosing the pectoral, are nearly identical. In both statues, small lions decorate the sleeves of the goddess.

The most striking feature of the Farnese and d'Este figures is the serried rows of protuberances that cover their torsos.[21] No known ancient statue of Artemis is depicted with nipples, which adds weight to the suggestion that the swollen, bulbous forms were originally meant as testicles, as Seiterle and others have claimed.[22] Their identification as breasts, in other words, dates only from the Renaissance, when the cult image of Artemis was adapted to fountain design.[23]

In both statues, the goddess wears a tight-fitting, sheath-like skirt. Six rows of lions, griffins, horses, bulls (which further suggests the identification of the protuberances as scrota), bees—some of which are depicted pollinating flowers—and sphinxes adorn the skirt of the Farnese Artemis. The tiered animals of the d'Este figure are too worn to identify with certainty.

Figure 23. Gillis van den Vliete, Fountain of Nature, 1568. Villa d'Este, Tivoli. Photo: Luke Morgan.

The d'Este fountain is not the first or only image of Nature as Artemis from the Renaissance. The personification of Nature as a nude lactating woman or as a woman endowed with many breasts seems to have been invented in Naples in the 1470s. Katherine Park has attributed the new image of Nature to the collaboration between the humanist Luciano Fosforo and the miniaturist Gaspare Romano, who worked together on an edition of Pliny's *Natural History*.[24] Their now lost image inspired numerous subsequent prints, book illustrations, and paintings. The similarity of the fresco of Artemis of Ephesus for the Vatican *loggie* (c. 1518–1519), by the Raphael workshop, suggests both that Fosforo and Romano's invention had become well known by the second decade of the sixteenth century and that the Farnese Artemis exerted a significant influence on artists (though the basic attributes of ancient images of the goddess seem to have remained remarkably stable).[25]

An Artemis appears in Raphael's Stanza dell'Incendio in the Vatican.[26] Lorenzo Lotto and Giorgio Vasari also depicted the figure on more than one occasion.[27] The idea of a "many-breasted" Artemis fountain had, likewise, occurred to at least two other artists prior to Pirro. Giulio Romano made designs of an Artemis figure spouting water from her breasts for the Villa Madama in Rome, prior to 1524.[28] Niccolò Tribolo's *Allegoria della Natura* (1529), which was sent to Francis I as a decoration for Fontainebleau, is an inventive (rather than an "archaeological") variation on the theme.[29]

Claudia Lazzaro has interpreted the d'Este fountain as an image of "the generative and fertile properties of nature," which "are expressed through the nourishing sexual characteristic of the female form."[30] Indeed, Pirro himself described the figure as the "multimammary goddess and wet-nurse to all living beings."[31] The Fountain of Nature is, undoubtedly, a powerful image of fertility. Her capacity for nourishment is clearly signified by what the Renaissance regarded as her many breasts. The animals adorning the lower half of the goddess's body can be understood as sustaining themselves from the spurting rivulets of water, symbolizing milk. Cesare Ripa recommended in his *Iconologia* (1593) that in visual personifications of Benignity artists should show how the figure "presses the milk from her breasts, which many animals drink, because the effect of benignity, together with charity, is to spill lovingly that which she has by nature."[32] This idea was exploited by the Jesuit polymath Athanasius Kircher in the seventeenth century, who made a design for an automaton in the form of the goddess, from whose many breasts warm milk spurted.[33] The fertility of nature is further emphasized in Pirro's source—the Farnese Artemis—by the relief images of bees pollinating flowers.

According to Lazzaro, the lactating breasts of the d'Este figure also symbolize the generation of rivers and streams in the bowels of the earth.[34] Again,
Pirro had written extensively on this theme in his treatise on rivers and water.[35]
In its original location at the center of the Fountain of the Organ, therefore,
the Fountain of Nature would have appeared to initiate the Deluge, which
was intended to culminate in an unrealized statue of Neptune riding a chariot
drawn by four sea horses at the other end of the axis.[36] Two familiar themes
of Renaissance landscape design are present here: first, the animistic idea of
Nature as mother (as well as model) and, second, the celebration and display
of water, which was an essential requirement for the construction of a large
pleasure garden during the period.

The d'Este goddess may be an image of Nature's bounty, but she is also a
figure of excessive physiology. From a sixteenth-century medical perspective,
she would have appeared as a blighted, abnormal specimen of monstrous generation. Pirro's invention portrays, of course, a goddess rather than a human
subject, a point that those who visited the Villa d'Este garden would have
immediately grasped. Yet supplementary meanings and alternative readings
remain. The Fountain of Nature hardly corresponds to the contemporary
conventions of female beauty that govern other representations of women in
Renaissance landscape design, such as the figure of Venus in the Boboli Grotta
Grande, where she appears as Venus Pudica, or at Castello (now Petraia),
where she is Venus Anadyomene. Not only does the d'Este goddess possess
too many "breasts," she also unceasingly secretes bodily fluid. She is at once
more "abnormal," given the excessive protuberances of her torso, and more
realistic, owing to the artist's integration of actual running water. She is, in a
word, "grotesque."

One of Mikhail Bakhtin's main arguments is that the grotesque body is
unfinished or in a state of perpetual "becoming," in contrast to its static, idealized, and autonomous classical counterpart.[37] Bakhtin claims that the grotesque body and the world interpenetrate: "The unfinished and open body
(dying, bringing forth and being born) is not separated from the world by
clearly defined boundaries; it is blended with the world, with animals, with
objects."[38] The d'Este Fountain of Nature clearly fulfills these criteria. It is,
on a literal level, a postpartum figure, whose breasts flow with milk, offering
sustenance to the world and participating in the life cycle.[39] The Renaissance
adaptation of the archaic, hieratic Ephesian Diana to fountain design animates her image, suggesting life, growth, and mutability. Her lactating breasts
"blend" her with the world and its inhabitants, as is implied by the animals

adorning her lower body. To reiterate, however, if she is more lifelike, she is also more physiologically abnormal—what the period would have defined as "monstrous."

The Fountain of Nature is not the only representation of bodily emission in Renaissance landscape design. There are, for instance, several other examples of female figures with overflowing breasts, from the Fontana Papacqua in Soriano nel Cimino to the hybrid creatures of the Villa d'Este. The numerous grotesque heads that ornament fountains and *scale* or *catene d'acqua* can, similarly, often be understood as disgorging or spewing water (for example, those of the Fontana dei Mostaccini in the Boboli Gardens).[40] Pissing boys also appear in several places, from the *Hypnerotomachia* to the Villa Medici in Pratolino, as do river gods. Like those of Giulio Romano's fresco *Proof of the Wool* in the Sala di Psiche of the Palazzo Te in Mantua, river gods are sometimes depicted urinating great torrents of water.[41] Michel de Montaigne's remark about the "sweat and tears" of Bartolommeo Ammannati's *Appennino* in Castello, who clasps his sides in a futile attempt to keep warm, might be recalled here as well.[42] At the foot of the scala d'acqua in the garden of the Palazzo Farnese in Caprarola, jets of water pour from the eyes and nostrils of a melancholy *mascherone* (figure 24), as if it were crying (recalling the Italian expression "piangere come una fontana").

Bodily fluids could have different meanings in different contexts during the Renaissance. Bakhtin argues that urine was both "debasing and generating," through its association with the genital organs.[43] In Rabelais's *Gargantua and Pantagruel*, for example, Pantagruel's urine creates all the medicinal springs of France and Italy.[44] Urine, like other fluids and functions of the body, is an ambivalent signifier that may amount to more than an ironic (and rather juvenile) joke.[45]

An unusual fountain sculpture (c. 1544) by Pierino da Vinci, originally installed in the garden of the Palazzo Pucci in Florence, of a putto urinating through a grotesque mask suggests debasement (figure 25). As in much grotesque literature and imagery, the nose of the mask here substitutes for the phallus.[46] The arresting effect of the figure depends on the deliberate contrast between the innocent glee of the young boy and the lecherous grin of the mask (a satyr?), whose lips are stretched wide by the boy as he relieves himself through them. This mixture of high and low motifs or genres is a standard trait of grotesque realism. Pierino's is an essentially comic image not unlike the fountain figure of a boy in the *Hypnerotomachia Poliphili* who urinates in Poliphilo's face, leading to gales of laughter all round.[47]

Figure 24. *Mascherone*. Palazzo Farnese, Caprarola. Photo: Luke Morgan.

In contrast to Pierino's figure, Lorenzo Lotto's painting *Venus and Cupid* (c. 1520–1540) implies the generative aspect of urine, as an equivalent of male ejaculate (figure 26). Lotto depicts Cupid peeing through a myrtle wreath, a well-established marital symbol, onto the reclining body of a smiling Venus. The picture probably celebrates a marriage, which may explain the portrait-like appearance of the faces of both figures, making it a private joke perhaps.[48] Certainly, the direction and depiction of Cupid's emission implies sexual intercourse and hoped-for procreation.

Most important, the representation of bodily fluids in Renaissance landscape design foregrounds the body as a living, breathing, organic entity, not unlike, in fact, the garden itself. Milk, vomit, urine, sweat, and tears were all depicted in gardens, most often in the medium of fountain design. They are signs of the body's imperfection—its condition as a leaking, weeping, mortal vessel, grotesque in its emissions and operations. The water pouring from the breasts of the d'Este fountain remains, certainly, a metaphor for Nature's fertility and people's dependence on it, but this does not mean that the more ambivalent early modern symbolism of bodily fluids is irrelevant to the figure's meaning.

Figure 25. Pierino da Vinci, Putto Urinating Through a Grotesque Mask, c. 1544. Museo Nazionale d'Arte Medievale e Moderna, Arezzo. Courtesy of Alinari Archives, Florence.

Figure 26. Lorenzo Lotto, *Venus and Cupid*, c. 1520–1540. Courtesy of Metropolitan Museum of Art, New York. Purchase, Mrs. Charles Wrightsman Gift, in honor of Marietta Tree, 1986 (1986.138).

The Renaissance addition of water to the multimammary Ephesian Diana animates her, creating the illusion of a living body in motion rather than a static and reified "classical" idealization. This animation of the figure implies another category of early modern monstrosity—the lifelike image or automaton. Extreme verisimilitude to the point where it is difficult not to infer life was sometimes described as "monstrous."[49] Indeed, by the sixteenth century, the reputation of automata had "been tarnished by a strong association with sorcery."[50]

Antonella Pietrogrande has recently argued that the revival of the image of Diana of Ephesus in the sixteenth century reflects the renewed interest in ancient myths and cults of the "Great Mother."[51] Pietrogrande draws attention to Venturi Ferriolo's cosmological reading (in 2002) of the Villa d'Este garden, in which the Fountain of Nature becomes the latest in a succession of female deities of the earth and nature that stretches back to prehistoric religion.[52] The "pre-Olympian," even anticlassical character of the d'Este "Diana Efesia Multimammia" is thus a consequence of both the historical origins of the goddess's image in remote antiquity and a neopagan sacralization of the landscape.[53]

This interpretation implies an animistic attitude toward landscape features, which suggests that the sixteenth-century garden should be understood less as an outdoor sculpture gallery *all'antica* than as a neopagan anthropomorphic landscape inhabited by deities, spirits, and prosopopoeiae. The bodies of these figures are in a constant state of exchange (or interpenetration) with the encompassing landscape (or world): in some cases they are open and can be explored; in others they pour forth their contents in the form of lactation, micturition, sweat, and tears. The Renaissance garden thus proposes in microcosm that the world is itself a giant body, sometimes literally and sometimes analogically.

Park has demonstrated that in the sixteenth century the old medieval idea of Nature as a dignified, tutelary figure of morality and law was superseded by a humanist concept of Nature as indifferent to human needs—possessing her own indecipherable volition: Nature as "wet-nurse," to quote Pirro again, rather than mother.[54] This new, enigmatic quality is epitomized by the d'Este Fountain of Nature.[55] In a sense, the revival of the image, if not the cult, of a preclassical pagan fertility goddess as a surrogate for Nature as a whole, necessarily entails the revival of an idea of nature as premoral. Equally, if in the embryonic empirical science of the sixteenth century, nature was laid partially bare as it were but nonetheless continued to conceal its secrets, the seminaked but no less mysterious figure of the Ephesian Diana was an appropriate choice for the personification of nature.

In summary, the d'Este Diana can be regarded as a transitional or threshold figure. She is a revival of an ancient figurative type, but reimagined on the basis of the later period's different concept of Nature. The sixteenth century was itself a period of transition from an episteme dominated by the topoi of resemblance, analogy, and the perceived bond between signs and things to one in which empirical evidence, natural causes, and an acknowledgment of the incommensurable gap between words and phenomena ultimately prevailed. It ushered in the shift, not quite an epistemic "break," as Michel Foucault claimed, from an animistic to a mechanistic worldview.[56] In the garden, there is a comparable shift from the survival of an idea of the landscape and the world as a giant body—nature as maternal anthropomorph—to Descartes's comparison of the human body to the mechanisms of the grotto automata that he admired.[57]

The d'Este Diana expresses the earlier view of nature, though without the hybrid sexual attributes of its ancient prototypes. She is firmly female—a majestic wet nurse. Yet, some of the anxiety or indecisiveness of a period in which basic concepts were being challenged and rethought may be present in her appearance of indifference. Nature is yet to become a fully exploitable resource—the grist to science's mill—but she has already abdicated her role as tutelary divinity, lawgiver, and mother.

Deficiency: The Hell Mouth, or Anthropophagy

> Monstrosity is the accidental and conditional threat of incompletion or distortion in the formation of form.
> —Georges Canguilhem[58]

The Hell Mouth in the Sacro Bosco (figure 27), like the Fountain of Nature, depicts a "body in the act of becoming," though it is, strictly speaking, *dis*embodied or lacking a body.[59] If the d'Este fountain and the statues of urinating boys in gardens allude to bodily emission, the Hell Mouth presents an image of bodily ingestion. Emission and ingestion are, however, two sides of the same coin. In both cases, the prosaic functions and necessities of the mortal body are foregrounded. Neither is ideal or timeless but is, instead, grotesque in Bakhtin's sense. The two works also implicate the observer, who is enjoined to partake of the goddess's water or to enter the maw of the Hell Mouth (in a reciprocal or imitative act of ingestion).

There are, however, few other similarities between the two figures. Where the expression of the Fountain of Nature is inscrutable, reflecting the persistent inscrutability of nature itself, the Hell Mouth appears as enraged or (less feasibly), astonished.[60] Physiologically, the d'Este goddess is a figure of excess. The Hell Mouth, lacking a body altogether, is in contrast a figure of deficiency. The one sustains, while the other devours. Indeed, the anthropomorphic appearance of the Hell Mouth implies the theme of cannibalism or anthropophagy, a theme that appears in more than one Renaissance garden.

The identity of the artist of the Hell Mouth, like that of the Sacro Bosco as a whole, is uncertain. Many different attributions have been proposed, from

Figure 27. Hell Mouth, 1552–1585. Sacro Bosco, Bomarzo. Photo: Luke Morgan.

Pirro and Ammannati to, according to a local legend, a group of Turkish prisoners captured during the Battle of Lepanto and brought back to Bomarzo.[61] This problem seems unlikely to be resolved in the near future, although the latter suggestion is almost certainly the result of a historical confusion.[62] In any case, the Hell Mouth is not a unique invention (at least outside garden design), which makes its authorship of less importance than a reconstruction of its visual and cultural sources.

The Hell Mouth belongs to an old visual tradition that has its origins in Anglo-Saxon England. In his study of the motif, Gary D. Schmidt has argued that the image of a disembodied head with a gaping mouth, into which the damned are thrust, emerged in tenth-century Britain out of a coalescence of four distinct visual ideas: hell conceived as an open pit, Satan depicted as a roaring, devouring lion, Satan as a fire-breathing dragon, and the cavernous mouth of the sea monster Leviathan.[63]

Most of these separate images have analogues in Renaissance garden design. Bianca Capello's festa in the Orti Oricellari included a hellish pit of the kind discussed by Schmidt.[64] Three of the gaping anthropomorphic fireplaces in the Villa della Torre in Fumane di Valpolicella are unmistakably leonine in appearance.[65] Dragons likewise appear at a number of sites, most memorably, perhaps, in the garden of the Villa d'Este , where the Fountain of the Dragons belched black water, according to an early seventeenth-century visitor.[66] Sea monsters were also part of the conventional imagery of Renaissance garden fountains.

The new image of the Hell Mouth that emerged in Anglo-Saxon England from these various traditions had an explicitly spiritual purpose. It was intended as an illustration of damnation and the wages of sin.[67] As Schmidt points out: "A sense of orality dominates . . . most hell mouth illustrations; to be damned is to be swallowed—a linking of the spiritual and accordant physical torment."[68] This meaning is preserved in the Orsini Hell Mouth through the deliberately inaccurate quotation of Dante inscribed on its lips. Orality, the gaping mouth, and eating or devouring are also, of course, fundamental to grotesque realism.

The Hell Mouth in the Sacro Bosco clearly belongs to a cultural context different from that of the earlier Anglo-Saxon and medieval illustrations, one in which the threat of the hellish pit or maw no longer provoked the anxiety that it once did. Capello's temporary simulation of hell in the Oricellari and Vicino Orsini's monstrous grotto are both witty variations on a previously deadly serious theme.[69] They retain a vestige of the symbolism of their predecessors but are more startling than they are hortatory. Both are also associated with eating. The Hell Mouth was a dining room, but so too was Capello's hellish pit, once the demons had been banished.

The Satanic, leonine Mouth of Hell is a common motif in postmedieval northern European art.[70] Ernst Guldan, for instance, has traced the theme in Flemish manuscript illustrations and paintings, though he does not mention the relevant fact that Orsini was a prisoner of war in Flanders from 1553 to 1556.[71] It is plausible that Orsini encountered the image in Protestant broadsheets during his involuntary exile. Guldan and, later, Horst Bredekamp both reproduce a sixteenth-century woodcut that depicts a group of cowled Catholic monks enjoying a meal at a table inside the mouth of a colossal demon.[72] The monks appear either unconcerned or unaware that at any moment the jaws of the monster will close and they will be devoured. That this is a Protestant satire is emphasized by the fact that the demon sits upon a papal bull, which serves as a rug. There is a clear relationship between this image and the Hell Mouth in the Sacro Bosco, but the latter was surely not intended to convey the satirical and political meaning of the antipapal print.

The Hell Mouth has Italian antecedents as well. Orsini may, for example, have intended it as a reminiscence of the plaster *boccaccione* (mask) that he had seen paraded through Rome in the annual Carnivale that Pope Paul III reinstated in 1545.[73] This may itself have been a revival of the Hell Mouth of the medieval mystery plays. The Orsini Hell Mouth also recalls the grotesque masks of Italian architectural decoration. These motifs have their probable origins in Hellenistic and Roman fountains and drain covers, and are commonplace in Renaissance garden design.[74] The chthonic symbolism of the Hell Mouth is not dissimilar to that of the central cistern drain cover of the internal courtyard of the nearby Villa Farnese in Caprarola, which was built by Orsini's close friend Alessandro Farnese (figure 28).[75] In his discussion of the cover, Loren Partridge notes: "Traditionally, the wild Dionysian expression and uncontrollable hair on such *mascheroni*, representations of fluvial or marine deities appropriate for the fountains or drains where they were used, signified flux, metamorphosis, and transformation within the terrestrial world, or the unreasoning, instinctual, animalistic side of nature."[76] Though it is not a fountain, the Hell Mouth also suggests flux, metamorphosis, and transformation, or that state of "becoming" that is typical of the grotesque. It is, likewise, an image of unreason, a theme that the inscription makes explicit: "Lasciare ogni *pensiero* voi ch'entrate."[77]

The old local superstition that the Hell Mouth will reveal the details of the death of anyone who stands inside it on a particular day of the year suggests another relationship.[78] The best-known prophetic *mascherone* is the ancient Bocca della Verità (Mouth of Truth), in the narthex of Santa Maria in Cosmedin in Rome (figure 29). From at least 1450, the Bocca served as a test of chastity or fidelity, becoming by the 1800s a general lie detector. As Fabio Barry puts it: "All modern tourists . . . are heirs to an animistic myth that regarded this massive relic of antiquity as a terrible demon who cautioned against perjury on pain of amputation."[79]

The Hell Mouth's range of allusions includes literary as well as visual sources. Besides the misquotation of Dante, Francesco Colonna's *Hypnerotomachia Poliphili* again provides a precedent. In the course of his quest, Poliphilo encounters a colossal head "of terrible Medusa [that] was boldly and perfectly carved, howling and snarling to show its fury, with frightful eyes sunk under lowering brows, the forehead furrowed and the mouth gaping wide. The latter was hollowed out into a straight passageway with a vaulted roof which penetrated as far as the centre. . . . One climbed to this mouth-opening

Figure 28. Grotesque Drain Cover. Palazzo Farnese, Caprarola. Photo: Luke Morgan.

by way of the curling hair, which was formed with unimaginable cleverness and artistry, and extraordinary invention on the part of its maker, so that one could easily make the ascent to the gaping jaws by means of a regular staircase."[80] Although Medusa is the subject, Colonna's description has much in common with the later Hell Mouth in the Sacro Bosco. The latter is depicted as if "howling and snarling." It also has a furrowed forehead and "gaping wide" mouth. In the Sacro Bosco the jaws are entered by way of ascending stairs.[81] Indeed, the *Hypnerotomachia* provides numerous examples of what might be called a "participatory grotesque," in which the beholder has an active role. The analogies between, for example, Colonna's groaning, lovesick giant and the *Appennino* at Pratolino, both of whose interiors can be explored, and, in this case, the colossal head of Medusa and the Hell Mouth demonstrate the influence of the *Hypnerotomachia*; or, at least, its significance as an evocation of the ambience and experience of the sixteenth-century garden.

Another possible literary source should be mentioned here. There is a strikingly direct relationship between a scene in Rabelais's *Gargantua and*

Figure 29. Bocca della Verità. Santa Maria in Cosmedin, Rome. Photo: Luke Morgan.

Pantagruel and the Hell Mouth. In the novel, Rabelais describes how Alcofrybas spends several months exploring Pantagruel's digestive tract, devouring morsels of the meals ingested by the giant.[82] In the Sacro Bosco, upon entering the Hell Mouth the visitor is, like Alcofrybas, swallowed. However, he or she then participates in the act of devouring and digesting (as depicted in Giovanni Guerra's drawing), just as Alcofrybas does. The close similarity of effect—what was described earlier as a mise en abyme of swallowing—combined with the fact that Orsini knew Rabelais's work raises the possibility that the Hell Mouth may be, if not a depiction of the giant, influenced by Rabelais's book.

The Hell Mouth in the Sacro Bosco clearly recalls a wide range of traditions, but it does not belong exclusively to any one of them. Its sources include the satanic jaws of hell of Anglo-Saxon imagery, the gaping mouths of northern European antipapal propaganda, the boccaccione of the Roman carnival, the grotesque masks of ancient and postclassical architecture, and the prophetic Bocca della Verità. In Bomarzo, however, the Christian theme of damnation is undermined by the deliberate misquotation from Dante and the function of the mouth as a novel dining chamber. Similarly, it is unlikely that the resemblance of the Hell Mouth to Protestant prints, if not coincidental, is motivated by shared religious convictions. Even the mascheroni of Italian visual traditions provide only partial precedents for Orsini's invention. Colonna likewise describes an experience that resembles that of the Hell Mouth, but the relationship between the two motifs is, strictly speaking, one of homology rather than analogy. (The experience of Alcofrybas and that of the visitor to the Sacro Bosco are, however, remarkably similar.)

The Hell Mouth is the key example of the theme of devouring and, by extension, anthropophagy in Italian Renaissance landscape design. This implies a broad discursive context that includes non-Western visual traditions and cultural practices, to which the Orsini garden also alludes. In his late sixteenth-century agricultural treatise, for example, Giovanvettorio Soderini compared the Hell Mouth with Indian sculptures carved from living rock.[83] It may not be a coincidence that an inhabitant of Bomarzo, Biagio Sinibaldi, had traveled extensively in India, Ceylon, Japan, and China.[84]

The numerous inscriptions in the Sacro Bosco also imply a global context or range of reference. One of the two sphinxes is inscribed with the following lines: "Whoever without raised eyebrows / and pursed lips / goes through this place / will fail to admire / the famous / seven wonders of the world."[85] The presence of the inscription below the figure is particularly appropriate given that, prior to Oedipus, those who failed to solve the Theban sphinx's riddle were devoured. This monster was half lion and half woman. It crouched on top of a rock asking travelers the answer to a riddle in order to safely pass: "What animal is that which in the morning goes on four feet, at noon on two, and in the evening upon three?"[86] Both sphinxes in the Sacro Bosco closely resemble the Theban sphinx: they have the bodies of lions and the heads and breasts of women. They also crouch on rocks and pronounce, if not a riddle with potentially dire consequences, enigmatic exhortations to the visitor.[87]

The allusion to the ancient wonders of the world is repeated, with greater specificity in an inscription near the colossal sculptural group of the fighting giants: "If Rhodes of old was elevated by its colossus / so by this one my wood is made glorious too / and more I cannot do. I do as much as I am able to."[88] The Orsini *bosco* is, in other words, a miniature microcosm of wonders. The archaic culture of the Viterbo region itself is also evoked in the garden. John P. Oleson has argued that the Sacro Bosco "resembles an Etruscan necropolis with its large masses of worked stone surrounded and animated by uncultivated vegetation" and contains several Etruscan motifs.[89]

The Orsini garden may also gesture toward the New World. Horst Bredekamp has suggested that the giant tortoise symbolizes Central America. He draws attention to the visual relationship between the figure of Fame astride the tortoise in the Sacro Bosco and an illustration of Mars riding a tortoise pulled by four lions from G. Benzoni's *America* (1594). In this image, Mars is depicted protecting Christopher Columbus from the "cannibal sea gods of America."[90] Bredekamp also points out that examples of Aztec art (jewelry, idols, and gravestones) could be found in European collections, including that of Cosimo I de' Medici during Orsini's period at his court in Florence.[91] The Mask of Madness (figure 30), with its headdress, globe, and castle (emblem of the Orsini da Castello, Vicino's family), may thus be indebted to mask sculptures from the Aztec kingdom of Tenochtitlan, examples of which Vicino had probably seen.[92]

India, ancient Greece, Egypt, and Etruria as well as the Aztec civilization of the New World are all potentially invoked in the Sacro Bosco. This is an unusually wide range of reference for a sixteenth-century Italian garden, and may have been motivated by Orsini's interests in antiquity, including the local history of the Viterbo region, and contemporary voyages of discovery. Many accounts of the newly discovered (by Europeans) continent emphasized the foreign customs of its inhabitants, which extended to cannibalism. The longstanding European traditions of the "exotic races" and the "marvels of the East" thus began to intersect with contemporary travelogues.

A good example is provided by the cynocephali. From antiquity to the early modern period, cynocephali were classed among the so-called marvels of the East, the monstrous races of foreign lands. Ktesias wrote the first detailed account of these people in the fourth century B.C.E. He located them in India and claimed that they "did not use articulate speech but bark[ed] like dogs."[93] Much later, in the thirteenth century, the artist(s) of the Hereford Map depicted two cynocephali communicating with each other in the way described by Ktesias. Interest in the legendary dog-headed people of the East had not abated by the Renaissance. The English translator of Konrad Gesner's learned *Historia Animalium* (1551–1587), Edward Topsell, included cynocephali with satyrs and sphinxes in the species "ape."[94] Il Sodoma also included a cynocephalus in his frescoes for the cloister of the abbey at Monte Oliveto near Siena in 1505–1508.

The *Travels of Sir John Mandeville* (c. 1356), which saw numerous editions until well into the sixteenth century and was translated into all the major European languages, includes the following description of the cynocephali:

Figure 30. Mask of Madness with "Aztec" Headdress. Sacro Bosco, Bomarzo.
Photo: Luke Morgan.

Thence one travels by sea to another land, called Natumeran [the
Nicobar Islands]. It is a large and fair island, whose circuit is nearly a
thousand miles. Men and women of that isle have heads like dogs, and
they are called Cynocephales. These people, despite their shape, are
fully reasonable and intelligent. They worship an ox as their god. Each
one of them carries an ox made of gold or silver on his brow, as a token
that they love their god well. They go quite naked except for a little
cloth round their privy parts. They are big in stature and good warriors;
they carry a large shield, which covers all their body, and a long spear in
their hand, and dressed in this way they go boldly against their enemies.
If they capture any man in battle, they eat him.[95]

Like many writers before and after him, Mandeville attributed cannibalism to
the monstrous races (a practice especially associated with the anthropophagi—
that race of men whose heads were in their chests). Cannibalism was also attributed to the newly encountered human inhabitants of the Americas.

Columbus was instrumental in "the creation of monsters of the Latin American imaginary."[96] He had read Mandeville and Marco Polo as well as numerous other accounts of the monstrous races of the East. As Persephine Braham has noted: "When he arrived in the Caribbean Sea, Columbus was convinced that he had arrived in the mythical East . . . he reported encountering three *serenas* (sirens) [on today's Haiti], and described them matter-of-factly as 'not so beautiful as they are painted, though to some extent they have the form of a human face.'"[97]

Columbus also heard reports of cynocephali and anthropophagy from local inhabitants. Bartolomé de Las Casas includes these stories in his diary of the first voyage: "Fourth of November: [Columbus] also understood that, far away, there were men with one eye, and others with dogs' noses who were cannibals, and that when they captured an enemy, they beheaded him and drank his blood, and cut off his private parts."[98] Columbus himself was apparently skeptical of the existence of these cynocephali, but anthropophagy nonetheless loomed large in the European imagination and became a key feature of tales of the Cannibal Sea. Indeed, Philippe Galle personified the entire continent of America as a cannibal woman in circa 1581.[99]

Carlo Ginzburg has drawn attention to Michel de Montaigne's equal fascination with Brazilian cannibals and Italian garden grottoes. Ginzburg claims that Montaigne's extraordinary receptivity to diverse and especially bizarre phenomena, both familiar and foreign, belongs to a specific historical context provided by the culture of the Wunderkammer. More to the point here, however, is Montaigne's comparison of his own essays to "grotesques, that is to say, fantastic paintings whose only charm lies in their variety and extravagance. And what are these essays but grotesque and monstrous bodies, pieced together of different members, without any definite shape, without any order, coherence, or proportion, except they be accidental?"[100] As Ginzburg argues, Montaigne's terms— "grotesques" and "monstrous bodies"—have a "positive connotation. . . . But their aesthetic implications have not yet been fully explored."[101]

It is possible that the Renaissance garden and the New World cannibal have more in common than even Ginzburg intuited. The Orsini Hell Mouth as well as those in the gardens of the Villa Aldobrandini (figure 31), the Giardino Giusti, and the Villa della Torre (figure 32), all occupy a threshold between tradition and projection. On the one hand, they suggest a vestigial fascination with the chthonic symbolism of the monstrous gaping maw. The portal to hell is relocated to the secular environment of the mannerist garden, where its potency as a demonstration of the consequences of sin is, nonetheless, muted.

Figure 31. Grotesque Grotto. Villa Aldobrandini, Frascati. Photo: Luke Morgan.

On the other, the gaping mouth in the garden implies a peculiar transaction with the visitor. Like Alcofrybas in Rabelais's *Gargantua and Pantagruel*, upon entering the mouth one willingly (perhaps even ritualistically) submits to one's own consumption, replicating the process in miniature inside the grotto.

On the level of aesthetics, the effect is grotesque. Indeed, the Hell Mouth at Bomarzo epitomizes Bakhtin's definition of the grotesque body as an incomplete body perpetually on the brink of transformation.[102] It appears as if permanently frozen in the moment of swallowing, devouring, rending, and change, its appetite never sated. On the level of cultural reference, however, the Hell Mouth may allude to ancient and contemporary fantasies about human-flesh-eating monsters, once hypothesized as inhabiting the unknown outer edges of the world (as in Sodoma's fresco), but by the end of the sixteenth century, thought to actually exist in the Americas. Orsini's exposure to Aztec artifacts, along with his demonstrable interest in travelers' tales, suggests another possible context for his Hell Mouth. Without contradiction or constraint, Orsini's curiosity could embrace, as could Montaigne's, cannibalism

Figure 32. Grotesque Fireplace. Villa della Torre, Fumane di Valpolicella.
Photo: Luke Morgan.

and garden grottoes. These two apparently quite different themes are combined in the Sacro Bosco, a designed landscape that makes reference to the visual culture of the Americas. As the European world expanded, the allusions of the garden, as microcosm, followed suit.[103]

Like the disproportionate figure of the Pratolino *Appennino*, and the disorderly Polyphemus of the Oricellari, the grotesque motif of the gigantic anthropophagous maw serves to undermine the putative rational (or "classical") logic and harmony of the landscape. The discordant note of "anti-Renaissance" unreason that these colossi introduce into the design as a whole is also characteristic of the hybrid or composite figure.[104]

Hybridity: Harpies or Gender

> Now what came to their ears but a rush of wind all stirred up by those ghastly wings—and in flew those loathsome, those unspeakable harpies, lured from the sky by the smell of the food. / They were a swarm of seven, all with pale, wasted women's faces, emaciated and wizened by constant hunger, ghastlier than death's-heads. Their clumsy great wings were hideously deformed; they had rapacious hands, hooked claws, a swollen, fetid belly, and a long tail which curled in and out like a snake. / One moment they could be heard flying in; the next moment saw them all snatching the food off the table and upsetting the dishes. And they kept defecating so abundantly that one simply had to hold one's nose—the stench was insupportable.
>
> —Ludovico Ariosto[105]

The harpy is, in some stories, a cannibal.[106] Although in very early Greek myth harpies appear as wind spirits, in all later stories they are associated with food and especially with hunger. In the Argonaut epics, for example, the blind Phineus is terrorized by harpies who "swoop down like the black cloud of a whirling tornado" every time he sits down to eat.[107] Aeneas later encounters them on the Strophades in the Aegean, where they behave in a similar way.

In Renaissance mythography the symbolic meaning of the traditional hybrids such as the harpy is overwhelmingly negative. According to Natale Conti, the "bodies of Harpies exactly expressed the souls of misers."[108] They are, for obvious reasons, often associated with the deadly sin of Gluttony. For the natural historian Ulisse Aldrovandi, the harpy signified rapacity, voraciousness, and filthiness.[109] In art, harpies sometimes symbolize avarice, being "weak with a hunger they cannot appease."[110] In all cases, they are creatures to be feared.

Historians of the Renaissance garden have rarely noticed these negative connotations of the hybrid creature. Lazzaro, for example, observes that the hybrid is an important sign of the fusion of art and nature in Renaissance landscape design, but her account does not address the potential additional association of composites with evil (although it should be acknowledged that Lazzaro's essay is primarily an exploration of gender in Renaissance gardens rather than of hybridity).[111]

Margaretta J. Darnall and Mark S. Weil's ingenious attempt to explain the meaning of the Sacro Bosco is a notable exception. Darnall and Weil associate the three colossal "harpies" of the hippodrome (figure 33) with Ariosto's description of the punishment of the Ethiopian king Senapo (Prester John) for his youthful attempt to discover the source of the Nile. He was plagued by harpies, who stole or defecated on his food every time he sat down to eat.[112]

According to Darnall and Weil, the harpies contribute to the moralizing message of the Sacro Bosco as a whole: the descent into hell, followed by an ascent to heaven, which they mainly derive from *Orlando furioso*: "The message of the tale of Prester John is much like that of the Sacro Bosco. Prester John lives in an earthly hell brought on himself by the prideful sins of his youth, just as Orlando, Vicino, and all men live in hells of their own making. They can be rescued from their suffering only through the miracle of Divine Grace."[113] The harpies are, in this reading, a kind of necessary rather than intrinsic evil: they provide an opportunity for faith to be tested and ultimately to prevail. In Ariosto's story they are banished to hell by Astolfo, who rescues Prester John, a Christian. Darnall and Weil conclude by pointing out that "the Mouth of Hell is at the foot of the Mountain of Paradise in *Orlando Furioso* just as the Mouth of Hell in the Sacro Bosco is in the side of the hill below the Hippodrome and the Temple."[114]

Darnall and Weil develop a compelling interpretation of what they believe is the narrative structure of the garden, which neatly incorporates the harpies and the Hell Mouth into the progression of the story.[115] Two objections to their approach are possible, however: first, it assumes that the garden was organized as a linear narrative, which may be a retrospective expectation rather than one that is found in the Renaissance; and, second, it neuters the harpies,

Figure 33. Harpy. Sacro Bosco, Bomarzo. Photo: Luke Morgan.

making them less strange or disturbing than they might otherwise appear to be, temporary monsters, easily and inevitably dismissed in a garden that turns out to have a Christian, moralizing message.[116]

In his chapter "Certain Monstrous Animals That Are Born Abnormally in the Bodies of Men, Women, and Small Children," Paré states that women sometimes give birth to harpies.[117] One of Paré's sources is the physician Laurent Joubert, who argued that in these instances the harpy was a self-engendered excrescence. But one of Joubert's own sources was literary—Ariosto's *Orlando furioso* in fact—epitomizing the admixture of fact and fiction that characterizes accounts of abnormality during the period.[118] For Joubert and subsequently Paré, Ariosto's story was clearly as legitimate a source as empirical observation; hearsay and myth could sometimes suffice in the absence of natural or physiological reasons for monstrous births. Elsewhere in his book, for example, Paré gives a quite different explanation for the generation of harpies: "The women of the realm of Naples are very subject to this [the birthing of harpies] because of the bad food they eat, for they have from time immemorial preferred to eat fruit, grasses [and/or herbs] and other bad-tasting and unnutritious things, which generate such animals through putrefaction, than to eat good nourishing food, just in order to be sparing and to be elegant and trim."[119] The harpy thus emerges from Paré's account as a real phenomenon with natural causes. Aldrovandi, too, attempted a medical explanation of the harpies' antisocial behavior, drawing attention to the fact that they could not retain their food and befouled everything that they touched. He suggested that these symptoms indicated a medical condition that contemporary physicians referred to as the "dog-like appetite."[120] It is plausible that a sixteenth-century visitor would have approached the representation of harpies and other hybrids in gardens with ideas of this kind in mind. The figure of the harpy transcends myth, where it is, nonetheless, an almost entirely negative and malevolent figure.

Simona Cohen has argued that the "threat of female sexuality to the male victim is reasserted as a leitmotif in legends of the sphinx, the harpy, the siren, and various conflations thereof, from classical antiquity to the renaissance."[121] Indeed, the "monsters" of the Renaissance garden are predominantly female in gender. The harpies of Bomarzo, the sphinxes of Bomarzo and Tivoli, and the figure of Amalthea in Soriano nel Cimino all derive their gender from the Greek myths. The Fountain of Nature in Tivoli likewise reflects the ancient and contemporary personification of nature as female (and grotesque). Even the motif of the Hell Mouth has been associated with female sexuality. In the twelfth century, for example, the mystic Hildegard of Bingen described her vision of "Mother Church" being assaulted by the Antichrist:

> And from her waist to the place that denotes the female, she [Mother Church] had various scaly blemishes; and in that latter place was a black and monstrous head. It had fiery eyes, and ears like an ass,' and nostrils and a mouth like a lion's; it opened wide its jowls and terribly clashed its horrible iron-colored teeth. And from this head down to her knees, the figure was white and red, as if bruised by many beatings; and from her knees to her tendons where they joined her heels, which appeared white, she was covered with blood. And behold! That monstrous head moved from its place with such a great shock that the figure of the woman was shaken through all her limbs. And a great mass of excrement adhered to the head; and it raised itself up on a mountain and tried to ascend the height of heaven.[122]

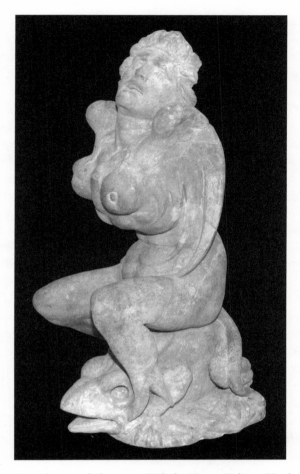

Figure 34. Niccolò Pericoli, known as Tribolo, Harpy Riding a Toad, c. 1530–1540. BLU | Palazzo d'Arte e Cultura Pisa, property of Fondazione Pisa, © Gronchi Fotoarte.

In a lost medieval manuscript illustration of Hildegard's vision, Mother Church is portrayed with a leonine toothy head in place of her genitals, which resembles the portrayal of the Hell Mouth in the Sacro Bosco.[123] The effect is not unlike that of Pierino da Vinci's fountain sculpture for the Palazzo Pucci in Florence, though the tone is quite different. Where the fountain is witty and playful, the manuscript presents a disturbing image of the entrance to hell as a *vagina dentata*.

Why were monsters usually depicted as female? One answer is simply that the monsters of Greek myth were predominantly female. It has been argued by Cohen and others, however, that the sphinx, harpy, and siren reflect male fears about the dangers of uncontrollable female sexuality. The siren, for example, is a seductress before she turns murderess. The harpy's insatiable hunger can, similarly, be interpreted as a metaphor for unbridled lust.

Moreover, the grotesque body is, more often than not, a female body. The porosity, mutability, and openness of the grotesque body are opposed to the completed, static, and closed classical body. The lactating Ephesian Diana and the female hybrids of the Villa d'Este garden and elsewhere thus imply the grotesque in their corporeality and interpenetration with the world.[124]

Niccolò Tribolo's *Harpy on the Back of a Toad* (c. 1530–1540), which was probably commissioned as a garden fountain ornament for the Palazzo Lanfranchi-Toscanelli in Pisa, is suggestive of both meanings of the female hybrid monster (figure 34). In Tribolo's work there is a deliberate contrast between the swollen breasts and open sex of the figure and the pitiful, beseeching expression of her face (which is similar to that of Tribolo's figure of Nature at Fontainebleau).[125] The harpy's face also recalls Ariosto's description of the "pale, wasted women's faces, emaciated and wizened by constant hunger, ghastlier than death's-heads." Tribolo's sculpture is generally suggestive of the Neoplatonic concept of the body as a *carcere terreno* (earthly prison), but here the shackles might be interpreted as explicitly sexual in nature. This harpy seems entrapped by the urges of her body, which she cannot control despite herself.

As Claudio Pizzorusso has observed, the harpy's "zoomorphic extremities appear almost amputated."[126] Indeed, Tribolo's figure does not correspond to the usual appearance of harpies in art. It is, rather, yet another inventive variation on the theme of the harpy in the garden, a subject that particularly lent itself to creative revision. Her wings, like those of the "harpies" of the Isolotto in the Boboli Gardens, are highly abbreviated. In place of lion's paws or bird's talons, she has fins. It is difficult to envisage her either flying or walking, given the apparent inadequacy of her wings and fins, which serves to further suggest her powerlessness to resist the dictates of her sexuality. Whether or not it is a harpy, however, the hybridity of the figure and the overt prominence of its sexual characteristics mark it as grotesque.[127]

Tribolo's harpy is depicted astride a toad, a creature traditionally associated with witchcraft.[128] This implies another potential attribute of the female hybrid. Although the harpy is invariably a foul, rapacious, and evil creature, other composites, such as the siren, appear in literature and myth as alluring temptresses.

Many of the fictional gardens of Renaissance literature, from Ariosto's *Orlando furioso* (1532) to Edmund Spenser's *Faerie Queene* (1590, 1596) are portrayed as the realms of seductive enchantresses and, consequently, have negative connotations not unlike those that adhered to automata. In his classic study of the sorceress Acrasia's "Bower of Bliss" in Spenser's poem, for example, Michael Leslie emphasizes the precedent of the Italian enchantresses Alcina in *Orlando furioso* and Armida in Torquato Tasso's *Gerusalemme liberata* (1581).[129] In all three cases, the effect of the sorceresses' magic arts is to seduce, stupefy, and emasculate the hero. The garden is revealed in these epic poems to be a false paradise, a charming but perilous illusion, which has the Circean propensity to ensnare and entrap the unwary or the weak. The poems thus further problematize the received idea of the garden as a straightforward locus amoenus (pleasant place). The association of the artificial garden with a malevolent sorceress certainly contrasts with other, more enthusiastic appraisals of the imitation of nature by art (by Claudio Tolomei, for example) in landscape design of the period.[130]

These ideas from contemporary literature, like those to be found in medical and teratological treatises on abnormality and monstrosity, must have informed the responses of visitors to gardens during the Renaissance. They also influenced design. The inscription in the Sacro Bosco—"You who have traveled the world longing to see great and stupendous marvels, come here, where there are horrendous faces, elephants, lions, bears, orcs and dragons"— may refer to the passage in Tasso's *Gerusalemme liberata* in which Rinaldo is tempted to linger on an island that is a "love trap" conjured by the sorceress Armida.[131] Annibal Caro's suggestions about appropriate grotto imagery are also relevant here. Caro thought that the sorceress "Circe turning the men under Ulysses into animals" would be an ideal subject.[132]

It is clear that there are other possibilities of meaning and signification in the garden besides the paradisiacal or Arcadian. The postpartum goddess of nature of the Villa d'Este implies both the grotesque and an animistic view of the earth as a living body. The Orsini Hell Mouth is suggestive not only of the grotesque but also of unreason, cannibalism, and the New World. The hybrid figures of the garden might plausibly have recalled the evil female creatures of Greek myth or, more generally, the literary motif of the enchanted but false bower, which the hero must somehow resist (like Ulysses, who stopped up his ears with wax and tied himself to the mast of his ship so as not to succumb to the song of the sirens).

All of these figures are the gendered products of an unequal society. The hybrid female monster and the sorceress, in particular, are indicative of male anxieties about the sexuality of women. During the period, female nature was frequently opposed to male culture.[133] The binary implies what was perceived to be a fundamental difference between men and women. If men were defined by their rationality and capacity for logical, even transcendent thought, women were, not unlike Tribolo's harpy, creatures of sensuality, emotion, and the body. According to Mary D. Garrard, the necessary application of reason (or *disegno*) to the task of laying out a garden so as to produce a new order thus becomes a metaphorical exploitation of the female body.[134] Thought prevails over unthinking, irrational matter; mind exploits its corporeal opposite. Garrard claims: "It is true that the notion of the metaphoric interdependency of a gendered art and nature flourished in garden theory as it did not in Renaissance art theory. Still, it is art that is calling the shots. If, as Lazzaro claims, nature is the 'female voice in gardens,' its protagonist, then it is the same kind of female protagonist we find in Cellini's Medusa and Vasari's Diana of Ephesus—passive and captive, a masculinist creation. As John Shearman noted, 'the sixteenth-century garden is more obviously a product of man than of nature . . . it has no life that he does not give it.'"[135] But this reinstates the historiographical fallacy that in the Renaissance garden art triumphed over nature. Garrard's views recall those of Ugo Ojetti as well as Shearman. As Lazzaro herself writes in the article that Garrard cites, "Twentieth-century writers selected the words of one Renaissance sculptor [Baccio Bandinelli] intimating that architecture was superior to planting, to embody the essence of the Renaissance garden, while they ignored countless other comments."[136]

The status of gender in the Renaissance landscape is complex. On the one hand, although the harpies, sirens, and sphinxes of the garden were undoubtedly expressions of male anxieties about women, they were surely not always "passive and captive." Tribolo's harpy is enslaved by her urges, which may reflect masculinist assumptions about women, but she is a threatening figure whose presence is disruptive and disturbing. It is difficult to imagine her submitting to the imposition of any kind of order or control, let alone that of (male) culture. The harpy is a figure of disorder, uncontrollable urges and, ultimately, evil. The fact of her gender is important for what it reveals about male prejudices, but there is, at least in Tribolo's rendition, no reassuring suggestion of her eventual containment and submission. The harpy signifies bestiality and chaos.

On the other hand, although, as Garrard observes, some Renaissance images of Diana of Ephesus imply the dominance of art and male culture, the concept of nature implied by the Ephesian Diana in Tivoli and the giants of the Renaissance garden suggest something different. The archaic, hieratic appearance of *La Natura* evokes the unknowable goddess, upon whom all depend, rather than an idea of nature as a yielding, exploitable, female body; nature as enigmatic wet nurse rather than pliable courtesan.

Pietrogrande has claimed, "There is a clear connection between the Mediterranean Great Mother, and expert in the *pharmaka* (cures and poisons) and in an all-feminine pharmacopeia drawn from nature, and the sorceresses-enchantresses of literature, the mistresses of splendid gardens."[137] This is, surely, one of the guises of the goddess in Tivoli: the d'Este figure also belongs to the literary tradition of the enchantress.

La Natura thus unites in her person several distinct ideas about nature, gardens, and the female. She is suggestive of the fundamental dependence of men and women on nature; of the mysteries of natural processes, which, on the cusp of an "epistemic shift," remained opaque; of an animistic attitude toward the landscape, conceived of as a living organism; and of the enchanted bowers of epic poetry—ideal landscapes under the sign of the sorceress. In none of these images is female nature depicted as "bound," suppressed, or exploited by male reason. Rather, nature exceeds the mind's capacity to understand. If the harpy's agency derives from its excessive appetites and uncontrollable urges, the agency of nature, personified in the garden as the Ephesian Diana, derives from an enigma. Both are forms of power.

The frontispiece of Fortunio Liceti's *De luminus natura et efficentia libri tres* (1640) shows a woman with a physique approximately similar to that of the d'Este Fountain of Nature, but she now appears as a piteous exhibit (figure 35).[138] She is denuded not only of her garments but also of her attributes—emblems of her now forsaken power. She stands in a tentative *contrapposto* on a pedestal. Depicted around her, leering and grimacing, are several monstrous and grotesque figures—the subjects of Liceti's book. To her right, an imperious male figure, Liceti's surrogate, dramatically draws back a curtain to reveal Nature as she really is. If, therefore, in the garden of the Villa d'Este, Nature, though partially revealed, nonetheless retains her enigmatic majesty, a hundred years later, she has indeed become just another specimen of abnormality. Her physiology, which is, however, significantly reduced (she now has only five supernumerary breasts), renders her pathetic—a poor creature whose condition will be submitted to analysis. For Liceti, nature concealed mechanical causes rather than numinous secrets. By the mid-seventeenth century, in other words, Pirro's "multimammary goddess and wet-nurse to all living things" has become a resource for analysis and exploitation, as Garrard and others have argued, but this does not apply to the same degree to the Renaissance garden.

F. LICETVS
DE
MONSTRIS.
H. Bary sculp.

Figure 35. Fortunio Liceti, Frontispiece from *De luminus natura et efficientia libri tres,* 1640. Courtesy of Wellcome Library, London.

Chapter 4

"Rare and Enormous Bones of Huge Animals"

The Colossal Mode

When he noticed me he asked me:
"Where have you come from Alcofrybas?"
And I replied,
"From your gorge, my Lord."
"And how long have you been in there?" he asked.
"Since you set out against the Almyrodes," I said.
"That was more than six months ago!" he said. "How did you manage? What did you eat? What did you drink?"
"My Lord," I replied, "the same as you. I exacted a toll on the most delicate morsels that passed through your lips."
—Rabelais, *Gargantua and Pantagruel*

Alcofrybas's account of life inside the giant Pantagruel's gullet recalls Poliphilo's exploration of the viscera of the lovesick colossus in Francesco Colonna's *Hypnerotomachia Poliphili*, with an important difference.[1] In Rabelais's novel, the interior of the giant is a complete landscape in itself. After traveling for "two leagues" across Pantagruel's tongue, for example, Alcofrybas wanders around "as one does in Sancta Sofia in Constantinople," encountering mountains (his teeth), meadows, forests, and cities the size of Lyons or Poitiers.[2] There are even gardens. Alcofrybas enjoys four months among the "countless summer-houses in the Italian style scattered over fields full of delights."[3]

Alcofrybas's comparison of the vast cavity of Pantagruel's mouth with the Hagia Sofia also provides a literal example of Filarete's analogy between bodies and buildings. In *Gargantua and Pantagruel,* "the building is truly a living man."[4] The giant's internal proportions, however, clearly exceed architectural plausibility. More than twenty-five inhabited kingdoms are located inside his body, not to mention deserts, oceans, and mountain ranges.[5]

Rabelais inverts the traditional relationship between giants and the natural environment. Pantagruel internalizes his environment or, more precisely, his interior constitutes another—alternative—world.[6] More commonly, as Susan Stewart has observed, "the gigantic becomes an explanation for the environment, a figure on the interface between the natural and human. Hence our words for the landscape are often projections of an enormous body upon it: the mouth of the river, the foot-hills, the fingers of the lake, the heartlands, the elbow of the stream. The gigantic reading of the landscape is often supplemented in folklore by accounts of causality."[7] In the Renaissance garden, giants were explicitly associated with the natural environment, especially local landscape features, which were frequently personified as anthropomorphic figures. Giambologna's colossal *Appennino* for the Villa Medici in Pratolino, for example, transforms the mountain range into a crouching giant. Bartolomeo Ammannati's earlier and more melancholy version of the theme in Castello personifies the Apennines as a shivering man who clasps his sides in a futile attempt to keep warm. The many river gods of the sixteenth-century garden also typically personify local tributaries. Adjacent to the Rometta in the garden of the Villa d'Este in Tivoli, for instance, a weathered figure of the river Anio (Aniene) is supported by an unusual *Appennino,* depicted as a beardless young man. Below him, a more conventional reclining image of the Tiber appears in a grotto (figure 36).

The ancient identification of landscape features as the fragments, effluence, or imprint of a giant's body on the environment is in this way recalled in the Renaissance garden. If it was once believed that the landscape was formed by giants, in the sixteenth-century garden the landscape was reimagined as inhabited by, or even composed of giants. (In his analysis of Giambologna's *Appennino,* Michael W. Cole writes, evocatively, that at Pratolino "nature itself has generated a giant, using water that rose, fell, and congealed into its form.")[8] The close association of the giant with nature would have made it an appealing motif to designers fascinated by the threshold and exchange between the natural and the artificial. As Stewart writes, the giant is "a figure on the interface between the natural and the human," and the same applies to the

Figure 36. Anio, Appennino, and Tiber. Villa d'Este, Tivoli. Photo: Luke Morgan.

"third nature" of the early modern garden. Both occupy the interstice between two categories.

It is not surprising, therefore, that the garden was an important site for the sixteenth-century revival of the colossal sculptural mode. At least fifty colossal statues or sculptural groups were made in Italy between 1500 and 1600, many of which were intended for or ended up in gardens.[9] Classical literary references to ancient colossi, such as Pliny's descriptions of the Colossus of Rhodes and the giant bronze figure of Nero that once presided over the Domus Aurea in Rome, as well as the extant remains of ancient statuary, especially the Quirinale *Dioscuri* and the Capitoline collection of giant figures and fragments, provided equal inspiration to sixteenth-century artists.[10]

With certain notable exceptions, however, such as Michelangelo's *David*, Benvenuto Cellini's *Perseus*, and Giambologna's *Rape of the Sabines*, the Renaissance interest in colossi has received little scholarly attention. Indeed, Virginia Bush's doctoral thesis, which she completed in 1967, remains the only dedicated study despite the fact that, as Cellini claimed, the construction of a colossus was regarded as "the most difficult and admirable task of all."[11]

Giambologna was arguably the most accomplished and successful sculptor of colossi during the second half of the sixteenth-century. His *Appennino* (figure 37) realizes, finally, the ancient dream of Alexander the Great's architect Dinocrates—to carve a mountain into the shape of a man—and can consequently be regarded as the climax of the Renaissance revival of the colossal tradition.[12] Yet the *Appennino* is a more ambivalent figure than has been acknowledged. It may be gargantuan in comparison with conventional sixteenth-century sculpture, but it amounts, nonetheless, to a miniaturization of its subject—the mountain range.[13] Also, it has little in common with the triumphant supermen of ancient sculpture or those devised by Michelangelo, Bartolommeo Ammannati, Baccio Bandinelli, and Cellini. The attitude of the *Appennino* seems weary and melancholic, which may allude to the great age, in geological time, of the mountain range (in addition to what Una Roman d'Elia has described as the topos of the "suffering landscape").[14]

The *Appennino* is not alone in its ambivalence. Giants have always been antinomic figures. Rabelais's Pantagruel fondly refers to Alcofrybas as his "noble comrade," but he is also responsible for catastrophic outbreaks of plague when his body emits deadly, noxious gases after he eats a meal smothered in garlic sauce. Pantagruel combines two traditional types of the giant: the giant as an anthropomorphic hero and the giant as a threatening, even hostile figure.[15] Both appear in the Renaissance garden, personified, for example, as Hercules and the Cyclops Polyphemus.[16] The latter's predilection for anthropophagy is a major motif of the Renaissance garden. The colossal grotesque mouths in Bomarzo, Frascati, Verona, and Fumane di Valpolicella all indirectly recall Polyphemus.[17] These variations of imagery and meaning in the representation of giants are epitomized by three key figures of early modern garden design: the Castello Hercules, an embodiment of the idea of the giant as a benevolent manlike hero, the Oricellari Polyphemus, a malevolent figure of debauchery and evil, and the Pratolino *Appennino*, an anthropomorphic reinstatement of the ancient giants of the landscape.[18]

This chapter argues that the giants of the sixteenth-century garden belong to more than one tradition. They clearly provide further evidence of the period's revival of classical artistic modes and genres. It is undeniable, for example, that the *Appennino* was informed by classical accounts of colossi. Yet, from the point of view of a reception history of the garden, figures such as the *Appennino* may also have evoked the many popular legends of the giants. Just

Figure 37. Giambologna, *Appennino*, 1579. Villa Medici (now Demidoff), Pratolino. Photo: Luke Morgan.

as, therefore, the monsters of the Renaissance garden would potentially have been understood by contemporary beholders in medical, legal, and natural historical terms, so too may people have responded to the giants on the basis of received ideas from what would today be called "popular culture." The giants of the garden thus suggest two interpretative frameworks: the art historical and the folkloric. The *Appennino* may be a colossus in the *aesthetic* sense, but it is also a giant in the *popular* sense.

The Colossus

In garden design, as in other mediums, there is a difference between giant representations and the representation of giants. In the Sacro Bosco in Bomarzo, for example, sirens, nymphs, and other figures are "gigantified" or depicted as giants, but generally not for established historical, literary, or mythological reasons.

Figure 38. Bartolomeo Ammannati, Hercules and Antaeus, 1559–1560. Villa
Medici, Castello. Photo: Luke Morgan.

In contrast, the figure of Hercules squeezing the life out of Antaeus in the garden of the Villa Medici in Castello (figure 38) is, like Giulio Romano's fresco of Jupiter defeating the giants in the Palazzo del Te in Mantua, a familiar image of gigantomachia.[19] Antaeus, the son of Poseidon and Gaea, was a Libyan half-giant whom Hercules defeated by lifting into the air to prevent him acquiring strength from contact with the earth. In Castello, both figures are identifiable as giants or, at least, as gigantic men, which accounts for their scale.[20] Colossal personifications of landscape features, such as rivers and mountains, are related to this group: the giant figure of the river god or man mountain logically evokes the scale of the subject in the environment at large.

Another point needs clarifying. Novelli's Polyphemus and Giambologna's *Appennino* are unambiguously colossal in scale, but Ammannati's Hercules is significantly smaller. What, then, constituted a colossus (*colosso*) in early modern Italy?

Pliny the Elder's use of the term was particularly important for the Renaissance. In *I commentarii* (c. 1447), for example, Lorenzo Ghiberti quoted Pliny's remark "We see enormously huge statues devised, what are called Colossi, as large as towers."[21] Leon Battista Alberti, in his *De statua*, imagined colossal statues two hundred feet high or as big as mountains; a scale that Costantino de' Servi emulated when he proposed a *gigante Notuno* (giant Neptune) for Prince Henry's Richmond Palace on the Thames in London more than a century later.[22]

During the sixteenth century, the word *colosso* was used with greater precision. In 1504, for example, Pomponio Gaurico defined three categories of over-life-size statue: "large or 'majestic' (up to one and a half times life size), larger (up to twice life size), and largest or 'colossal' (three times life size)."[23] For Cellini a colossus was, likewise, at least three times larger than life.[24] By this measure, the Hercules would be "majestic" compared with the "colossal" *Appennino* and Polyphemus. Gaurico himself states that this size is the most appropriate for Hercules, Theseus, and other "heroes."[25] As Bush points out, however, "by the latter part of the Cinquecento the term colossus was applied to many statues less than three times life size."[26] Gian Paolo Lomazzo, for instance, considered statues twice the size of life to be colossi.[27] Most of the giants discussed in this chapter are at least this large.

In Alberti's opinion, an *istoria* (history painting) was a more impressive technical achievement than a *colosso*—skillful composition being of greater value than sheer scale.[28] However, most sixteenth-century writers on the subject acknowledged the unique challenges of the colossus as worthwhile in their own right. To sculpt a giant was, of course, to emulate and compete with the ancients. Cellini, for example, believed that colossal sculpture was the most "difficult and miraculous" of all the works of the past ("opera la più difficile e la mirabile di tutte le passate"); difficulty being a virtue in the sense that the task of the artist was to overcome problems with apparent ease or aplomb.[29] For Vasari and other writers, the colossal statue or statuary group also embodied *gran maniera* (grand manner).[30] These two ideas—the perceived value of difficulty and prestige of large scale—inform sixteenth-century theories of and responses to the colossal image. They are as relevant to the giants of the Renaissance garden as they are to the colossal statuary of buildings and civic spaces.[31]

Many of the colossi of the sixteenth-century garden are personifications of natural forms and features. In these examples there is an unusually direct relation between the size of the figure and the size of the motif. The colossal mode of the river gods of Caprarola, Bagnaia, Tivoli, Pratolino, and Bomarzo is easily explicable as an allusion to the size and importance of local water sources.[32] These giant personifications of the Tiber, Arno, Mugnone, and other rivers also symbolize the importance of an abundant water supply to landscape design. Sixteenth-century garden visitors were particularly interested in the volume of water and the effects that it made possible. Michel de Montaigne, for example, remarks on the "gushing of an infinity of jets of water" in the garden of the Villa d'Este in his *Travel Journal* of 1580–1581.[33] He makes a point of comparing the waterworks of gardens that he visits. According to him the Villa d'Este was built in deliberate rivalry of Pratolino: "As to the richness and beauty of the grottoes, Florence [i.e., Pratolino] is infinitely superior; as to abundance of water, Ferrara [by which he means the garden in Tivoli of Ippolito d'Este, cardinal of Ferrara]; in variety of sports and amusing mechanisms derived from water, they are equal, unless the Florentine has a little more elegance in the arrangement and order of the whole body of the place; Ferrara excels in ancient statues, and in the palace, Florence."[34] Although Montaigne does not mention the organic elements of the gardens in Tivoli and Pratolino, these too would have required significant quantities of water for their ongoing viability.

The *Appennino* may also have started life as a colossal river god. Herbert Keutner has argued that the two leading modern historians of Pratolino—Webster Smith and Luigi Zangheri—omitted publishing sixteenth-century documents in which Giambologna's figure is referred to as "fiume Nilo" (river Nile).[35] Keutner believes that it is an open question whether Giambologna has represented a "Dio montagna o un Dio fluviale" (mountain god or a river god).[36] The *Appennino* may not recline as was usual in the representation of river gods, but the artist had already experimented with unusual poses in his designs for the figures of the Euphrates, Ganges, and Nile that ornament the shaft of the Fountain of Oceanus in the Boboli Gardens in Florence. The twisting pose of the *Appennino* is, in fact, indebted to the pose of one of these river gods. If the personified mountain is actually the Nile, then the "monstrous head" (as Lazzaro calls it) that it presses down upon could be identified as a crocodile or even, Keutner claims, a hippopotamus.[37] The Nile, as a generalized symbol of fertility and abundance, would not necessarily be out of place in the garden at Pratolino.[38] It is represented as one of the river gods of the Fontana dei Giganti in the garden of the Villa Lante in Bagnaia, for instance.

This is an ingenious argument, but it does not entirely convince. The evidence indicates that whatever ideas Giambologna may have entertained at the beginning of the project, his colossus ultimately became a man mountain rather than a river god.[39] Keutner's interpretation does, however, draw attention to the "monstrous head." Keutner may not be right about the identity of Giambologna's figure, but his attempt to be more specific than other historians about the identity of the head surely is.

As Keutner points out, the head that the *Appennino* pushes down upon is only ever described as "the Monster."[40] It must, however, have a more precise significance than this. Giambologna's concept for the colossal ensemble relies upon personification. If, therefore, the gigantic figure of a crouching man is a personification of the Apennines, it seems likely that the problematic head is also a personification. Indeed, the *Appennino* may refer to the many stories in which giants created the landscape prior to the advent of people.

Giambologna's colossus might, from this perspective, be interpreted as a primeval, demiurgic giant depicted in the act of creation. The monstrous head would then be a personification of the landscape itself—still inchoate, and spewing water as it acquires definition and emerges from the primordial ooze.

Alternatively, the head may depict the source of the landscape's rivers and streams in the mountain range. Notably, the *Appennino* and the artificial lake before it (into which water pours from the monster's mouth) act as a reservoir, providing water to the rest of the garden at Pratolino. The figure can therefore also be interpreted as a literal, rather than as an allegorical or prosopopeic, representation of the Apennine mountain range as a water source, serving the peninsular as a whole.

The Pratolino colossus is, in summary, a personification of the Apennines, an identification that is strengthened by the original presence of a sculpted mountain behind the figure (the dragon by Giovan Battista Foggini that today stands in its place is a later alteration dating from 1690). It is also a personification of place, albeit a mountain range rather than a river—a monumental genius loci. In addition, it is clearly indebted to the classical tradition of the colossus, from Dinocrates's project for a city constructed in the shape of a man to Michelangelo's related dream of an anthropomorphic mountain.

The Giant

Sixteenth-century artists may have relished the artistic challenge and the opportunity to compete with the ancients that a colosso offered, but from the point of view of the audience for this kind of statuary, colossi also potentially evoked the folkloric tradition of stories about the legendary actions of the giants. The figure of the giant is obviously not unique to the field of art and architecture.

Gargantua and Pantagruel, for example, are indebted to long-standing popular traditions, such as those of the Italian heroic-comic giant (Luigi Pulci's Morgante, a "good" giant, is perhaps the best-known example),[41] the permanent "town giants" of the medieval period, and especially the "popular-festive giants" of fairs, carnival parades, and Corpus Christi processions.[42] According to Mikhail Bakhtin, "We may conjecture that the popular-festive giants were the most important in his [Rabelais's] eyes. They enjoyed immense vogue, were familiar to everyone, and were saturated with the free atmosphere of the marketplace. They were closely connected with the popular conception of material-bodily wealth and abundance. The image and atmosphere of the giant appearing at the fairs doubtless contributed to the shaping of the gargantuan legend of the 'Great Chronicles.' The influence of popular giants of fairs and marketplaces on the first two books of Rabelais' novel is quite obvious."[43] Bakhtin notes that in *The Great Chronicles of Gargantua*, a 1532 chapbook that perpetuates an oral tradition in print, the emphasis is firmly on the giant's appetite and capacity to devour enormous amounts of food. Rabelais, Bakhtin argues, exploited the "strong grotesque bodily character" of his source in his own work. He also claims that the legend of the giants has always presented "an essentially grotesque image of the body."[44]

Gargantua and Pantagruel are, in Bakhtin's reading, popular giants of revelry and vast but ultimately unthreatening appetites—comedic figures of conviviality and excess. The infant Pantagruel's consumption of thousands of cows and bears or his later devastating bodily emissions are suggestive of the giant's body as unruly and imperfect, not unlike an ordinary human body. The body of the giant thus exemplifies Bakhtin's concept of "grotesque realism."

The vulnerable corporeality of the hybrid structures of the Renaissance garden—or at least that of their interiors—is equally suggestive of this notion of the giant as a superhumanly massive, but flawed, anthropoid. Like the love-sick colossus of the *Hypnerotomachia Poliphili*, for example, the *Appennino* in Pratolino can be entered and explored. As Alessandro Vezzosi has noted, the structure of the *Appennino's* interior evokes the "fabric" of the human body. The iron skeleton is the backbone, the bricks are the flesh, and the plaster is the skin.[45] Giambologna's figure was also, like Colonna's, a "grand hydraulic machine," containing numerous fountains and automata.[46]

Stewart has extended Bakhtin's analysis, arguing that "whereas the minia-ture represents closure, interiority, the domestic, and the overly cultural, the gigantic represents infinity, exteriority, the public and the overly natural."[47] She endorses Bakhtin's narrative of the historical progress of the giant from its ancient identification with the landscape to the world of carnival.[48] Like Bakhtin, Stewart stresses the popular symbolism of the giant as a figure of dis-order, superabundance, and excessive consumption. "The giant is frequently seen as a devourer, and even, as in the case of Cyclops, as a cannibal."[49]

The gigantic figure of a dipsomaniac Polyphemus in the Orti Oricellari might be recalled here. From Stewart's perspective, Novelli's giant may seem to embody both the idea of carnivalesque disorder, precipitated by excessive imbibing, and that of consumption or devouring (both actual and potential). Such an interpretation would, however, have the effect of rendering the giant less threatening. The colossal monocular cannibal is safely dispatched to the Bakhtinian category of carnival, a category in which violent and transgressive acts are, as subsequent critics have made clear, merely temporary and free of lasting adverse consequences.[50]

In his critique of Bakhtin, Walter Stephens argues that the historical evi-dence indicates that there was no firm line or dialectical relationship between popular and elite cultures in medieval and early modern Europe. The giant meant much the same thing in both contexts. Stephens relies here on Richard Berrong's argument that "current historical research has made it progressively more apparent that what we term the popular culture of the Middle Ages and Early Renaissance was in fact *every* man's culture—peasant, craftsman, bour-geois, noble."[51] What this means is that Bakhtin's understanding of the giant as the manifestation of an historical popular culture may no longer convince, but arguably his characterization of Gargantua and Pantagruel as exemplars of grotesque realism remains persuasive. The interior cavities of anthropomorphic garden structures, from the lovesick colossus of the *Hypnerotomachia Poliphili* to the *Appennino*, imply the grotesque. The motif of the Hell Mouth also obviously corresponds to the idea of the giant as a "devourer." Most important of all, however, the lack of a distinction between "high" and "low" culture strengthens the hypothesis that a contemporary beholder would have understood the giants of the Renaissance garden in both art historical and folkloric terms.

Stewart's reading is at its most Bakhtinian when she traces the later history of the giant: "The gigantic continues its secular life in the submerged world of the carnival grotesque; its celebrations of licentiousness and lived bodily reality are truly the underbelly of official life."[52] Stewart suggests that the parades of later official culture efface the participatory experience of their agrarian carnival antecedents, contributing to the construction of what Guy Debord called the "society of the spectacle."[53]

This historical process may also have an analogue in garden history. The "participatory grotesque" of the Italian Renaissance garden, in which anthropophagy is a major theme and giant bodies are open for exploration, involves multisensual experience—what Poliphilo frequently refers to as "voluptuousness." In contrast, the Le Nôtrean gardens of the seventeenth century can be described as "jardins de voyage," to borrow a phrase from Thierry Mariage.[54] The gardens of the Château de Versailles, for example, contribute to an expansive designed landscape that was meant to be experienced visually from the detached confines of a dedicated carriage.[55] In this reading, Versailles would be in the same relation to Pratolino as the modern parade is to the premodern carnival. The participatory dimension is lost or, at best, significantly contracted in favor of the visual.

Stewart's exploration of the theme of the giant as an avatar of nature is particularly relevant to landscape design. The third nature of the garden and the giant both occupy the interstices, a third space, between the natural and the cultural. The river gods and man mountains of the sixteenth-century landscape are literal expressions of the idea of the giant as a personification of nature. The *Appennino*, for example, recalls Stewart's argument that "the giant is represented through movement, through being in time. Even in the ascription of the still landscape to the giant, it is the activities of the giant, his or her legendary actions, that have resulted in the observable trace. In contrast to the still and perfect universe of the miniature, the gigantic represents the order and disorder of historical forces."[56] Giambologna's colossus can be understood as depicted in a moment of perpetual creation, squeezing water out of its peaks and crevasses. As I have suggested, it alludes to the many legends in which giants create the landscape prior to the advent of people. The *Appennino* is at once, therefore, a prosopopeic representation of a major Italian geological feature, scaled to the garden, and an allusion to the popular legend that giants once roamed the earth.

The not infrequent discovery of what were thought to be giant bones during the fifteenth and sixteenth centuries suggests the durability of these legends. Giovanni Boccaccio, for example, described one such discovery near Trapani in Sicily. Peasants digging in the foundations of a house excavated a room in which a giant figure sat enthroned, holding a staff "as tall as the mast of a ship." The giant soon crumbled to dust, however, leaving behind three gigantic teeth, parts of the skull and thighbone, and the staff.[57] Cardinal Cristoforo Madruzzo's gift of a gigantic bone, which was believed to have once belonged to a giant, to his neighbor Pierfrancesco "Vicino" Orsini—whose Sacro Bosco was full of colossal figures carved from the "living" rock—provides another example of the fascination of the period with giants.[58]

The legends of the giants have a particular relevance to the Sacro Bosco. In 1498 the local scholar Annius of Viterbo (Giovanni Nanni), published his *Antiquities*, in which he argued, on the basis of forged documentary sources, that Viterbo was the cradle of an Etruscan civilization founded by a race of noble and erudite giants descended from Noah.[59] This Viterban civilization, Annius claimed, surpassed Rome in antiquity and dignity.[60] The fact that Orsini's friend Francesco Sansovino translated the *Antiquities* into Italian and published them with commentaries suggests the relevance of Annius's fabricated gigantology, in which giants appear as positive agents of creation, to the sixteenth-century garden at Bomarzo.[61]

The colossal anthropomorphic "living" rocks of Bomarzo express a recurring theme of sixteenth-century garden design (albeit one that is rarely as explicit as it is in the Sacro Bosco): the animistic, indeed neo-pagan, attribution of life to the landscape. As a deity of the earth, for example, the Goddess of Nature of the Villa d'Este revives pre-Olympian cults of the "Great Mother." Her hieratic and enigmatic appearance implies a corollary concept of nature itself as premoral, unpredictable, and unknowable.

It follows that the giants of the Renaissance garden—instruments or embodiments of nature—contribute to this symbolism. Giambologna's

Appennino is a personification of the Italian mountain range—a representation of a major geological feature—but it is also portrayed as landscape demiurge, creator of the peaks, valleys, and rivers (or, in Bakhtin's terminology, the "towers" and "abysses"). This complex figure is sui generis, both the creator of the landscape and the landscape itself.

The personification of significant landscape features as giants in gardens recalls the analogy between the human body and the body of the earth in sixteenth-century natural history. Leonardo da Vinci provided one of the clearest statements of the idea: "We can say that the earth has a spirit of growth and that its flesh be the soil, its bones be the arrangement and connection of the rocks of which the mountains are composed; its cartilages are the tufa, its blood the veins of water, the lake of blood that lies around the heart is the ocean sea, and its breathing, and the increase and decrease of the blood in the pulses, is represented in the earth by the flow and ebb of the sea."[62] Leonardo's analogy between the earth and the living body has a long history, from Plato's *Timaeus* to Pirro Ligorio.[63] In the Renaissance garden, the flow of water through the landscape (a vital prerequisite to the ornaments and effects of the garden) is analogous to the flow of blood through the body. In Pratolino, the *Appennino* not only anthropomorphizes the landscape but also depicts the generation and flow of water, which spews from the "mouth" of the monstrous figure that the giant presses down upon into an artificial pond. There are, in effect, two bodies here: the mountain range and the water source. The implication is that water emerges or, rather, is (violently) forced from the body of the earth by the giant depicted as, again, landscape demiurge. The intellectual context for this colossal image is provided by the ideas of natural historians. Giambologna's *Appennino* is, first and foremost, a remarkably literal image of the earth as living body.

The *Appennino* is, therefore, an avatar of creative nature. Its size signifies the scale of the encompassing landscape—mountains and rivers. If we are "enveloped by the gigantic, surrounded by it, enclosed within its shadow," as Stewart claims, then the exploration of the interior of Giambologna's giant is a symbolic reenactment of our most basic relation to the landscape environment.[64] In a phrase, the giant *is* the environment (quite literally at Pratolino). That environment is not, however, blank or mute. In the case of the *Appennino* the colossal mode is a vehicle for a wide range of cultural convictions: ancient folkloric stories about the giants who formed the earth through their actions or through the fragmentation of their bodies ("rare and enormous bones of huge animals" in Alberti's phrase),[65] classical and early modern fantasies about anthropomorphic cities, the sustenance that the geography of the Italian peninsular provides its inhabitants, and—as the Renaissance progresses—the amoral character of nature.

By the later sixteenth century, the giant, in its identification with nature, was recategorized as neither benevolent nor malevolent. It had no morality, just as the old idea of nature as a moral force whose rules had to be followed at all times became increasingly outmoded. As was argued in the previous chapter, the medieval tradition of Nature as a dignified, robed female figure "who was delegated by the Christian God to shape individual beings through the physical process of generation, to guide her creatures, and to maintain order" was superseded by the image of Nature as a nude or seminude lactating woman or as a woman with multiple breasts.[66] To reiterate: this is a shift from a concept of Nature as an exemplary, occasionally stern, mother to one of Nature as a fertile, but largely indifferent, wet nurse.

A relevant example of the late sixteenth-century concept of Nature is provided by Cesare Ripa's influential emblem book *Iconologia* (1593). Nature is depicted as a "naked woman, with her breasts full of milk and holding a vulture in her hand."[67] According to Ripa, the swollen breasts signify Nature's active, formative role, "because form is that which nourishes and sustains all created things, as woman with her breasts nourishes and sustains infants." In contrast, the vulture symbolizes Nature's capacity for destruction. The vulture, "by its appetite for form, moving and altering itself, destroys little by little all corruptible things."[68] Ripa's Nature is both creator and destroyer, sustainer and devourer. She is as responsible for nourishment and perpetuation as she is for corruption and decay.

Katherine Park argues that "in Renaissance allegories and emblems, nature retained her power but lost her voice."[69] Her power, in other words, became inexplicable, enigmatic, and no longer a medium for the articulation of moral lessons, which is also the case with the nature of Ovid's *Metamorphoses*, in which events of terrifying violence, transformation, and death take place in serenely indifferent sylvan landscapes. This concept of nature has implications for the figure of the giant and, more specifically, for the colossi of the Italian Renaissance garden.

The giant is an embodiment of natural forces, as Stewart has argued. Giants are precivilized equivalents of nature, often imagined as dwelling in the mountains, caves, and ravines. The characterization of the giant as an avatar of nature is by no means unique to Italian and French traditions. In his *Deutsche Mythologie* (1844), for example, Jacob Grimm claims that "giants and Titans are the old gods of nature."[70] A few years later, Wilhelm Müller described giants as "the personifications of the untamed forces of nature."[71] Nature is also one of the principal themes of sixteenth-century landscape design—as raw material (or medium perhaps) and as subject matter. The giant, however, signifies a concept of nature different to that celebrated in accounts of the garden as a locus amoenus. It implies instead a nature that, as in Ovid, is amoral, capable of nonchalant destruction, and potentially frightening in its obliviousness to human scale and safety.

If the premise that a history of the early modern garden necessitates the reconstruction of contemporary habits of thought is accepted, then Giambologna's *Appennino* may have had the potential to provoke a response along these lines (in addition to the acknowledgment of its location within an art historical tradition of colossal statuary). A sixteenth-century beholder would conceivably have experienced trepidation when confronted with Giambologna's giant figure of the *Appennino*.[72] The figure of the giant, as a personification of nature, may reflect people's actual experience of the natural world, which could be both positive and negative. If the giant, as a sort of tutelary divinity of the sixteenth-century garden, conveys a message, it would be that nature is not always amenable.

The Giant as a Figure of Alterity

> The truly archaic Giants of folklore, and their verifiable descendants
> in civic pageantry, were figures of a terrible and hostile alterity, a
> menace to "us" and domestic culture.
>
> —Walter Stephens[73]

The Oricellari Polyphemus (figure 39) is a unique survival from early modern landscape design. Unlike Giambologna's *Appennino*, a genius loci on the margins of the Medici garden in Pratolino, Novelli's giant is installed at the center of Giovan Carlo de' Medici's garden. The Cyclops is depicted drinking from a wine skin, which in Homer's *Odyssey* eventually leads to the drunken stupor that allows Odysseus and his men to escape. The one-eyed, cannibalistic giant is an unequivocally menacing figure in the Homeric narrative and thus, given that this is Novelli's principal source, also in the Orti Oricellari.

Polyphemus is no less malevolent in Ovid's *Metamorphoses*. Sick with perverse desire for the beautiful shepherdess Galatea, the Cyclops kills her lover

Figure 39. Antonio Novelli, Polyphemus, 1640–52. Orti Oricellari, Florence. Photo: Attila Györ.

Acis with a boulder. In both stories Polyphemus "is, like Caliban, symbolic of a deviant eroticism and the raw natural forces that oppose reason. He is also a sign of the metaphysical evils that may beset humankind."[74]

The Oricellari colossus is a simpler figure than Giambologna's *Appennino*. Novelli's statue is a straightforward representation of a notorious and wholly malevolent giant from Greco-Roman myth. Yet Polyphemus is an intriguing choice for the central feature of a garden. The Cyclops is a creature of violence, perversity, and evil. It would be difficult to think of a more discordant motif.

Giants frequently appear as figures of disorder and disproportion. Bakhtin drew attention to the role of "town giants" in early modern carnival culture, but in most of the literature of giants their proportions and actions serve to destroy order. Early in the *Metamorphoses*, for example, the giants "assailed the kingdom of the gods and, piling mountains together, built them up to the stars above,"[75] an act of catastrophic hubris that precipitates the gigantomachy and their eventual defeat. Polyphemus is a clear affront to natural order with his one eye, his bloodthirstiness (in Homer), and his perverse desire (in Ovid). The titan Chronos, another ancient Greek enemy of men and women, most memorably depicted in the nineteenth century by Francisco Goya in his *Saturn Devouring His Children* (c. 1820), might also be mentioned here. Goya depicts Chronos/ Saturn eating one of his offspring, in a powerful image of the cannibalistic giant or the giant as devourer. Many more examples could be added, from the Italian comic giants of Pulci and Teofilo Folengo to Pantagruel and Jonathan Swift's Gulliver, who, as a giant to the Lilliputians, turns into a destructive "beast of consumption."[76]

Novelli's Polyphemus is not, strictly speaking, a Renaissance colossus. It belongs to the mid-seventeenth-century redevelopment of the Oricellari. Devouring and anthropophagy, however, are important themes of Renaissance landscape design. The sixteenth-century motif of the colossal Hell Mouth is a thematic antecedent of the Oricellari Polyphemus. Like the monster in the garden, neither can be easily reconciled with the concept of the locus amoenus.

In folklore and legend, giants have often played the same cultural role as monsters: both have frequently been conceptualized as abnormal, as freakish, and as moral outsiders. Janis L. Pallister claims, for example, that in general giants "are mythical monsters falling largely into the category of an evil force ultimately suppressed by an almost superhuman strength or great astuteness on the part of some virtuous 'hero,'" as in the gigantomachia of Hercules and Antaeus.[77] If the monster is a necessary fiction of what Foucault calls the "juridico-biological domain," then the giant's excessive size and strength potentially makes him just as definitive a figure of alterity.[78] The giant is, of course, more complex than this—physical size can also signify valor or strength of character rather than depravity and moral turpitude: Hercules or St. Christopher rather than Antaeus or Goliath.

Jeffrey Jerome Cohen has argued that giants are hybrid figures, which exhibit some of the characteristics of the monster in early modern teratological and medical treatises. He links the medieval giant—a "foundational monster"—with the monsters of Anglo-Saxon England, which "became a kind of cultural shorthand for the problems of identity construction, for the irreducible difference that lurks deep within the culture-bound self."[79] This is a familiar argument: the giant, like the monster, is abjected or excluded as diametrically "other" to sociocultural or physiological norms. Identity construction, in other words, requires the figure of the monster or the giant. For Cohen, monsters and giants are constantly with us, are indeed an intrinsic part of us, "because a signification based upon exclusion depends upon the continued presence (if only a presence in death) of the thing it exiles."[80] Richard Bernheimer has proposed a similar theory of the medieval "wild-man," but Cohen's position recalls most closely the concept of monstrosity that emerged from Canguilhem's and Foucault's studies.[81]

For Canguilhem, however, a giant cannot be classified as a monster. In his view, a gigantic man is still in the end a man rather than a monster.[82] According to Canguilhem, "We may say of a rock that it is enormous, but not of a mountain that it is monstrous, except in a mythical universe of discourse in which mountains may possibly give birth to mice."[83] This point clearly applies to Giambologna's *Appennino*, which is a mountain but cannot be convincingly interpreted as a monster. Stephens's reading of the early modern giant as a figure of alterity may, likewise, not seem readily applicable to the colossal personifications of the Renaissance garden. Although the motif of the Hell Mouth—conceivably the fragment of a gigantic body—is an unambiguously hostile one, as is Novelli's Polyphemus, the image of the *Appennino* is, again, not as straightforwardly legible along these lines.

With the exception of well-known mythological giants such as the Oricellari Polyphemus or the figure of Antaeus in Castello, the early modern garden giant is not quite other to either its environment or the beholder. It is, rather, a representation or personification of nature as well as being recognizably extrapolated from the human form. In the garden, the legendary figure of the giant does not, as Canguilhem realized, enact the same cultural role as that of the monster. The *Appennino* may be abnormal in scale, but there is nothing unusual or troubling about its anatomy. Unlike the harpy, whose combinatory or composite anatomy and negative symbolism mark it as unnatural or "outside" nature, as Ambroise Paré wrote, the giant is fundamentally a figure of nature. In the context of Renaissance landscape design, which was conceived as a collaboration between nature and art—a revelation rather than an imposition of order—the giant would not have been understood in the same way as the harpy. The giant, in contrast to the monster, does not violate the laws of nature. Giants are avatars of nature.[84]

In the garden, the giant serves two principal functions besides the deliberate revival of an ancient sculptural mode. First, and perhaps most important, it provided one of the Renaissance designer's main means of representing nature—both the local topography of the region and the vast scale and grandeur of the natural world. The disproportionate size of the giant expresses the disproportionate size of nature itself in comparison with the human subject. As a consequence, the giant in the garden has the same capacity to provoke a pseudo-sublime or interrupted sublime as the giants of Dante's *Inferno*.[85] The giant implies the familiar reality, at least to agrarian societies, that nature could be both kind and cruel.

Second, the figure of the giant makes a significant contribution to the grotesque realism of the garden—Bakhtin's "downward movement." In most traditions, giants are envisaged as having colossal appetites and of being capable of ingesting vast amounts. This capacity to devour and envelope is connected to ancient fears about nature's destructive potential as well as being a distinctive feature of the grotesque. Pantagruel's appetite, for example, was uncontrollable. The Orsini Hell Mouth epitomizes this theme of devouring.

The figure of the giant is, in conclusion, a natural inhabitant of the Renaissance landscape. In its occupancy of the interstice between two categories it is a kind of analogue of the third nature of the garden. As Stewart writes: "The gigantic becomes an explanation for the environment, a figure on the interface between the natural and human." This is the giant's primary significance within the garden: as a prosopopeic incarnation of amoral nature. Although the garden giant may not be the figure of hostile alterity that Stephens argues is characteristic of its literary and mythological equivalents, its presence contributes little to the concept of the garden as a locus amoenus. Indeed, the giant embodies nature's two opposed faces, the one amenable and creative and the other forbidding and destructive. More perhaps than any other single figurative type, therefore, the giant expresses the dramatic duality between pleasure and fear that is a crucial feature of Renaissance landscape design.[86]

Chapter 5

"Pietra Morta, in Pietra Viva"

The Sacro Bosco

Monsters and giants you (I know) shall beat
if no more foolish whim turns you aside.
— Torquato Tasso, *The Liberation of Jerusalem*

The Sacro Bosco in Bomarzo is an object lesson in the difficulties of interpretation that attend the study of historical gardens. It is not unlike the early
seventeenth-century Hortus Palatinus in Heidelberg (c. 1613–1619), in that
there are few documentary sources to guide the historian. The problem is
compounded by the nearly complete absence of records of response to the
Sacro Bosco until the twentieth century (besides the allusions to the garden in
Pierfrancesco "Vicino" Orsini's own correspondence).[1] Those references that
do survive from the sixteenth century, though valuable, offer little in the way
of specific information.

One consequence of the lack of information from the period has been
that the Sacro Bosco, like Salomon de Caus's Hortus Palatinus, has served as a
kind of tabula rasa upon which scholars have projected their own preoccupations.[2] Some have declared the Sacro Bosco to be an "irrational" or incoherent garden that cannot, by definition, be interpreted in any meaningful way.[3]
Others have identified literary texts from the period that, they believe, clarify
and explain the iconography of the garden.[4] Another group has argued that
the Sacro Bosco is an autobiographical statement, even a *psychomachia*, which
allegorizes the events of Orsini's life and depicts his state of mind.[5] Still others have sought to explain specific motifs, an approach that has been most

productive in relation to the "Etruscan" elements of the garden.[6] Hermetic, alchemical, astrological, cross-cultural, and Epicurean themes have been uncovered.[7] The influence of the local scholar Annius of Viterbo's fabricated but immensely popular "histories" of the archaic civilization of the Alto Lazio and the philosopher Francesco Patrizi's theory of *meraviglia* (wonderment) have been proposed as possible contexts.[8] Yet there remains little or no consensus about the meaning of the Sacro Bosco.[9]

This disagreement extends to basic facts about the site. There has, for example, been a long-running argument in the literature about the original location of the entrance to the Sacro Bosco, which, in turn, has implications for any attempt to interpret the garden as a narrative. Most writers argue that the entrance was at the northern end of the wood near the Casa Pendente.[10] Margaretta J. Darnall and Mark S. Weil, however, locate the entrance at the bridge to the south of the wood, near what has since been identified as the dam and the lake.[11] In their interpretation, the first major motif encountered by the visitor would have been the colossal fighting giants (figure 40). This reflects their main hypothesis: that the structure of Dante's *Divine Comedy* is replicated in Bomarzo, "where the path leads down into a false paradise before ascending to a Temple of Divine Love."[12] The standing giant is identified as Orlando, who, Ariosto relates, was driven mad by earthly love, just as Orsini himself was supposed to have been. Moreover, the figure of Orlando tearing a woodsman apart (from canto 19 of *Orlando furioso*) indicates that this level of the design is a place of earthly pleasure and pain. As Darnall and Weil write: "The animal nature of man was immediately present."[13]

If, however, the entrance was located at the other end of the wood, then the first major monument (after the two sphinxes) would have been the Casa Pendente, which is dedicated to Orsini's friend and neighbor Cardinal Cristoforo Madruzzo.[14] The meaning of the Casa Pendente is altogether different from that of the Orlando and Woodsman group. According to Darnall and Weil, the house offers a "cure for Vicino's irrational desire," which is suggested by one of its inscriptions: "If quieted the soul acts in a wiser fashion."[15] The cure is contemplation.

The narrative structure of the garden, as hypothesized by Darnall and Weil, thus requires the entrance to be located near the Orlando and Woodsman group. The journey from the lower, more bestial realm to the Tempietto, which symbolizes the achievement of the state of grace that is the purpose of the visit, cannot logically proceed in the opposite direction. The Casa Pendente is a turning point, directing the visitor toward enlightenment.

Figure 40. Fighting Giants. Sacro Bosco, Bomarzo. Photo: Luke Morgan.

Figure 41. Casa Pendente. Sacro Bosco, Bomarzo. Photo: Luke Morgan.

Much therefore depends on the location of the entrance. In Darnall and Weil's interpretation, however, even more depends on the a priori assumption that the Sacro Bosco *has* a narrative structure. The "Itinerary of the 'Sacro Bosco'" is, for Darnall and Weil, linear, progressive, and very closely based on Orlando's own itinerary in Ariosto's poem. Their reading is impressively erudite but, in its unwavering adherence to the prior text, stretches credibility. Although they refer to a range of literary sources, Darnall and Weil strive to establish *Orlando furioso* as the single point of origin for the imagery and symbolism of the garden. Consequently, their reading is a prime example of the "narrative expectation" of a certain type of garden history, which closely resembles the postwar "iconological" interpretations of, especially, Anglophone art history.[16]

Like that of many of the art historians who adopted Erwin Panofsky's methods, Darnall and Weil's approach implicitly privileges texts over works of art. The underlying assumption is an essentially Hegelian one: literary texts, like philosophical propositions, are generative of works of art (including gardens). The Sacro Bosco thus owes its existence and meaning to Orsini's reading of Ariosto and his self-identification with Orlando. This has the adverse effect of reducing the garden to illustration; more seriously, it leaves out everything that makes a garden a garden rather than a text or a painting. In this situation, interpretation risks resembling little more than a "mere technique of deciphering."[17]

As I argued in chapter 1, the narrative allusions or topoi of historical gardens may be less important than their status as unstable, multisensual environments in which the visitor is enjoined and empowered to make his or her own decisions. Reception should, as a result, probably be thought of as subjective, idiosyncratic, tendentious, partial, magpie-like, fallible, and biased. It may be more accurate to liken the experience of gardens to "browsing" rather than "reading." Indeed, if gardens are heterotopic spaces, then they should be seen as accommodating, indeed promoting, inconsistency without resolution.

The physical realities of the site of the Sacro Bosco also militate against the presence of a strict linear narrative to which visitors inevitably adhered. The fact that much of the colossal statuary was carved out of "living rock" suggests a haphazard, additive approach to the layout and design of the landscape. Some preexisting rocks would have been better suited to particular designs than others. The Orlando and Woodsman group, for example, would have required a certain scale and dimension for its conception and execution. Rather than being carefully plotted so as to conform to the sequential narrative of Ariosto's text, therefore, it is more likely that the figures of the bosco were simply carved out of the available materials. The site itself, in other words, determined the locations of the figures to a large extent rather than a predetermined narrative program. (This does not mean, however, that there are not allusions to *Orlando furioso* in the Sacro Bosco.)

Another general characteristic of the site deserves comment. Arguably, the Sacro Bosco is not, from a typological perspective, actually a garden. It is, rather, a wood. (Its name, Sacro Bosco, is taken from an inscription on one of the walls of the xystus: "Yield both Memphis and every other marvel, which formerly the world held in esteem, to the Sacred Wood which is only itself and resembles no other.")[18] It has been suggested that a more conventional "Italian" garden was laid out on the slope of the hill leading down from the Palazzo Orsini to the Sacro Bosco.[19] If so, then the wood would have to be understood as a bosco (or *boschetto*) that was once adjacent to a garden, not unlike the bosco of the Villa Lante in Bagnaia perhaps. There is, however, no contemporary evidence for this layout.[20] The inscription, which describes the wood as "only itself" and as resembling "no other," also suggests that it was conceived as a self-sufficient entity and not as part of a larger complex from which it would derive meaning.[21]

If the Sacro Bosco is approached as a wood rather than a garden, it can be seen to belong to an essentially literary tradition of the sacred grove.[22] The sacred grove at Rome, described by Virgil (*Aeneid* VIII, 342–58), has been identified as a possible source of inspiration.[23] There are many other contenders, however, such as the "savage" forest in which Dante loses his way at the beginning of *Inferno*, the "dark wood" where Poliphilo becomes "incapacitated by terror" in Colonna's *Hypnerotomachia Poliphili*, and the description of the "sacred wood" in chapter 10 of Jacopo Sannazaro's *Arcadia*.[24] In one case, it has been proposed that the influence ran in the opposite direction: Maurizio Calvesi and Josephine von Henneberg have argued that Torquato Tasso's description of the enchanted wood in *Gerusalemme liberata* (canto 18) (1581) may have been inspired by a visit to Bomarzo with his father, Bernardo Tasso.[25]

Dark woods, like many aspects of the uncultivated or wild landscape ("first nature," in the terminology of the sixteenth century), often provoked fear—in life, as in literature. In Bartolomeo Taegio's *La Villa* (1559), for example, Vitauro claims that villa gardens "produce much more delight" than their equivalents in the city "because of the proximity of their opposite: for often *in villa* one sees threatening mountains, serpent's lairs, dark caves, horrid cliffs, strange crags, steep precipices, fallen rocks, hermits' huts, rough rocks, mountainous deserts, and similar things that, although one can hardly gaze upon them without horror, nevertheless render more complete the joys and happinesses of the villa."[26] Hervé Brunon has argued that in the later sixteenth century, frightening landscapes of this kind are incorporated *within* gardens, instead of remaining safely exterior to them.[27] Giambologna's *Appennino* in Pratolino, for example, can be interpreted as an anthropomorphic representation of a threatening, mountainous landscape located within the garden of the villa.

The Sacro Bosco contains several of the elements mentioned by Taegio. It offers no contrast to the external threat of untamed nature due to the absence of a conventional geometrical garden, representative of "third nature," to serve as foil. Moreover, its reference to wilderness is not confined to a single motif, however gargantuan, as it is in Pratolino. As a bosco, the landscape in Bomarzo literally, though not exclusively, consists of the "dark caves, horrid cliffs" and "strange crags" of Taegio's description.

As in Tasso's poem, the imagery of the Sacro Bosco is dominated by "monsters and giants."[28] There are harpies, for example—hybrid figures whose foul behavior, negative symbolism, and dreadful medical condition (according to physicians such as Ambroise Paré and Ulisse Aldrovandi) were discussed in chapter 3. There are voracious disembodied heads (the Hell Mouth, the Mask of Madness, and a sea monster), images of deficiency and grotesque hunger. Many of the figures would, likewise, have been defined as "colossal" by Pomponio Gaurico or Giovanni Paolo Lomazzo, but these giants are antiheroes, closer to the tradition of the giant as a hostile figure of menacing alterity. There are, in addition, two scenes of violence: the gigantic figure identified as Orlando, who is depicted tearing a woodsman apart, and the dragon being attacked by a lion and a dog.

"One can hardly gaze upon them without horror," Taegio noted of the features of the wild landscape outside the villa garden. The same applies to the statuary of Orsini's Sacro Bosco. As a wood, however, the presence of these "threatening" and "horrid" figures is appropriate and suggestive of sixteenth-century fears of untamed (and unknowable) nature. Consequently, the experience of the wood would have been more like that of the dark and savage forest (locus horridus) than that of the ornamental garden (locus amoenus).

The themes of this book thus come together in the Sacro Bosco: monsters, giants, the opposition of the grotesque and the "classical" (the latter primarily represented at Bomarzo by the Tempietto), the motif of violence, and the dramatic duality of sixteenth-century landscape design are all present. This chapter builds on the earlier discussion of these themes in the Renaissance garden to further develop the "horizon of perception" or "period eye" of the Sacro Bosco's contemporary audience. The account presented here seeks to suggest plausible responses to a selection of the sculptural and architectonic motifs of Orsini's wood, as well as a handful of other sites (such as the Grotta Grande in the Boboli Gardens in Florence), on the basis of the premise that garden experience is unlike reading.[29] It is not intended to be comprehensive or conclusive.

Particular attention will be paid to two unusual features of the Sacro
Bosco The first derives from Orsini's practice of having his "monsters and giants" carved from the "living" rock of Bomarzo, a phenomenon that has not
previously been considered in any detail. The second concerns temporality.
The Sacro Bosco, like the surrounding landscape of Alto Lazio, incorporates
ruins. The fragment of a faux Etruscan tomb, for example—a "folly" *avant
la lettre*—implies a concept of time or, more precisely, of plural temporalities
that deserves closer attention.

Living Rock

In the late sixteenth century Giovanvettorio Soderini compared the Hell
Mouth to Indian sculptures carved from local rock:

> Nor should one forget to mention that in some of these palaces of
> India in the meadows which surround them issue out of the ground
> some lumps of natural rock from which they have carved their
> idols and some figures of statues of their very fantastic animals. So
> should there be such rocks in our region, they could be transformed
> into finely carved statues, colossi, or some other happy idea; as at
> Bomarzo are seen those carved out of natural rocks of more than a
> huge pebble which depicts a mask in which the mouth makes the
> door and the windows are the eyes and within the tongue serves as a
> table and the teeth are seats, so that when the table is set for supper
> with lights among the dishes from afar it appears a most frightening
> mask.[30]

The "natural rock" from which the Hell Mouth was carved is called *peperino* and is a volcanic tuff found in the region of Viterbo. The name refers to
the black grains that give the stone its peppercorn-like appearance. It is one of
the most ancient building materials of the area, much used by the Romans for
example, who called it *lapis albanus*.

The properties of peperino were also well known to the Renaissance. One
of the most informative discussions of the stone can be found in Giorgio
Vasari's text on artistic technique, which was originally published as an introduction to the 1550 edition of his *Lives of the Artists*. He describes the "stone
named piperno or more commonly peperigno" as a "blackish and spongy

stone, resembling travertine, which is excavated in the Roman Campagna."
According to him, "It is used for the posts of windows and doors in various
places, notably at Naples and in Rome; and it also serves artists for painting
on in oil. . . . This is a very thirsty stone and indeed more like cinder than
anything else."[31]

Vasari's reference to painters' use of peperino is of particular interest. In
a letter of 9 September 1575 to Giovanni Drouet, Vicino Orsini informed his
friend that he had "already applied the color to several statues of the grove."
He adds that he has learnt a secret for enhancing the durability of the paint,
which involved tempering the pigment with milk. As a result, he writes that
the colors have lasted well, even after four to five months.[32] Vasari's comments
about the artistic uses of peperino indicate that Orsini's decision to paint some
of the colossal figures of the Sacro Bosco (traces of paint are most clearly visible on the Mask of Madness) was not an eccentric whim but followed an
established practice. As Vasari notes, peperino was regarded as suitable for
painting.

Precedents for carving figures out of living rock are more difficult to find
in fifteenth- and sixteenth-century Italy, although the methods that Orsini's
sculptor(s) must have employed, and the style of the extant statues, are suggestive of Florentine practices. The Orlando figure, for example, recalls Baccio Bandinelli's post-Michelangelesque classicism.[33] The sculptors of the Sacro
Bosco also employed a subtractive technique of the kind favored by Florentine
artists and theorists of sculpture from Leon Battista Alberti to Michelangelo.[34]
In *De statua*, Alberti divided sculptors into three types. First, there are those
working in wax or clay, who add and take away. He calls these artists "model-
ers." Second, there are those who are exclusively concerned with subtraction,
such as those working in marble and other stones. These, he calls "sculptors."
Third, there are those who only add, such as silversmiths.[35] More than a hundred years later, in his terse response to Benedetto Varchi's famous questionnaire to artists of 1547, Michelangelo echoed Alberti in defining sculpture
succinctly as "work which is fashioned by dint of taking away."[36]

This was the method employed in the Sacro Bosco. Each rock, in the
familiar Renaissance topos (most closely associated with Michelangelo),
contained its ideal and unique *concetto*, which, in a kind of operative Neoplatonism, it was the sculptor's task to release. The decision to use the local
peperino would also have provided one of the major constraints of the project.
To reiterate: the size and shape of the rocks scattered across the site would have
influenced the size, shape, and identity of many of the figures to be carved.

Soderini's reference to colossi carved out of "natural rock" is suggestive of another aspect of Michelangelo's legacy: his unrealized (and perhaps never seriously contemplated) project to carve giant figures directly out of the Carrara mountains (many centuries before Mount Rushmore). In his *Life* of Michelangelo, Ascanio Condivi relates how on one occasion

> Michelangelo stayed in those mountains with two assistants and a mount, but with no provision other than foodstuffs, for over eight months. While there, he looked out one day over the whole expanse from a mountain that rises above the coast and conceived the idea of making a colossus that would be visible to mariners far out at sea. He was encouraged in his notion by the enormous mass of rock, which could be easily carved, and by the example of the ancients who, perhaps moved just as Michelangelo was after landing at some opportune spot, or perhaps to escape idleness or for who knows what reason, left their own rough-carved memorials as mementos of their work.[37]

Michelangelo probably had the story of Dinocrates's project for Mt. Athos in mind, besides the ancient carved figures that were still visible at Carrara in the early sixteenth century.[38] In Bomarzo, a more readily available precedent for peperino carving in situ was provided by the remains of the Etruscan civilization that litter the region.

The rock-cut forms of Etruscan tombs must have been a major source of inspiration for Orsini's Sacro Bosco. Eugenio Battisti was one of the first to suggest that the Hell Mouth should be seen as an "Etruscan tomb . . . transformed . . . into a banquet hall."[39] Subsequent writers such as John P. Oleson and, most recently, Katherine Coty have pursued this line of inquiry.[40] Coty has argued persuasively that the Sacro Bosco is related to the surrounding landscape of ancient Etruscan ruins, carvings, and fragments, from which it drew inspiration. From this perspective, Orsini's creation appears as a sacred wood within sacred woods. More to the point here, however, is the fact that the familiar remains of Etruscan civilization (at least to inhabitants of Bomarzo, Soriano nel Cimino, and the Viterbo region) provided numerous local examples of architectural and sculptural forms carved from living rock.

The sculpted facade of the simulated Etruscan ruin in the Sacro Bosco, for example, "is a full-sized, substantially accurate reproduction of the rock-cut, Etruscan aedicule tomb, a tomb type that was popular in southern Etruria during the second and third centuries B.C."[41] It resembles the facades of the Tomba della Sirena and the Tomba del Trifone in Sovana, which is near Pitigliano, another seat of the Orsini family (and which has its own examples of rock-cut figures, probably inspired by those of the Sacro Bosco).[42]

In sixteenth-century Italy, the phrase (and concept of) "living rock" (*pietra viva*) appears in art and architectural treatises, poetry, and natural history. In his description of Sanmichele's Pellegrini Chapel in the Church of San Bernardino in Verona (1520s), for instance, Vasari mentions the "white and living stone (*pietra viva e bianca*) which, because of the sound it makes when it is worked, is called in that city *bronzo*."[43] Andrea Palladio also discusses the characteristics of "pietra viva durissima" in book 3 of *I quattro libri dell'architettura* (1570). During the period other architectural structures such as walls and bridges are sometimes described as being made of pietra viva.[44] The sculptor Benvenuto Cellini likewise referred to "un sasso di pietra viva."[45]

Francesco Petrarch's metaphorical use of the phrase "pietra viva" in the *Rerum vulgarium fragmenta* (c. 1327–1368) is probably the best-known poetic image of living rock from early Italian poetry.[46] In "Di pensier in pensier, di monte in monte," he evokes the pain of unrequited love:

The wilder the place is,
the more barren the shore where I may be,
the more lovely do my thoughts depict her image;
but when the truth dispels
that sweet mistake, right then and there I sit
down cold as dead stone set on living rock (*pietra morta, in pietra
  viva*),
a statue that can think and weep and write.[47]

Petrarch's beloved Laura appears here as a Medusa-like figure, capable of transforming the lovelorn poet into dead rock or a statue (the image is also a play on Petrarch's own name which derives from *petra* or *pietra*). In art this idea is again associated with Michelangelo. In his Petrarchan poem about Michelangelo's first *Pietà*, later quoted in full by Vasari, Giovan Battista Strozzi wrote that "pain, pity and death are alive in dead marble" ("in vivo marmo morte"), which reverses the terms of Petrarch's "pietra morta, in pietra viva."[48] It also, of course, recalls Michelangelo's subtractive and "Neoplatonic" practice.

It is highly likely that Orsini had Petrarchan ideas of this kind in mind during the course of his work on the Sacro Bosco.[49] It has frequently been pointed out, for example, that the wood is on one level a memorial to his deceased wife, Giulia Farnese. Indeed, the Sacro Bosco was understood in this way during Orsini's own lifetime. In his dedication of Sannazaro's *Arcadia* (1578) to Orsini, for example, Francesco Sansovino refers to the "theatre, the lake and the temple dedicated to the happy memory of the most illustrious lady Giulia Farnese, your former consort."[50] Sansovino emphasized the dedication of the temple to Giulia in two later publications: *Ritratto delle più nobili et famose città d'Italia* (1575), and *Della origine et de' fatti delle famiglie illustri d'Italia* (1582).[51]

Whether or not Orsini was a faithful husband to Giulia, which Coty doubts, and irrespective even of whether Sansovino was referring to the Tempietto in the Sacro Bosco or to the nearby Church of Santa Maria della Valle, there is a striking correlation between the principal medium of the wood— living peperino rock carved in situ—and the Petrarchan poetic metaphor, which, moreover, alludes directly to sculpture.[52] It is not difficult to imagine Orsini himself sitting "down cold as dead stone set on living rock, a statue that can think and weep and write" in his Sacro Bosco or, more precisely, it is not difficult to imagine him imagining himself along these lines. In fact, he seems to echo Petrarch's metaphor in a melancholy letter to Drouet:

> When I consider that from now on there are no more installations to be made in my boschetto, other than contemplating deeper and higher things, this has the effect on me of leaving me insensible, with *a soul like a statue's.* I do still hope to have the sweet company of many men, women as well, and their conversation, and songs and music at meals and so on; I believe my spirit might enjoy that. You may ask "Why then don't you act like that, at your age?" To which I say that I pay for it with my life, for an upset stomach or strong sexual pleasure could be the cause of sending me to join my fathers or—which would be much worse—of getting me maimed and bedridden. Now you could answer me "Do everything in such a way that neither of these things happens." To that I say that nights of love would then be so seldom that I'd forget how it goes, though they're natural things; on the other hand too frequent activity would bring about a condition beyond control. So it is better to forget it all and see if one can find some pleasure in a melancholy life, and if pleasure isn't to be had, at least to minimize the pain, hence *a human being minus pleasure and pain is changed into a statue.*[53]

These sentiments do not, however, necessarily imply an unwarranted romanticization of Orsini's grief over the passing of his wife; only that the Petrarchan concetto is well suited to the unique characteristics of the wood at Bomarzo and the recent events of Orsini's life. Orsini's depth of feeling for his wife (the references in his letters to his dalliances with other women before, during, and after his marriage prove little either way) is of less relevance than the appropriateness of Petrarch's metaphor to Orsini's artistic aims. The point, in short, is that the rock-cut statuary of the Sacro Bosco is perfectly adapted to Petrarch's image of "pietra morta, in pietra viva" and, moreover, that Orsini's late frame of mind seems distinctly Petrarchan.

One further implication of the idea of living rock in the sixteenth century is relevant to the Sacro Bosco. Natural historians believed that all things, including rocks, "grew" in the bowels of the earth. A passage from Scipione Capece's *De principiis rerum* (1546) is representative: "The cave under the great chain of hills, where the native of Lucca, rich in fat oxen, ploughs with the crooked plough, oozes drops of water. We may observe that the moisture oozing there has turned into hard stone, and that soft water, with the passing of time, becomes hard [rock]. In like manner, when a cold wind blows vigorously over the earth, moisture falling from the roofs or from the weeping boughs, though until now it has flowed like a liquid, changes into ice and hangs down in the form of a hard icicle."[54]

In garden design, these ideas are most familiar from grottoes and their ornamentation.[55] The Grotta Grande in the Boboli, for instance, depicts various states of generation, growth, and metamorphosis in the formation of form—from inchoate *materia* to completed figures and landscapes. It is worth recalling that in 1585 Michelangelo's emergent and half-formed *Prigioni* were installed as telamons in Buontalenti's grotto, as if to underline the point.[56] The living rocks of the Sacro Bosco imply something similar. They emerge from the earth—quite literally—in differing states of completion, albeit in the open air rather than inside grottoes, which were interpreted as microcosmic representations of the interior of the earth and its processes.[57] As a wood rather than a garden, the Sacro Bosco is also suggestive of interiority, enclosure, and even, perhaps, microcosmic symbolism.

The artistic precedents of the living rocks are, in summary, in post-Michelangelesque sculptural practice and ancient Etruscan rock-cut funerary monuments. They belong to the same poetic world as Petrarch's poem "Di pensier in pensier, di monte in monte." They also refer to two compatible creation myths—one "scientific" and the other mythical or folkloric. The first is the natural historical explanation for the generation of form in the bowels of the earth. The second is associated with the archaic figure of the giant as both avatar and amanuensis of nature—creator of the landscape.

It should, finally, be obvious that the concept of the earth as a *living* body implies a concept of the earth as a *grotesque* body. It is, as in Bakhtin's definition, a "body in the act of becoming. It is never finished, never completed."[58] This applies as much to the Hell Mouth as it does to the living rocks of the Sacro Bosco and, indeed, the landscape in general. The concept is also implied by the porous bodies of the Renaissance garden, which vomit, lactate, and micturate water. The living earth is a major theme of the Renaissance garden, but it is always an imperfect, metamorphic, generative, and ultimately grotesque earth.

Substitutions: The Garden in Time

In his essay "Of Other Spaces," Michel Foucault stated: "Heterotopias are most often linked to slices in time—which is to say that they open onto what might be termed, for the sake of symmetry, heterochronies."[59] He gives the example of a cemetery in which the subject is both absent and present. The deceased is consigned to a "quasi-eternity in which her permanent lot is dissolution and disappearance."[60] In modernity, Foucault continues, museums and libraries can be defined as heterochronic in their accumulation of time in a place that is itself outside time.

Arguably, however, heterochronism is not an exclusive characteristic of modern spaces and institutions. The Fontana Papacqua in Soriano nel Cimino, near Bomarzo, for example, accomplishes similar "time-bending" effects in which multiple pasts or temporalities coexist in a perpetual present. In Soriano, the mythical goat-woman Amalthea—a grotesque human-animal hybrid from whose breasts water pours (figure 42)—is implausibly accompanied by the Old Testament patriarch Moses (figure 43). This juxtaposition may not be historically and culturally defensible—Amalthea and Moses belong, of course, to quite different traditions—but in Soriano their presence reflects the influence of Annius's complex Viterbocentric genealogies of the gods and the Etruscan civilization.[61]

Pseudo-Etruscan letters are inscribed on the base of the rock upon which Amalthea reclines. Coty suggests that "the presence of the epigraphy playfully gives the impression that the nymphaeum is of Etruscan manufacture,

Figure 42. Amalthea. Fontana Papacqua, Soriano nel Cimino. Photo: Luke Morgan.

as though a product of an earlier, Arcadian time when the region's 'human stock was not yet separated from the goat-footed ones.'"[62] This pretense of great antiquity links Madruzzo's nymphaeum to Orsini's Sacro Bosco. In the latter, for example, there is a faux Etruscan *tomba a fossa* and the ruin of an "Etruscan" tomb.

The nymphaeum in Soriano and the tombs in Bomarzo would amount to little more than idiosyncratic expressions of the personal taste of Orsini's circle were it not for a local tradition of forgery of Etruscan antiquities. Annius substantiated his claims about the ancient history of Europe through his "discovery" of a cache of "vases, bronzes, and marbles incised with old letters" near Viterbo.[63] These "proved" the existence and accuracy of the testimony of the Chaldean sage Berosus, whom Annius had invented. Annius's phony antiquities, which he actually buried and then excavated, thus corroborated his texts, and vice versa, in a mutually reinforcing hermeneutic circle.

Not all of Annius's evidence was forged. The so-called *Marmo osiriano*, for example, had for many years been visible in the Duomo at Viterbo (originally

Figure 43. Moses. Fontana Papacqua, Soriano nel Cimino. Photo: Luke Morgan.

a Temple of Hercules, according to Annius). In Annius's words: "Our fore-fathers . . . in order to keep the eternal memory of the antiquity of this city before our eyes, placed before the *rostra a columnula*, that is, an alabaster tab-let, monument to the triumph of Osiris."[64] Annius interpreted the medieval lunette with two profile heads (of, he claimed, Osiris and his cousin Sais Xan-tho) in the spandrel, as a fragment of a column erected by Osiris and thus proof that the Egyptian god had visited Italy.

Annius's acknowledgment that the monument might be a replica of a lost original is of more significance than his spurious interpretation: "Whether this is truly the tablet or a substitute for it—the original having collapsed through age—we cannot yet be certain. Either way, we consider the tablet to have survived."[65] His acceptance of the *Marmo osiriano* as ancient, and as extant, despite the very real possibility that it was in fact a copy is a clear example of what Alexander Nagel and Christopher S. Wood have called the early modern "principle of substitution." This is also an important principle of the Sacro Bosco.

Nagel and Wood contend that a work of art is "a strange kind of event whose relation to time is plural."[66] On one level, this is fairly self-evident. The work of art during the Renaissance often refers to a prior point of origin—in mythology or divinity—but it also, like all durable art, addresses its future audiences. Nagel and Wood give their premise greater specificity, however, when they identify and describe two competing models of the temporality of the work of art in the fifteenth and sixteenth centuries. The first is the substitutional model, of which the *Marmo osiriano* is an example: "Under this model, the work did not merely repeat the prior work, for repetition proposes difference, an altering interval. Rather, the work simply *is* its own predecessor, such that the prior is no longer prior but present."[67]

The Byzantine icon tradition provides a straightforward example of this argument. For centuries, indeed millennia, this visual tradition underwent almost no stylistic changes: each image of the Madonna looks like prior images of the Madonna. The stability, even stasis, of the depiction of the Virgin ultimately derives from a legend—that St. Luke painted her portrait (she appeared before him in a vision). The concept of the sacred image as likeness ensured the remarkable longevity of the ancient conventions governing the depiction of the Madonna. Each subsequent icon was not, however, a copy or repetition but a "true" portrayal or, in Nagel and Wood's terminology, its own predecessor. The "real presence" of the Virgin was in this way preserved.

The second model of the temporality of the work of art during the Renaissance was based on a principle of authorship associated with the "mystery of the artist's talent."[68] According to Leonardo, for example, "[The painting] cannot be copied, as happens with letters, where the copy is worth as much as the original. It cannot be cast, as happens with sculpture where the impression is like the original as far as the virtue of the work is concerned. It does not produce infinite children, as do printed books. Painting alone remains noble, it alone honors its author (*onora il suo Autore*) and remains precious and unique and never bears children equal to itself. This singularity makes painting more excellent than those [sciences] which are widely published."[69] In this "authorial" or "performative" model, the origin of the work of art is not in some temporally distant event or artifact but in the performance of the unique *ingenium* of the individual artist and cannot be replicated. (This resembles Vasari's notion of artistic genius, which modern art history inherited.) The result is that "the painting's resistance to duplication allows it to dominate time."[70]

Nagel and Wood add one further element to this conceptual framework. They note that the time-collapsing propensity of the work of art was not discovered or invented in the Renaissance. What was new, however, was the period's "apprehensiveness about the temporal instability of the artwork, and its re-creation of the artwork as an occasion for reflection on that instability."[71] The clash of the two models of the temporality of the work of art, in other words, provoked an anxiety that was manifested as an exploration of time. In this way, the artistic project of the Renaissance comes to resemble that of early twentieth-century modernism in that both were periods of artistic innovation motivated by an intense interest in the capabilities, peculiarities, and limits of the mediums of art.[72]

"Anachronic" thus describes the strange, even disturbing, temporal effects of the Renaissance work of art. As Nagel and Wood put it:

> To anachronize is to be belated again, to linger. The work is late, first because it succeeds some reality that it re-presents, and then late again when that re-presentation is repeated for successive recipients. To many that double postponement came to seem troublesome, calling for correction, compensation, or, at the very least, explanation.
>
> The work of art when it is late, when it repeats, when it hesitates, when it remembers, but also when it projects a future or an ideal, is "anachronic." We introduce this term as an alternative to "anachronistic," a judgmental term that caries with it the historicist assumption that every event and every object has its proper location within objective and linear time.[73]

Anachronism is linked to the substitutional model, which was increasingly troubled and ultimately superseded by the performative or authorial model of artistic production. (Nagel and Wood's account of anachronism concludes with Raphael's Vatican *Stanze* frescoes, which "mask so successfully any possible doubts about their own authority"—the triumph of the author over the anachronic.)[74]

Nagel and Wood argue that their conceptual model could potentially be brought to bear on "anything built or pictured between the fourteenth and sixteenth centuries," including, presumably, gardens.[75] However, not all of their readers have been so sure. In one of the most thoughtful early reviews of *Anachronic Renaissance* (2010), Frank Fehrenbach wondered "how one would define the substitutionality of, say . . . Buontalenti's *Grotta Grande* (1583–93) in the Boboli Gardens? Where is the 'sameness' with a past original (or an a-temporal norm) that . . . [the grotto] . . . would self-reflectively juxtapose to artistic performance?"[76]

Yet the Grotta Grande (figure 44) might actually be regarded as paradigmatic of the principle of substitution in sixteenth-century gardens. Renaissance landscape designers, as we would now call them, were even more poorly informed than architects. Nagel and Wood note that "in the fifteenth century a consuming interest in Vitruvius arose among a new class of author architects and architectural cognoscenti who read the treatise as a guide for reconstructing ancient architecture but found themselves stranded between, on the one hand, the elliptical and in part incomprehensible text and, on the other, the fragmentary material evidence."[77]

At least architects had access to physical fragments—ruins and *spolia*—however partial or vestigial they may have been. Landscape designers were forced to rely on attenuated references to ancient gardens in textual sources, such as Pliny the Elder's epistolary descriptions of his Laurentium and Tusculum villas and, in an even more general sense, the landscape descriptions in Ovid's *Metamorphoses*. If one of the aims of Renaissance architecture was "projective reconstruction," then this was even more true of the development of the garden in the same period.[78] In fact, a better analogy than architecture for the relation of Renaissance gardens in general to the ancient world may be provided by a late work of Alessandro Botticelli. His painting *The Calumny of Apelles* (1494) was explicitly based on Lucian's exegetical account of a lost ancient painting (as redacted by Alberti).[79] Botticelli's picture was therefore a "substitution" of an absent original, mediated by text. The same might be said to apply to sixteenth-century gardens, which likewise "substituted" for lost and only dimly perceived originals.

Buontalenti's Grotta Grande succinctly expresses this relationship. As Naomi Miller recognized, it "is surely an example of a Renaissance grotto with Classical prototypes, its walls covered with chalky limestone and adorned with figures in scenes of painted stucco."[80] Yet its prototypes cannot be identified. The Grotta Grande substitutes for a "past original" that has no, and perhaps never had any, material existence. It is a projective reconstruction of an idea of the grotto found in ancient writings. In his discussion of pumice, for example, Pliny notes: "This name, of course, is given to the hollowed rocks in the buildings called by the Greeks 'Home of the Muses,' where such rocks hang from the ceiling so as to create an artificial imitation of a cave."[81] In the *Metamorphoses*, Ovid describes "a vale in that region . . . the sacred haunt of high-girt Diana. In its most secret nook there was a well-shaded grotto wrought by no

Figure 44. Bernardo Buontalenti, Grotta Grande, 1583–1593. Boboli Gardens, Florence. Photo: Luke Morgan.

artist's hand. But Nature by her own cunning had imitated art; for she had shaped a native arch of the living rock and soft tufa."[82]

Like Botticelli's *Calumny of Apelles*, the "substitutionality" of Buontalenti's Grotta Grande is dependent on textual description rather than a material original. This relationship is not, however, qualitatively different to that of the earlier example of the Byzantine icon in which, arguably, the original—the living, breathing figure of the Madonna—is also irretrievably lost (albeit historically mediated by the visual rather than the textual). Perhaps, then, the only point of difference is one of degree or, better, embodiment: the substitutionality of the Grotta Grande might thus be qualified as "virtual" or as "simulative" given the physical absence of any original. In this case, the grotto—emphatically—"simply *is* its own predecessor, such that the prior is no longer prior but present," as in Nagel and Wood's general definition of the anachronic artwork.[83] Indeed, it could be argued that nonlinear, anachronic time is a fundamental condition of the Renaissance garden, a medium of art whose reconstructions are necessarily *more* projective than those of other contemporary mediums.

Fehrenbach's second query concerns the juxtaposition of the two models of the temporality of the artwork—the substitutional and the authorial—which he implies is absent in the Grotta Grande. In one respect, however, the grotto contained a preeminent example of authorial performance—Michelangelo's four *Prisoners*, which entered Cosimo I de' Medici's collection during the period of the grotto's construction (and provided the impetus to its completion). It has frequently been observed that Michelangelo's unfinished figures, half trapped in their rocky bounds, harmonize with the naturalistic interior of the grotto. But from another perspective, the *Prisoners* are quintessential expressions of the Renaissance concept of artistic genius; of the idea that an artwork is the unique expression of a unified subject, whose artistic utterances "dominate time." Michelangelo is, after all, the presiding figure of Vasari's *Lives of the Artists*— "a genius universal in each art . . . seeming rather divine than earthly."[84] Instead, therefore, of seeing the sculptures as well adapted to and participatory in the rocky and rupestral décor of the artificial cavern, they can be regarded as initiating the dialectic between two competing models of the temporality of the artwork: the substitutional, however virtual, and the authorial.

Other elements of the Grotta Grande attest to the presence of this dialectical condition. It has already been suggested that Giambologna's Fountain of Venus, installed in the innermost cavity of the grotto complex in 1592, implies the "dramatic duality," as Brunon calls it, of sixteenth-century gardens between the (oscillating) categories of the classical and the grotesque. To reiterate: the former is signified by the figure of Venus Anadyomene and the latter by the leering satyrs who are depicted grasping the sides of the basin as they gaze lecherously up at the nude figure. According to Nagel and Wood, "Precisely because it is a performance, normativity or classicism can never be a long-term or stable state in the modern West. The performance of the classical is always quickly fed back into the recursive mill to become raw material for the next performance."[85] Their point is less relevant to the issue of temporality in the Grotta Grande than it is to that of the contingent and vicarious relationship between the classical and the grotesque, but it does underline the inherently dialectical structure of the grotto.

The contrast between the classical and the grotesque, or the rational and the disorderly, is also found in the Sacro Bosco, where an elegant Tempietto stands near the colossal group of fighting giants. Indeed, the concept of anachronism seems peculiarly well suited to the Sacro Bosco.[86] Like other sixteenth-century gardens, it lacks a definitive "author" (although it is generally assumed that Orsini was responsible for laying it out). The wood certainly cannot be interpreted as the performance of an identifiable author-artist, and, though idiosyncratic, it is not entirely unique. Another branch of the Orsini family seems to have followed Vicino's lead at Pitigliano, where worn rock-cut figures and benches are still (just) extant. The Hell Mouth was likewise duplicated at several sites—from the garden of the Villa Aldobrandini in Frascati to the Giardino Giusti in Verona.

Of more importance here, however, is the status of the "ruins" of the Sacro Bosco, and their relationship to the rock-cut Etruscan necropolises of the Bomarzo area. Oleson is right to point out that the Etruscan references in the Sacro Bosco have been neglected by scholars, especially the "reproduction" tomb (figure 45), but his understanding of them as straightforward derivations from local originals suppresses their complex relations to historical time.[87] These are anachronic monuments that reveal much about the Sacro Bosco as a whole.

The Etruscan tomb is a deliberate ruin or what, in the eighteenth century, would come to be known as a "folly."[88] As Oleson observes: "Although the block gives the impression of having broken free from a complete monument and tumbled down the slope, the left side of the façade never existed, and the worked base cannot have been buried in the earth as a foundation."[89] In contrast to the Tempietto (figure 46), in other words, it was never completed, but was designed, preemptively, to depict the ravages of time. (It even has a

Figure 45. "Etruscan Tomb." Sacro Bosco, Bomarzo. Photo: Luke Morgan.

"picturesque fracture.")[90] Like the other monuments of the Sacro Bosco, it was sculpted out of a local peperino boulder. The upper part of the monument has been carved to resemble a gabled facade with a niche and door, Corinthian pilasters, and corner volutes "reminiscent of Hellenistic Etruscan Aeolic capitals."[91] The bas-relief of the pediment depicts a monstrous hybrid figure with a human head, wings and a scaly fishtail carrying an oar.

The monument is a simulation of a third- or second-century B.C.E. rock-cut tomb from southern Etruria, but it is not based on a specific precedent. It is, therefore, not a representation, though it obviously refers to the local landscape of Etruscan ruins, but a substitution. As a faux antiquity, it is a simulation of a tomb without a function or referent. It entombs no one and has no specific source. Its relationship to the ancient Etruscan tombs of the region suggests Richard Brilliant's distinction between *spolia in se* (the reuse of material objects) and *spolia in re* (the reuse of virtual objects or reproductions).[92] The "doublethink" of the Renaissance with regard to spolia in re and objects like the *Marmo osiriano*, in which originals and copies inhabited the same conceptual territory, also applies to the tomb in the bosco.[93] From this

Figure 46. Tempietto. Sacro Bosco, Bomarzo. Photo: Luke Morgan.

perspective, Annibal Caro's puzzling description of the ancient (*antica*) "teatri, logge & stanze & tempi" of the Sacro Bosco seems perfectly apt.[94] It simply did not matter whether the "ancient" structures of the Sacro Bosco were originals or copies. Their significance and meaning were the same.

Orsini's "Etruscan" tomb is also literally "belated again," in Nagel and Wood's formulation. It is "late, first because it succeeds some reality that it re-presents, and then late again when that re-presentation is repeated for successive recipients." The ruinous state of the tomb, compared with the wood's other monuments, indicates that it was meant to be seen as older, that there is more than one temporality in the Sacro Bosco. But it also belongs to the future. It simultaneously substitutes for an ancient Etruscan tomb and anticipates the invention of the folly in the eighteenth century.

Orsini's faux tomb is at once, therefore, both behind and ahead of its time. It performs the "function of art under the substitutional system [which] was precisely to effect a disruption of chronological time, to collapse temporal distance."[95] This is a characteristic of the ruin in general (whether real, fabricated, or depicted), which at the simplest level is a metaphor for the passing of time.⁹⁶ The disruptive agency of the ruin could also be disturbing. Maria Fabricius Hansen has drawn attention to negative perceptions of ruins in the Renaissance: "If buildings were compared with bodies, ruins were perceived as repugnant forms of organic decay."⁹⁷ In 1398, for example, Pier Paolo Vergerio observed that the air close to ruins was detrimental to one's health. Later, Poggio Bracciolini characterized the city of Rome as "stripped naked of all ornament, lying prostrate like a giant rotten corpse."⁹⁸

In Hansen's summary: "A ruin was somehow shameful as it was deformed, unintegral architecture, a material structure lacking coherence and limits or definition."⁹⁹ Alberti's catalogue of architectural defects, Hansen points out, was representative: anything "distorted, stunted, excessive, or deformed in any way" (which recalls early modern attempts to categorize monstrosity). In Alberti's view, "no one can look at anything shameful, deformed or disgusting without immediate displeasure and aversion."¹⁰⁰ Ruination could still provoke fear in the late sixteenth century. In 1591, Francesco Bocchi observed that the seemingly ruinous state of the Boboli Grotta Grande "aroused delight, but not without terror, because the building seemed about to collapse to the ground."¹⁰¹

Once again, the grotesque lurks behind these various negative appraisals of the ruin, whether actual or fictive. In fact, the ruin and especially the ruined tomb in the Sacro Bosco might be seen as epitomizing the grotesque. It is an analogue of the dismembered body; a sign of incompletion, failure, and the anticlassical. (Although, at Bomarzo, the "classical" means something different to, for example, Roman or Venetian understandings of the term. In the Annian narratives, the "classical antiquity" of the Alto Lazio was Etrurian and mythic rather than Greco-Roman.) Bracciolini's prostrate Roman giant recalls the lovesick colossus of the *Hypnerotomachia Poliphili*, whose body could be entered and traversed. Likewise, the imputation of corporeality to the city and its architectural fragments by both Bracciolini and Raphael cannot help but suggest Filarete's comparison of a building to a body, which needs "to be nourished and governed," lest "through lack it sickens and dies like man." In this context, a detached fragment of a larger architectural whole—such as Orsini's ruined tomb—might connote illness, amputation, and deformity.

This association of the ruin with the grotesque is not merely rhetorical.¹⁰² First, grotteschi were in effect discovered *inside* a ruin—the Domus Aurea—at the close of the fifteenth century. The subsequent histories of ruins and grotteschi are intertwined. Ruins are, for example, depicted in the extensive grotteschi decorations of the ceiling of the east wing of the Uffizi by Antonio Tempesta and Alessandro Allori (1579–1581; figure 47). Second, ruins and

Figure 47. Detail of the Ceiling of the East Wing, Uffizi, decorated by Antonio Tempesta and Alessandro Allori, 1579–1581. Photo: Luke Morgan.

grotesque ornaments were explicitly associated in more than one garden building of the sixteenth century. (Hansen has pointed out that they were especially favored in threshold spaces such as corridors, passageways. and loggias opening onto gardens.)[103] A particularly relevant example, given its proximity to Bomarzo and the fact that Cardinal Gianfrancesco Gambara was a member of Orsini's circle, is the ceiling of one of the casinos of the Villa Lante in Bagnaia (commissioned by Gambara).

Ruins, then, like living bodies, are imperfect expressions of mortality, of temporality and, consequently, of the grotesque—the principal mode of the Sacro Bosco as a whole. From the early sixteenth century, ruins were often associated with grotteschi, which indicates that their connotations were understood as shared. As a fictive ruin, the "Etruscan" tomb in the Sacro Bosco appropriates and participates in this symbolism. As a substitution rather than a representation, albeit one without a referent (or "original")—an example of spolia in re—it is no less authentic than the ancient tombs of its environs.

"The Grotesque Is Everywhere"

This chapter has not proposed another interpretation of the Sacro Bosco. It has, rather, had the more limited aim of drawing attention to two of the most unusual features of Orsini's creation: the sculptures carved from living rock, and the fragment of an "Etruscan" temple. In the absence of any real history of reception, it has tried to reconstruct contemporary attitudes to rock-cut statuary and ruins. After all, to have attempted a comprehensive interpretation of the wood would contradict the initial premise: that the experience of landscape is more like browsing than reading. This chapter presents, in other words, an unashamedly partial account. Yet, arguably, this reflects the condition of the historical visitor to gardens, then as now.

A handful of the hypotheses explored here do, however, have a broader applicability. The Sacro Bosco that emerges from this chapter is certainly unusual, but it is not, as has sometimes been argued, a bizarre oddity or aporeitic outlier constructed in a personal idiolect analogous perhaps to that of the *Hypnerotomachia* in literature. As a designed space, it is itself a kind of fragment, not unlike its ruins, at least in the broader context of Italian Renaissance landscape design. Many of the most notable gardens of the period, such as the Villa Medici in Pratolino or the nearby Villa Lante in Bagnaia, incorporate *boschi* or *boschetti*, which the Sacro Bosco can be compared with. Orsini's exclusive focus on the motif of the perilous "dark forest," which so fascinated early Italian writers and poets, is related to the growing tendency in sixteenth-century design to incorporate wilderness within the walls. It points toward a developing interest in proto-sublime experience within the microcosm of the garden.

Another theme of Renaissance landscape design is manifest in the Sacro Bosco—what might be thought of as a strain of animism. The garden, as an experimental, heterotopic site—a kind of material reenactment of Ovid's *Metamorphoses*—was overtly pagan or neo-pagan in its imagery and symbolism. The anthropomorphic living rocks of the Sacro Bosco can thus be related to the survival of archaic beliefs about the maternal principle and the earth as a living entity or body. These ideas are found elsewhere in sixteenth-century Italy, besides the Villa d'Este garden, which was once presided over by the ancient Asiatic goddess, Diana Ephesia. The giants of Bomarzo, like those of Pratolino, Bagnaia, Caprarola, and the Oricellari, are also, ultimately, indicative of an implicit theme of gardens—the relation of the landscape to a host of seemingly contradictory origin myths. Madruzzo's nymphaeum at Soriano nel Cimino succinctly expresses this clash of origins.

These contradictions and antagonisms are rarely resolved in Renaissance gardens, however much one might want them to be. In fact, they proliferate. Animistic attitudes toward the landscape and popular legends of the giants as avatars or demiurges of nature are joined by natural historical hypotheses about the origin and growth of all things deep within the womb of the earth. Well-proportioned, functional buildings are compared with healthy, virile bodies, and ruins with sick or deformed limbs. Annius and Leonardo are not as far apart as one might imagine. The *campanilismo* of the charlatan scholar and the rational skepticism of the prototypical modern scientist are not only anthropocentric but also anthropomorphic. The stories of the giants are essentially about physical bodies, even if they are gargantuan ones with hypertrophied appetites and excessive agency. In sixteenth-century natural history, the earth itself was conceived of as a giant body. As Leonardo put it: "Its flesh be the soil, its bones be the arrangement and connection of the rocks of which the mountains are composed; its cartilages are the tufa, its blood the veins of water."[104]

This emphasis on the open, unfinished, living, and breathing body, which Renaissance gardens thematize in multiple ways, is a manifestation of the grotesque in the broad Rabelaisian sense rather than in the more technical sixteenth-century aesthetic sense of grotteschi. To quote Victor Hugo again: "The grotesque is everywhere: on the one hand it creates the formless and the terrifying, on the other hand the comic, the buffoon-like."[105] The grotesque body is inescapable in the Renaissance garden.

The Sacro Bosco draws attention to one further theme of sixteenth-century landscape design. Orsini's ruin may be an unusual early instance of a folly in a garden, but its implications for the status of temporality in the Renaissance garden are significant. Like the Boboli Grotta Grande, the "Etruscan" temple in the Sacro Bosco cannot be identified as a copy or representation of a prior structure. Neither is it a forgery or a fake. It is, rather, an anachronic monument, the modus operandi of which is substitutional. In this way, it reflects contemporary ideas about the persistent authority of ancient images, even in circumstances where the ancient prototype is no longer extant but has been replaced by a substitute.

The ruined temple is not alone in fulfilling the conditions of substitutionality in the Sacro Bosco. The Tempietto, for example, which David R. Coffin has demonstrated is closely based on Vitruvius's description of an Etruscan temple is, like the Grotta Grande in the Boboli Gardens, in a similar relation to "antiquity" as Botticelli's *Calumny of Apelles*.[106] All three were inspired by exegetical descriptions of lost originals. This raises, for the last time, the vexed issue of the relationship of so-called Renaissance gardens to their classical predecessors. What, in fact, are the grounds for describing the sixteenth-century garden as a manifestation of *rinascità*, rebirth or renaissance? The term seems ill chosen, given the almost complete absence of evidence for classical landscape design in early modern Italy.

On the other hand though, the substitutional model of transmission may go some way toward legitimating its continued usage, with one caveat. It seems obvious that it is an imagined antiquity that is revived in the sixteenth-century garden; an antiquity that again more closely resembles the world of the *Hypnerotomachia* than it does any excavated Greek or Roman garden.[107] Finally, even that statement needs to be qualified. The imagined antiquity of the Viterban, or Annian, Sacro Bosco, manifest in its substitutions, is not that of the Roman Villa d'Este or the Florentine Boboli Gardens, still less that of the Venetian Giardino Giusti. The rinascità of sixteenth-century gardens in Italy is much more variegated, localized, and differentiated.

Conclusion

Toward the Sublime

We want to have *us* translated into stone and plants; we want to take
walks *in us* when we stroll through these hallways and gardens.
— Friedrich Nietzsche, *The Gay Science*

In a letter to the Florentine traveler and merchant Benedetto Dei, Leonardo
da Vinci wrote that a giant had appeared from the Libyan desert.[1] This terrifying figure had

> swollen and red eyes set beneath the awful, dark eyebrows which
> might cause the sky to be overcast and the earth to tremble. And,
> believe me, there is no man so brave but that when the fiery eyes
> were turned upon him he would not willingly have put on wings
> in order to flee, for infernal Lucifer's face would seem angelic when
> compared with this. The nose was turned up with wide nostrils
> from which issued many large bristles; beneath these was the arched
> mouth with thick lips, and with whiskers at the ends like a cat's,
> and the teeth were yellow. He towered above the heads of men on
> horseback from the top of his feet upward. When the proud giant
> fell because of the gory and miry ground it seemed as though a
> mountain had fallen; whereat the country shook as with an earth-
> quake, with terror to Pluto in hell; and Mars fearing for his life took
> refuge under the bed of Jove.[2]

Leonardo relates that when the giant fell, the people, who believed that he
had been slain by a thunderbolt, proceeded to swarm all over his body and

through his hair like lice ("the minute creatures which are sometimes found harbored there"). Rousing himself, the giant shook off his puny assailants, killing multitudes.

Leonardo's fiction is the equivalent of his drawing *The Deluge* (figure 48), which depicts a vortex of water destroying everything in its path, including the structures erected by men and women. In the letter, nature is personified as a malevolent and enraged giant.[3] The melancholic demiurge of the Villa Medici in Pratolino—Giambologna's *Appennino*—may not possess the same frightening alterity, but it is nonetheless a personification of unruly natural forces. In Pratolino, the giant is depicted creating the landscape (personified as a "monstrous head"). Indeed, most of the colossi of the Renaissance garden signify nature, whether they are benign (the river gods) or malign (Polyphemus).

In folklore, the figure of the giant is defined by his or her appetites: he or she is a devourer and sometimes a cannibal. Leonardo may have had this popular tradition in mind when he imagined his own fate, "swimming with bent head through the mighty throat, and remaining buried within a huge belly, confused with death," at the end of his letter to Dei.[4] The implication is that the giant, or nature, has fatally ingested him. His lot recalls Poliphilo's (albeit voluntary) journey through the body of a colossus "down the stairs that were in his throat, thence into his stomach, and so by intricate passageways, and in some terror, to all the other parts of his internal viscera."[5] Leonardo's giant is also suggestive of Rabelais's Pantagruel, who "swallows, devours, rends the world apart."[6] Of course, Alcofrybas's experience inside the body of the giant with its "countless summerhouses in the Italian style scattered over fields of delights" is the opposite of Leonardo's suspended chthonic state.[7]

Walter Stephens has argued that the folkloric giant, far from being a benign embodiment of "us" or "our" culture as Bakhtin believed, is in fact absolutely "other" to "us."[8] In pre-Renaissance traditions the figure of the giant was conceived as a terrifying "enemy" and embodiment of danger.[9] Stephens draws on Susan Stewart's arguments about scale, but arrives at different conclusions:

> The question of scale may explain why the ultimate fascination of
> the Giant is with his appetite, his capacity to devour or "contain"
> even ordinary human beings. From the Cyclops to the maneaters
> of such tales as Jack and the Beanstalk, to Alcofrybas's explora-
> tion of his master's digestive tract, the Giant's capacity to devour
> and envelop—whether he actually does so or not—exerts a queasy
> charm over narrators and audiences of Giant tales. This capacity

Figure 48. Leonardo da Vinci, *The Deluge*, c. 1517–1518. Courtesy of Royal Collection Trust/© Her Majesty Queen Elizabeth II, 2014.

ultimately expresses our uneasiness at the disproportion between ourselves and our surroundings, and the hostility to things human which incidentally results from nature's vastness.[10]

Stephens's characterization of the giant recalls one of the premises of this book: that in Ovid's *Metamorphoses* and sixteenth-century writings, nature sometimes acts with cruelty and amorality and that this antagonistic theme often appears in Renaissance gardens alongside the more familiar imagery of the locus amoenus. In Stephens's interpretation and Leonardo's letter to Dei, the giant personifies the elemental forces of nature, which dwarf and belittle the human subject. The giant, as a symbol of the "overly natural," signifies the enveloping vastness and unpredictability of nature.[11]

Fear, topophobia, and antagonism are neglected concepts in landscape history. Yet there is evidence, besides the connotations of the giant, that early

modern gardens provoked these kinds of responses despite (or perhaps because of) their Arcadian aspirations. The vicious serpent or dragon that attacks the companions of Cadmus in the *Metamorphoses* within an archetypal
locus amoenus—"an ancient forest" with pleasant springs and cool grottoes—
provides a prototype. Dragons are likewise frequently depicted within the
idyllic spaces of the Renaissance garden, which so often drew on Ovid. Indeed, the violence of the *Metamorphoses* is echoed in numerous images of the
garden: Hercules crushing Antaeus to death in Castello, for instance, and the
enraged Orlando tearing a woodsman apart in Bomarzo.

The historical reception of the grotesque, which found a natural home
in the sixteenth-century garden, provides another example. From Vitruvius
to John Ruskin, the grotesque has appeared to some commentators as "depraved," "degraded," and "foul."[12] Edmund Wilson's horrified reaction to the
Sacro Bosco may be a twentieth-century response, but it has its antecedents
in earlier periods. The closely related category of the monstrous has similar implications. The monsters of the garden, expressions of *mescolanza* and
what Eugenio Battisti dubbed the *antirinascimento*, reflect contemporary
ideas about abnormality in medicine, teratology, and law, in addition to their
status as natural marvels or lusus naturae. The harpy, for instance, tortured
by what Ulisse Aldrovandi called its "doglike appetite," yet a conventional
figure of the sixteenth-century garden, is an entirely negative presence, with
no redeeming features. Or there is the image of the Hell Mouth, which is repeated in several late Renaissance gardens: a disembodied, cannibalistic monster with roots in pagan and Christian visual traditions of the underworld
and the wages of sin.

Some early modern commentators were explicit about their fear of the
natural environment, both inside and outside the garden. In the seventeenth
century, a British visitor noted that the Fountain of the Dragons at the Villa
d'Este in Tivoli belched water "of so black a colour, that it resembleth an ugly
smoke, fearful to behold."[13] In 1591, Francesco Bocchi commented that the
Grotta Grande in the Boboli Gardens in Florence "aroused delight, but not
without terror, because the building seemed about to collapse to the ground,"
which is indicative of contemporary attitudes toward ruins in general.[14] Bocchi's experience corresponds to Leonardo's own "contrary emotions," which
ranged from "fear of the threatening dark grotto" to "desire to see whether
there were any marvellous thing within it."[15] Yet another example is provided
by Taegio's *La Villa*, in which Vitauro describes the "horror" of external nature
with its "threatening mountains, serpent's lairs, dark caves, horrid cliffs."[16] In

the sixteenth century this wild and forbidding landscape was brought inside the confines of the garden.

The giant, the grotesque hybrid, the monster, the ruin, and the wilderness were thus figures of fear, yet they were all represented in Renaissance landscape design. Their presence suggests a possibility that has remained implicit until now: that the pleasures of the sixteenth-century garden—as much a locus horridus as a locus amoenus—may have resembled those of the sublime.[17]

The most important text for the idea of the sublime prior to Edmund Burke and Immannuel Kant's eighteenth-century aesthetic treatises was Longinus's *Peri hupsous* (*On the Sublime*) (c. CE 50). This work was widely disseminated in manuscript editions from the fifteenth century onward, despite the long-standing assumption that it was not well known until Nicolas Boileau's famous translation of it into French in 1674.[18] Notwithstanding direct influence, it is plausible that "in early modern Europe experiences that after 1750 would be characterized as 'sublime' did occur, but were labeled differently: as experiences of wonder or amazement, as mystical experiences of rapture, as horror or fear."[19]

In Burke's eighteenth-century distinction between the beautiful and the sublime, the latter is said to involve a pleasurable fear or dread.[20] The sublime is, of course, firmly associated with Enlightenment aesthetics, though there have been some recent attempts to reconstruct its historical genealogy.[21] Unsurprisingly, it is a concept that frequently appears in studies of giants and the gigantic, since it is, in the accounts of Burke and Kant, often defined as an overwhelmed response to vast size or scale in nature (such as mountain tops, ravines, and seascapes). The sublime is, for example, fundamental to Susan Stewart's understanding of the gigantic.[22] Similarly, for Jeffrey Jerome Cohen, although he is primarily interested in northern European medieval literature, "giants are figures of sublime dread."[23]

In a study of the giants of the *Divine Comedy*, Eleanora Stoppino has argued that a "gigantic pseudo-Sublime" or "interrupted Sublime" appears in Dante's *Inferno*.[24] She suggests that Kant's "mathematical sublime" offers a useful guide for the definition of the sublime in Dante's poem: "The form of Sublime that arises from the gigantic in canto XXXI of the *Divine Comedy* is an interrupted Sublime à la Kant, one that does not end either in the realization of infinity or in the annihilation of the self within it. In this episode there is indeed a representative failure of the imagination to comprehend the gigantic. What ensues and interrupts the movement toward the sublime is the management of the gigantic through either mathematical measurement or dismemberment."[25] The pleasure, in other words, derives from a process of containment rather than a sense of ecstatic helplessness in the face of the unfathomable. This, clearly, is not the later concept of the sublime, which entails an ultimately enjoyable annihilation of the self, but it does resonate with Renaissance concepts and experiences of the gigantic. The huge bones (of elephants and other animals), like those that Madruzzo presented to Orsini, were thought to have once belonged to giants; the colossal fragments of classical sculpture were familiar to artists both before and after Michelangelo; in literature, Francesco Colonna's Island of Cythera is littered with giant body parts; the monstrous hell mouths of the Renaissance garden are, similarly, disembodied heads, synecdochal signs of a presumably previously unified, though horrific, giant body.[26]

The fear that the giant in the garden, such as the *Appennino*, might have elicited in its observers was therefore probably of a curtailed kind; something like Stoppino's "interrupted Sublime." It was an effect of enormity, but this was never limitless—obviously so.[27] The interrupted sublime of the *Appennino* nonetheless looks forward to the later formulations of eighteenth-century philosophy. Giambologna's colossus is, after all, a mountain range.

More generally, many of the records of response to Renaissance gardens that have been discussed in this book imply sublime experience. Leonardo's conflicted state of mind at the entrance to a garden grotto is perhaps the most representative. "Fear" and "desire" are fellow travelers in the sixteenth-century experience of landscape. They imply a Longinian poetics in which opposing elements are juxtaposed despite the fact that this experiential phenomenon had not yet been codified as an aesthetic theory.[28] The dramatic duality between the locus amoenus and the locus horridus in the Renaissance garden can, in this light, be seen as a "vernacular" translation of Longinus's dialectical theory of rhetoric.[29]

Fear was also, of course, a common reaction to the grotesque and the monstrous. This book has argued that people's experience of monstrosity, abnormality, and otherness in multiple discourses, venues, and sites informed their experience of gardens; that a reception history of the Renaissance garden should seek to reconstruct a wide range of mentalités, "ways of seeing," or a "period eye" composed from varied sources. It is a commonplace that the early modern garden was a microcosmic representation of the world outside its walls. But if that is so, then the unpalatable, ostensibly anti-Arcadian themes of the exterior world must logically have intruded into the idyllic spaces of the garden. The presence of grotesque realism, mescolanza, monsters, and giants in the most important late sixteenth-century gardens indicates that this was indeed the case. The Renaissance garden was more than a locus amoenus.

Duality and dialectic are crucial to the modus operandi of landscape design, but conflict and difference are not necessarily resolved in or by the garden. Rather, as a heterotopic space, which simultaneously confirms and contests prevailing norms, gardens are capable of juxtaposing polarities or of holding conflict in a state of suspension. The garden holds a mirror up to its society, mimicking its preoccupations and simulating its forms. This is surely what Friedrich Nietzsche had in mind when he wrote: "We want to have *us* translated into stone and plants; we want to take walks *in us* when we stroll through these hallways and gardens."[30]

Nietzsche's observation is relevant not only to gardens but also to the figure of the monster. Monsters have always been sociocultural constructions that, like gardens, reflect the anxieties of their time and place. The monstrous is only monstrous in relation to a consensual but artificial norm. From this perspective, the monster is a necessary presence in art as in life. In the former, the norm is provided by a notion of the "classical," whereas in the latter it is the "natural" that is normative. According to this logic, grotteschi are unclassical, just as the excessive, deficient, and hybrid bodies of the sixteenth century are unnatural. Yet the binary conceals the fact that the grotesque, like the monstrous, is never a distant externality, safely "other" to the coherent, normative subject, be it a work of art or an individual. The monster is, rather, always within, however denied or repressed. To quote Michel de Montaigne: "I have seen no more evident monster or miracle in the world than myself."[31]

These points, finally, have implications for Arcadia as a cultural concept. In his introduction to the 1578 edition of Jacopo Sannazaro's *Arcadia*, Orsini's friend Francesco Sansovino wrote wistfully: "Reading the present volume, I have found there some descriptions of hills and valleys which, recalling the site of Bomarzo, have awakened in me the greatest longing for it."[32] Sansovino thus associates the Sacro Bosco with one of the most widely read early modern literary evocations of the "ancient *locus amoenus* of Arcadia."[33]

Sannazaro's Arcadia and Orsini's bosco are both "sacred" woods that memorialize a deceased lover: the writer's beloved, Phyllis, and the duke's wife, Giulia Farnese. But the similarities end there. The Sacro Bosco is a garden of monsters and giants, replete with images of violence and ruination. If it is a vision of Arcadia, then it presents, surely, an image of Arcadia as fragile and perpetually under threat. Yet perhaps this is what Arcadia has always been—a dualistic concept that, in its reflection on an ideal, requires its opposite. Without the threat of the dark wood, the rapacious harpy, the murderous giant, or the entrance to hell itself, Arcadia has no definition. If so, then the monsters and giants may be necessary to the idyll.

Notes

INTRODUCTION

Epigraph. Vinci, *Notebooks of Leonardo da Vinci*, 526.

1. "Questi, & molt'altri Mostri simili, & diversi, come quello, che se vede nella loggia dello Spedale della Scala, crediamo noi filosoficamente, che siano stati, & che possono essere." Varchi, *Lezzioni*, 98. Translated in Hanafi, *Monster in the Machine*, 21. See Findlen, *Possessing Nature*, 209–20, for a discussion of Renaissance anatomical demonstrations, including the one attended by Varchi and Bronzino. For the Orti Oricellari, see Bartoli and Contorni, *Gli Orti Oricellari*, and Morolli et al., *Il gigante*. Besides Hanafi, *Monster in the Machine*, 16–18, see also Battisti, *L'antirinascimento*, 133–34, for the entertainment in the Oricellari.

2. See Gilbert, "Bernardo Rucellai and the Orti Oricellari."

3. See the poem by Pietro Crinito, "Ad Faustum: De sylva Oricellaria," in his *Commentarii*, for a description of the plants in the Rucellai garden.

4. See Vasari, *Lives*, 2: 209, and Vasari, *Opere*, 4: 258.

5. Hanafi, *Monster in the Machine*, 17.

6. See Battisti, *L'antirinascimento*, 133–34, for a full description and the relevant sources.

7. Quoted in Panofsky, *Renaissance and Renascences*, 10.

8. Alberti, *Ten Books of Architecture*, 300.

9. For an account of the topos in Italian literature prior to the Renaissance, see Ricci, "Gardens in Italian Literature," and Giannetto, "Writing the Garden." The classic study of the idea of the locus amoenus is Curtius, *European Literature*, 183–202.

10. The phrase is Claudia Lazzaro's. See her *Italian Renaissance Garden*, 150.

11. According to Vasari: "From the mouth of Antaeus water issues in a great quantity, instead of his spirit." *Lives*, 3: 173. See Vasari, *Opere*, 6: 81, for the Italian text.

12. Tchikine, "*Giochi d'acqua*," 63. See also Tchikine, "*Galera, Navicella, Barcaccia?*" 314–17, for more on military motifs in Italian fountain design.

13. Brunon, "Songe de Poliphile," 7.

14. "Dopo l'inferno Cristiano, un paradiso mussulmano." Battisti, *L'antirinascimento*, 134.

15. Hunt, *Garden and Grove*, 42. For a general account of the influence of Ovid, see also Hinds, "Landscape with Figures."

16. Ovid, *Metamorphoses*, 111.

17. For the importance of the concept of metamorphosis in sixteenth-century thought, see Jeanneret, *Perpetual Motion*.

18. Ovid, *Metamorphoses*, 104.

19. Ibid., 102.

20. Ibid., 103.

21. Ibid., 103.

22. Ibid., 75.

23. Ibid.

24. Hunt, *Garden and Grove*, 44.

25. Segal, *Landscape in Ovid's Metamorphoses*, 75–76.

26. The categories of "topophilia" and "topophobia" are from Bachelard, *Poetics of Space*.

27. On fear in the Renaissance, see Scott and Kosso, eds., *Fear and Its Representations*.

28. On Virgil, nature, and compassionate sympathy, see Segal, *Landscape in Ovid's Metamorphoses*, 88.

29. Brunon, "Songe de Poliphile," 7.

30. According to Lazzaro, for example: "Statues of such hybrids are common in Renaissance gardens, encapsulating the fusion of art and nature and also expressing artistic license as is appropriate to the natural setting with its freedom from the strict requirements of both artistic conventions and behavioral norms." "Gendered Nature," 254.

31. Paré, *Monsters and Marvels*, 56.

32. Foucault, *Abnormal*, 55–56.

33. For the full text in Italian and English, see Taegio, *La Villa*, 58.

34. Frith, "Sexuality and Politics," 304.

35. Ovid, *Metamorphoses*, 104.

36. See Beck in Taegio, *La Villa*, 63, for this point.

37. For the case, see Greenblatt, "Fiction and Friction," Jones and Stallybrass, "Fetishizing Gender," 88–89, Daston and Park, "The Hermaphrodite and the Orders of Nature," and Long, *Hermaphrodites*, 80ff.

38. "Une fille nous a esté representé: Laquelle ayant esté baptisée, nommee, entretenue & tousiours vestue comme les autres filles de sa sorte, iusques à l'aage de vingt ans, à esté finallement recognue home: & comme tel à plusieurs & diverses fois en habitation charnelle avec une femme, qu'il avoit fiancée par paroles de present, avec promesse du mariage futur." For the translation, see Long, *Hermaphrodites*, 80.

39. See Jones and Stallybrass, "Fetishizing Gender," 89.

40. Foucault's comments on the Marcis case are worth quoting here: "The other reason for the importance of this case is that it clearly asserts that the hermaphrodite is a monster. We find this in Riolan's discourse where he says that the hermaphrodite is a monster because he/she is counter to the order and general rule of nature that has divided humankind into two: male and female. Thus, if someone has both sexes, the he/she must be regarded as a monster." Foucault, *Abnormal*, 68.

41. For a comparable case from Spain, see Burshatin, "Elena Alias Eleno." Like Duval,

Paré regarded gender assignment as essential. As he stated: "Male and female hermaphrodites are those who have both sets of sexual organs well-formed, and they can help and be used in reproduction; and both the ancient and modern laws have obliged and still oblige these latter to choose which sex organs they wish to use, and they are forbidden on pain of death to use any but those they will have chosen, on account of the misfortunes that could result from such." Paré, *Monsters and Marvels*, 27.

42. Francis and Hester, *Meaning of Gardens*, 4.

43. Elkins, "Analysis of Gardens," 189.

44. Foucault, "Of Other Spaces," 25.

45. Wilson, *The Devils and Canon Barham*, 203.

46. Ruskin, *Stones of Venice*, 236. See Singley, "Devouring Architecture," for a discussion of this passage.

47. Ruskin, *Stones of Venice*, 238.

48. Bakhtin, *Rabelais*, 25.

49. Claudia Lazzaro is one of the few historians to have raised the issue of the grotesque in relation to the Renaissance garden, albeit only in passing. See her prescient comments on the Fountain of Nature in the garden of the Villa d'Este in Tivoli: "Although the statue is based explicitly on an antique model, the large-scale, rough stone, pendulous breasts, and dripping water, invert, perhaps even subvert, the ancient model, transforming it into something approaching the grotesque in the sense discussed by Mikhail Bakhtin, the Rabelais scholar. The Goddess of Nature at Tivoli, in its distorted human form, with its multiple protuberances secreting bodily fluid, stands in opposition to the classical ideal. It suggests abundance, excess, and lack of restraint, all qualities also associated with female. Dislodged from the conventions of the classical by its subject and its garden location, the fountain is at the same time familiar and strange, playful and disturbing." "Gendered Nature," 251.

50. Bakhtin, *Rabelais*, 317–18. In a note he adds: "This grotesque logic is also extended to images of nature and to objects in which depths (holes) and convexities are emphasized." Ibid., 318, n. 6.

51. There was, in addition, a chamber for a small orchestra located in the head. My thanks to John Dixon Hunt for this point.

52. Bakhtin, *Rabelais*, 339.

53. For the sources, see Lazzaro, *Italian Renaissance Garden*, 148–49.

54. Seymour, *Michelangelo's David*, 34.

55. This was also noted by Roswitha Stewering, "World, Landscape, and Polia," 3–4.

56. Colonna, *Hypnerotomachia*, 35–36.

57. See Brunon, "Songe de Poliphile." Giambologna's *Appennino* may even be, as Brunon has proposed, the quintessential "anthropomorphic image of the *locus horridus*." Brunon, "Les mouvements de l'âme, 123.

58. No ancient garden had survived to serve as a model, and the few extant texts that had been transmitted from antiquity furnished little unambiguous information. Pliny, despite the general influence of his letters, is notoriously vague about what his gardens actually looked like, and Vitruvius has almost nothing of use to say on the subject. The

other main sources were the agricultural treatises of Cato, Varro, and Columella, which are largely concerned with propagation and husbandry. For a discussion of these sources, see Giannetto, *Medici Gardens*.

59. Baxandall, *Painting and Experience*, 29–108.

CHAPTER 1. THE LEGIBILITY OF LANDSCAPE

Epigraph: "Giardino architettonico con le piante mortificate dalle cesoie." Adolfo Callegari, "Il giardino veneto," 209–10 (my translation).

1. Coffin, ed., *The Italian Garden*, and Beneš and Lee, eds., *Clio in the Italian Garden*.

2. Coffin, "History of the Italian Garden," 33.

3. Ibid., 83.

4. Ibid., 33.

5. My comments on the historiography of Italian Renaissance gardens are not meant to be comprehensive. Their main aim is to situate this book and its aims within the field as it is currently constituted. The following essays should be consulted for detailed historiographical studies: Coffin, "History of the Italian Garden"; Beneš, "Recent Developments"; and Beneš, "Methodological Changes." For French scholarship, see Brunon, "L'essor artistique." For Italian scholarship, see: Visentini, "Storia dei giardini"; Zalum, "La storia del giardino italiano"; and Visentini, "Riflessioni."

6. Wölfflin, *Renaissance and Baroque*, 149.

7. Ibid., 144.

8. See Coffin, *Villa d'Este*; Coffin, *Gardens and Gardening*; Coffin, *Villa in the Life*; MacDougall, *Fountains, Statues, and Flowers*; Lazzaro, *Italian Renaissance Garden*. There is nothing intrinsically wrong with either approach. Note Beneš's comment: "In the field overall there have been two main interpretative approaches, architectural and iconographical, and they still have great validity." Beneš, "Recent Developments," 45.

9. To some extent, as Beneš has observed, this was corrected by the emergence of Marxist approaches to the Italian villa and its garden that "considered its social and especially its economic aspects." Beneš, "Recent Developments," 46. Lionello Puppi's "The Villa Garden of the Veneto from the Fifteenth to the Eighteenth Century," published in *The Italian Garden*, is a good example. Adopting a Marxist position, Puppi argued that gardens of the Veneto were *not* motivated by "a metaphysical nostalgia for a lost Eden beyond time, but [were] a response that was precise and also variable at times within the varied and complexly changing course of urban society. This means that the artificial formation of nature was guided by codes and rules belonging to a defined and totally documentable cultural world, a world that fostered an ideological self-awareness in the dominant class, to whom the possession of natural resources was pertinent." Puppi, "Villa Garden," 84. This passage is also discussed by Beneš, "Recent Developments," 47.

10. This despite the fact that in the Renaissance the "authorship" or design of landscape was already regarded as a collaborative enterprise, and not just in the sense that several

people were involved in the construction process. See Barthes, "Death of the Author," and Foucault, "What Is an Author?"

11. See Marin, *Portrait of the King*.

12. See, for example, Lefebvre, *Production of Space*, and Certeau, "Walking in the City."

13. Beneš, "Recent Developments," 67.

14. Coffin, *Villa d'Este,* 38. For other examples of the idea, see Lazzaro, "Gendered Nature," 270, n. 22.

15. The literature on the *Mostra del giardino italiano* is small, but growing. The main studies are: Cazzato, "I giardini del desiderio"; Lazzaro, "National Garden Tradition"; and Giannetto, "'Grafting the Edelweiss.'"

16. "Il continuo ordinato e visibile dominio dell'uomo sulla natura." *Mostra,* 23. All translations are my own unless otherwise indicated.

17. "Una natura fatta obediente e domestica." *Mostra,* 24.

18. *Mostra,* 209–10.

19. I have used the English edition, published a year later (1925): Dami, *Italian Garden,* 24.

20. Ibid., 21–22.

21. *Mostra,* 23.

22. Dami, *Italian Garden,* 29.

23. "Ma classici tempietti rotondi od ottagoni sorgevano ancóra nel folto dell'elegante foresta romantic come un rimpianto per l'architettura perduta." *Mostra,* 23.

24. "Anche questa Mostra intende rimettere in onore un'arte singolarmente nostra che dopo aver conquistato il mondo sembrò offuscata da alter mode o nacosta sotto nomi stranieri." *Mostra,* 23.

25. See Benjamin, "Work of Art," 242.

26. For Ojetti's "giardini dell'intelligenza," see *Mostra,* 24. For Dami's comment, see *Italian Garden,* 21.

27. "Ritorno della ragione nell'architettura." *Mostra,* 24.

28. Luchinat, "I giardini dei Medici," 48.

29. Dami, *Italian Garden,* 23.

30. Lazzaro, "National Garden Tradition," 161.

31. Ibid.

32. See Lazzaro, "National Garden Tradition," and Lasansky, *Renaissance Perfected.*

33. The *teatrini* have survived and are currently housed in the Villa Medici in Castello, where they have recently undergone a restoration. See Luchinat, "Il modello del giardino fiorentino."

34. The full entry is as follows: "Invenzione dell'architetto ENRICO LUSINI, ispirata al giardino di Castello quale appare nel disegno del Tribolo, con l'aiuto della descrizione che ne fa il Vasari nella Vita di lui. Alcuni elementi sono tratti dai lunettoni del Museo Storico Topografico di Firenze [themselves exhibited in rooms 4, 5, 6, and 7 of the Palazzo Vecchio] che riproducono I giardini di Castello e di Boboli. Le parti maurate derivano da creazioni dell'Ammannati." *Mostra,* 29. Vasari dedicates several pages to the Villa Medici at Castello,

more space than he devotes to any other garden or garden feature in his *Lives*. See Vasari, *Lives*, 3: 169–75, and Vasari, *Opere*, 6: 72–85. See Lazzaro, "National Garden Tradition," for a reproduction of the Utens lunette.

35. Lazzaro, "National Garden Tradition," 162–63.

36. Note Giannetto's argument that the Utens lunettes should not be regarded as accurate representations of the Medici villa gardens owing to their much later date. Giannetto, *Medici Gardens*, 26–27.

37. See Lazzaro, "National Garden Tradition," 164.

38. Something similar occurred in the restoration of Renaissance paintings during the 1930s. The face of Giorgione's Benson Madonna, for example, was "restored" by the unfortunately (or perhaps aptly) named conservator Bogus, to make it conform more closely to the contemporary ideal of beauty promoted by Estée Lauder and other fashion houses, but this surely had little or nothing to do with Fascist ideological positions. My thanks to Jaynie Anderson for discussing the restoration of the Benson Madonna with me. See her *Giorgione* for more detail.

39. Alberti, *Ten Books of Architecture*, 196.

40. Ibid., 300.

41. See Lazzaro, *Italian Renaissance Garden*, 44, for Martini's approach to garden design.

42. Wittkower, *Architectural Principles*, 7.

43. Chandra Mukerji has made a similar point about bourgeois gardens of the Renaissance in France. See her "Bourgeois Culture and French Gardening," 178–79. See my *Nature as Model* for more on the idea of revelation in relation to science and design. Note also D. R. Edward Wright's comment that "the literature on Italian gardens is characterized by a hierarchized opposition of Art versus Nature which needs to be deconstructed." Wright, "Some Medici Gardens," 34.

44. See Francis and Hester, eds., *Meaning of Gardens*, 4.

45. "Le cose che si murano debbono essere guida e superiori a quelle che si piantano." *Mostra*, 23.

46. See Nielsen, "*Diana Efesia Multimammia*," 461, for this interpretation.

47. "Mescolando l'arte con la natura, non si sa discernere s'elle è opera di questo o di quella; anzi or altrui pare un naturale artifizio ora una artifiziosa natura." Translated in Taegio, *La Villa*, 61. Beck provides a careful study of these statements and their relationship to Taegio's text in the same volume. For the concept of the "three natures" in general, see Hunt, "*Paragone* in Paradise."

48. See Lazzaro, *Italian Renaissance* Garden, 58.

49. For a prior account of the *Hypnerotomachia Poliphili* as a document of garden response, but with emphases different to my own, see Hunt, "Experiencing Gardens and Landscapes."

50. Colonna, *Hypnerotomachia*, 15.

51. Ibid., 19.

52. Ibid., 15.

53. Ibid., 17, 56, 99, 117.

54. Ibid., 80, 83, 57, 64, 64.

55. Ibid., 177, 224.

56. Ibid., 358.

57. "É nel mezzo di questo giardino un salvatico d'altissimi e folti cipressi, lauri e mortelle, i quali girando in tondo fanno la forma d'un laberinto circondato di bossoli alti due braccia e mezzo, e tanto pari e con bell'ordine condotti, che paiono fatti col penello." Vasari, *Opere*, 6: 74. For the translation, see Vasari, *Lives*, 3: 170.

58. For a useful survey of some of these issues in relation to landscape history, see Harris and Ruggles, "Landscape and Vision." See Jay, "Scopic Regimes," for a well-known account of ocularcentrism in Western culture since the Renaissance.

59. Translated in Johnson, "Touch, Tactility, and the Reception of Sculpture," 69. For the Italian text, see Barocchi, ed., *Scritti d'arte* 1: 518.

60. It is worth pointing out that, more perhaps than any other example, the garden of the Villa Medici at Castello emphasizes sensual response. Besides the figure of Antaeus being squeezed to death by Hercules, there were the strong scents of the large and important citrus collection and the figure of the shivering *Appennino*.

61. Colonna, *Hypnerotomachia*, 293.

62. Ibid. 128.

63. Ibid., 138.

64. See Tchikine, "*Giochi d'acqua*," 57–58.

65. Bacon, *Philosophical Works*, 794.

66. See Tchikine, "*Giochi d'acqua*," 63.

67. David R. Coffin's study of the uses of Roman Renaissance villas and their gardens, *Villa in the Life*, is a major precedent, though "use" does not necessarily correspond to "reception." Michel Conan writes in his introduction to the edited volume *Baroque Garden Cultures* (p. 1): "Repeated calls have been made in the last five years for the study of the social reception of gardens as a step in renewing an understanding of garden culture. By taking up this challenge, we are trying to negotiate a turning point in garden history. To a large extent, garden history has been concerned up to now with establishing the intentions of patrons and garden designers, and with linking these intentions to broader cultural trends in order to account for changes in garden design."

68. Hunt, *Afterlife of Gardens*, and Conan, ed., *Baroque Garden Cultures*. The most substantial work on the subject is the former. Note also Hunt's earlier statement: "We need, above all, a history of the reception or consumption of gardens that acknowledges that they yield as much a dramatic as a discursive experience. There is a virtual dimension to the designed landscape: despite its palpable objectivity, it needs an addressee, as it were, to receive it—a spectator, visitor, or inhabitant, somebody to feel, to sense its existence and understand its qualities. To use or to inhabit a landscape may be regarded as a response to its design, and to study such responses will bring us to a better understanding of design history. So we need to track how people have responded to sites in word and image. And especially since one of the essential features of a landscape architectural site is its fragility,

its changefulness, even the unpredictability of natural elements notionally brought under
the control of a designer, one way in which to capture this evanescent character is to plot
the succeeding responses to it, or to understand by what different processes visitors of different kinds have accessed the garden experience under different conditions. Further, this
reception history will not be concerned, it will even be freed from the obligation, to ask
whether a 'reading' or experience of a garden is right or acceptable . . . rather, we should
seek to know how that reading process occurred and was conducted." Hunt, "Approaches
(New and Old)," 89.

69. Conan, ed., *Baroque Garden Cultures*, 15.

70. Ibid., 32–33. See also Conan's introduction to *Performance and Appropriation*, in
which he discusses the social history of the Tuileries, Paris, in the seventeenth century. As
he says (p. 4), this history "raises a question about how rituals established the cultural significance of gardens, and it questions the reliance on a study of a garden's iconography as a
major source for discussing its meanings."

71. Roy Strong's work exemplifies this approach. See, among his other books, *The
Artist and the Garden*.

72. Wright, "Some Medici Gardens," 35.

73. Ibid., 41.

74. Baxandall, *Painting and Experience*. The approaches of Conan and Wright also
resemble the "histoire des mentalités" pioneered in France by the Annales school of history.
For a brief discussion of the unexplored utility of this approach in garden and landscape
studies, see Beneš, "Recent Developments," 65–66. See especially her comments "It is to
this type of work and to the extensive foundations that it has laid that the current and next
generations of scholars of Italian gardens will be looking" (p. 66) and "So far in Italian
garden studies we do not find anything that is comparable to the fertile appropriation of
the French garden as a subject by French social and cultural historians and theorists, who
provide new insights into French gardens as part of social histories or histories of mental
conceptions" (p. 69). See also Beneš, "Methodological Changes," 31–32.

75. Foucault, *Abnormal*, 55–56.

76. As Giannetto has pointed out, the regional differences between Italian garden designs of the sixteenth century are much more pronounced than their similarity. Giannetto,
"'Grafting the Edelweiss,'" 60.

77. Hanafi, *Monster in the Machine*, 18.

78. Ibid.

79. Barisi, Fagiolo, and Madonna, *Villa d'Este*, 92.

80. See Bélanger, *Bomarzo ou les incertitudes de la lecture*.

81. See also Jeanneret, *Perpetual Motion*, Frascari, *Monsters of Architecture*, and Pontecorboli and Gentile, *La Fontana dei Mostri*.

82. Foucault, *Order of Things*, xviii.

83. The Borges story is "The Analytical Language of John Wilkins," in *Other Inquisitions*, 101–5. Foucault's quotation of it is on p. xv of *Order of Things*.

84. Johnson, "Foucault's 'Different Spaces,'" 76.

85. Foucault, "Other Spaces," 24.

86. Ibid., 25.

87. Ibid., 25–6.

88. Ibid., 26.

89. Quoted in Teyssot, "Heterotopias," 298.

90. Soja, *Thirdspace*, 162.

91. Urbach has provided a useful summary of the critical fortunes of heterotopia in architectural discourse after 1967. Important moments in the dissemination of the concept include Demetri Porphyrios's account of Alvar Aalto's oeuvre as heterotopic, which is here a "category of design methodology" or a "sensibility," a form of modernism that is opposed to the orthodox "homotopic" variety. Urbach is particularly skeptical of Charles Jencks's use of the term in his book *Heteropolis* (1993), which again converts Foucault's critical concept into a formalist prescription for a pluralist architectural language. Note that "Other Spaces" was first published in the journal *Architecture, Mouvement, Continuité* (1984) and reprinted in *Lotus International* (1985–1986). In the latter case, the concept served to legitimate the work of a group of contemporary European architects, which included Aldo Rossi, O. M. Ungers, and Vittorio Gregotti. Urbach, "Writing Architectural Heterotopia," 349. Note that this brief sketch cannot do justice to the vast literature in which heterotopia is deployed as a methodological concept. See Saldanha, "Heterotopia and Structuralism," for another survey, which focuses on the uses made of the concept in geography and cultural studies.

92. Genocchio, "Heterotopia and Its Limits," 38.

93. Ibid., 39.

94. Foucault, *Order of Things*, xv.

95. Strong, *Art and Power*, 143. Strong suggests that "it was as though a section of the ducal garden at Pratolino had been conjured by magic into the cortile."

96. Foucault, "Other Spaces," 27.

97. Ibid.

98. See Hunt, *Greater Perfections*, 76–115, for an overview of representation in gardens.

99. Lazzaro, *Italian Renaissance Garden*, 236.

100. It is worth reiterating here that in the broadcast Foucault specifically mentions the tents and dens that children erect in gardens. Similar structures were constructed in Renaissance gardens. The tree house in the garden of the Villa Medici at Castello is an example. This secluded room, partially constructed out of natural materials, would have provided both a vantage point—Vasari notes that the water running through the pipes could be turned on or off at will so as to drench unsuspecting visitors beneath the tree house—and a private space within the garden, which nonetheless remains part of the garden. Vasari, *Lives*, 3: 174, and Vasari, *Opere*, 6: 82.

101. Defert, "Foucault, Space and the Architects," 280.

102. There are many other examples: see, for instance, the head of the *Appennino* at Pratolino, which could house an orchestra or be used for fishing in the artificial lake below.

103. See my *Nature as Model*, 154–55, for an earlier discussion of "*topoi*," not narrative."

104. Flaubert, *Bouvard and Pécuchet*, 65.

105. Ibid., 65–68.

106. Lefebvre, *Production of Space*, 183.

107. See Stackelberg, *Roman Garden*, 31, for some comments on Lefebvre's relevance to garden history.

108. Elkins, "Analysis of Gardens," 189.

109. Vasari, *Lives*, 3: 174.

110. Montaigne, *Complete Works*, 931–32.

111. See John Dixon Hunt's comments on the "polysemy that lies at the heart of garden-making and thus of writing about gardens." Hunt, "Introduction: Making and Writing," 2.

112. See Thacker, "'Manière de montrer,'" and, for a more recent edition, Berger and Hedin, *Diplomatic Tours*.

113. Kelsall, "Iconography of Stourhead," 136–37.

114. Tschumi, *Cinégram folie*, viii.

115. Hunt, *Nature over Again*, 46.

116. Lefebvre, *Production of Space*, 142.

CHAPTER 2. THE GROTESQUE AND THE MONSTROUS

Epigraph. "Les grotesques comme les monstres peuplent les marges de la représenta-tion et de la connaissance." Morel, *Grotesques*, 180 (my translation).

1. The best account of the "marvels of the east," or Plinian monstrous races, remains Wittkower, "Marvels of the East." See also Friedman, *Monstrous Races*, 5–25.

2. For the identification of the figures in Sodoma's fresco, which are derived from Hartmann Schedel's *Nuremberg Chronicle* (1493), see Morel, *Grotesques*, 167. See also Chas-tel, *La grottesque*, 42–45.

3. This is one of Dacos's main arguments: "Si la découverte des peintures des grottes, dès 1480, leur assura aussitôt une grande diffusion, c'est que le goût y était préparé: les artistes avaient hérité de l'époque gothique l'intérêt pour le fantastique et le monstrueux et ils pouvaient déjà répartir ces éléments de part et d'autre d'un axe central. La découverte des grotesques ne fit donc que favoriser une préoccupation déjà existante, dont il était utile de dégager les éléments essen-tiels." Dacos, *Domus Aurea*, viii. See also Baltrušaitis, *Réveils et prodiges*.

4. See Morel, *Grotesques*, 167, for this point.

5. Note that the importance of the Domus Aurea to the Renaissance "rediscovery" of the grotesque may have been overemphasized. Hansen has argued: "It was not the accessi-bility of *one* recently discovered building with ancient frescoes which generated the success of this kind of interior decoration within Mannerism. Rather, the new interest in the study of Antiquity led to a comprehension of the visual evidence uninterruptedly available back from the time of the Roman empire. . . . The Mannerist grotesque was a pictorial strategy adopted from the medieval period and reincarnated in a classical body of form." "*Maniera* and the Grotesque," 257.

6. Summers has, however, pointed out that although Cellini "provides this explanation, he considers it mistaken, adding that the 'grottoes' in question are really rooms, and that the paintings should be called 'monsters' of the kind the ancients liked to make." "Archaeology of the Modern Grotesque," 42, n. 2. The terms "grotesque" and "monstrous" were clearly interchangeable to some extent, as they remain. In his biography of Giovanni da Udine, Vasari notes that grotesques were "so called from being found in grottoes." *Lives*, 4: 9, and Vasari, *Opere*, 6: 551.

7. Note Dacos's comment: "À la Renaissance, la grotte est chargée de mystère. Les incursions que l'on y fait conduisent au cœur de la terre et tendent à faire connaître les secrets qu'elle recèle. De cette notion à celle de fantastique, la distance est brève." Dacos, *Domus Aurea*, 12.

8. For this point, see Zamperini, *Ornament and the Grotesque*, 95.

9. See Dacos, *Domus Aurea*, 130–31.

10. Payne has drawn attention to the importance of Ovid's *Metamorphoses* to architectural thinking in the Renaissance. According to her: "Thus alongside Horace, Ovid's *Metamorphoses* gave the metaphor even greater currency in a culture deeply committed to its reading, for here the concern with multiple beings, with human, vegetal and animal simultaneity and the act of passage from one realm of being into another, through layers of existence, borders on fascination. Moreover, Ovid and Ovid-related literature signaled a richer, more nuanced context for reading heterogeneous mixtures for his metamorphic beings and monsters constitute the origin of things." Payne, "*Mescolare*," 284–85. Pirro Ligorio also emphasizes the importance of the principle of hybridization and metamorphosis in grotesque paintings. See Dacos, *Domus Aurea*, 132. For a general account of the principle of metamorphosis in sixteenth-century culture, see Jeanneret, *Perpetual Motion*.

11. Vitruvius, *Ten Books*, 91.

12. See Summers, "Archaeology of the Modern Grotesque," 21, for a discussion of Horace's phrase.

13. Note that Rabelais uses the term "crotesque," as does Montaigne—two early instances of the migration of the term from the specialized field of Italian wall painting. See Dacos, *Domus Aurea*, 3, n. 2.

14. Cited in Bakhtin, *Rabelais*, 43. Note that what Hugo actually wrote was: "Dans la pensée des modernes, au contraire, le grotesque a un rôle immense. Il y est partout; d'une part, il crée le diforme et l'horrible; de l'autre le comique et le bouffon." Hugo, *Cromwell*, 14.

15. The best account of these debates, which I have inevitably relied upon here, is Dacos, *Domus Aurea*. See, in particular, part 3: "Fortune des grotesques au XVIe siècle," 121–35.

16. Doni, *Disegno*.

17. For a discussion of Doni's argument and its sources, see Dacos, *Domus Aurea*, 124–26, and Zamperini, *Ornament and the Grotesque*, 171. See also Jeanneret, *Perpetual Motion*, 139.

18. Vasari, *Opere*, 1: 193.

19. Quoted and translated in Summers, *Michelangelo*, 135–36.

20. "Selon lui, les grotesques doivent se conformer à l'ordre de la nature et par

conséquent aux règles de la pesanteur, à celles des proportions et à celles de la composition, qui doit être symétrique." Dacos, *Domus Aurea*, 130.

21. Payne, *"Mescolare,"* 285.

22. Vitruvius, *Ten Books*, 55.

23. Payne, *"Mescolare,"* 286.

24. "Mescolando l'arte con la natura, non sis a discernere s'elle è opera di questo o di quella; anzi o altrui pare un naturale artifizio ora una artifiziosa natura." The translation is by Beck. See Taegio, *La Villa*, 61, for Beck's discussion of this passage.

25. "La natura incorporata con l'arte è fatta artifice, e connaturale de l'arte, e d'amendue è fatta una terza natura, a cui non sarei dar nome." Taegio, *La Villa*, 58.

26. "Quivi sono senza fine gl'ingeniosi innesti, che con si gran meraviglia al mondo mostrano, quanto sia l'industria d'un accorto giardiniero, she incorporando l'arte con la natura fà, che d'amendue ne riesce una terza natura, la qual cosa, che i frutti sieno quivi piu saporiti, che altrove." See Taegio, *La Villa*, 58–59, for Beck's translation.

27. The article remained unpublished at Pirro's death. It is from his *Libro dell'antichità*, VI, fols. 151–61, which is preserved in the Archivio di Stato di Torino. Dacos published it in full for the first time. See her "Appendix II: Texte de Pirro Ligorio sur les grotesques," *Domus Aurea*, 161–82. I have used her transcription as the basis of my own comments.

28. See Coffin, "Pirro Ligorio and Decoration," 182. Pirro's moralizing views are close to Lomazzo's. Both are, of course, products of their time—the Counter Reformation. For them, the grotteschi were not aberrant chimeras or absurd, pagan monsters but constituted an allegorical language. See Jeanneret, *Perpetual Motion*, 140–41.

29. "Le pitture grottesche de gentili non siano senza significatione, et ritrouate da qualche bello ingegno, philosophico, et poeticamente rappresentate imperoche secondo, hauemo potuto uedere nelle istesse antiche pitture, sono di soggetto di consonantia, et conformemente; sono paralelle à guise d'una palinodia per replicate et correspondent . . . onde ad uso di lettere Hierogliphiche fatte, come per significare inciò uarij auuenimenti negli piccioli principij, che hanno le cose delli gouerni terreni quelle delle grandissime potentie, et nelli fatti et nelli comandamenti imperatorij." See Coffin, "Pirro Ligorio and Decoration," 183, for the translation.

30. Noted by Coffin, ibid. Jeanneret argues that the strategy of Pirro and Lomazzo, "amounts to neutralizing the grotesques by giving them hidden meaning; monsters are only signs of something else, and the imagination, far from being a threat to reason, works in its service." Jeanneret, *Perpetual Motion*, 140–41.

31. Coffin, "Pirro Ligorio and Decoration," 183. One of Pirro's direct sources here is Giovanni Piero Valeriano's *Hieroglyphica sive de sacris aegyptiorum literis commentarii* (Basel, 1556). See also Morel, who notes the "confluence et l'homologie structurale entre ces deux types de langage figure." *Grotesques*, 15.

32. Coffin comments: "In this discussion of grotesque painting Ligorio goes through almost the entire range of ancient mythology and subject matter, often attempting to reveal the moral or philosophical meaning which he believed was expressed by the different stories or subjects. For example, one subject, which had been used earlier to decorate the vestibule to the Casino of Pius IV designed by Ligorio himself in the Vatican, is that of 'the chariots

of cupids drawn by animals: by lions, by tigers, by elephants, by dragons, by camels, by ostriches, by bears, by hedgehogs, by tortoises, and by every type of bird. All show that a cupid is conqueror of each, and, as each animal runs to his delegated goal and all live under the yoke of love, they are extended. At the end they are led under the palm and victory of Cupid, who carries away the crown of all.'" Coffin, "Pirro Ligorio and Decoration," 184. Morel, *Grotesques*, 94, notes that Pirro's fundamental idea is encapsulated in his statement that "le pitture grotteschi de gentili non siano senza significatione."

33. See Dacos, *Domus Aurea*, 132, for this point. See Morel, *Grotesques*, 94–95, for the importance of metamorphosis to Pirro's interpretation of grotteschi.

34. For the Giardino Giusti, see the two essays by Visentini: "Il Giardino Giusti" and "La grotta nel cinquecento Veneto."

35. According to Morel, *Grotesques*, 195–98: "La fonction du masque dans les grotesques peut avoir on ce sens une valeur emblématique. Il est souvent précis dans son execution et ridicule à souhait. Il met en evidence ce qu'il y a de plus spécifiquement humain dans l'homme—le visage—, tout en l'attirant vers les limites de l'expression caricaturale, de l'apparance étrange voire inquiétante, et de la resemblance végétale en animale. Le traité *De humana physiognomonia* publié en 1586 par Giambattista della Porta explore de telles similitudes en y recherchant les marques visibles d'une plus intime parenté, les signes révélateurs de traits de caractère et de formes de temperament: 'Quelle que soit la similitude avec un home, ce dernier aura le même temperament que l'animal en question.'"

36. See, for example, the Fontana dei Mostri in the Boboli Gardens. A little known text by Maddalena Gentile is worth quoting here: "These gargoyles and monstrous heads, popularly called 'mostaccini,' show a manieristic stamp influenced by Buontalenti. They certainly do not embody the power and transcendence of the demons and gargoyles that adorn gothic churches; neither do they possess the good-natured, almost Disneyesque lavishness of the Bomarzo Garden monsters. They simply follow the ancient symbolism of water, a violent and beneficial natural force (which therefore can be anthropomorphized in fanciful, unrestrained couplings of wild animals with demons). There are monsters and demoniacal wild animals but ones with substantially good-natured expressions." Pontecorboli and Gentile, *Fontana dei Mostri*, 8.

37. Montaigne, *Complete Works*, 931.

38. On this analogy, see also Kohane and Hill, "The Decorum of Doors," 150.

39. Filarete, *Treatise on Architecture*, 12–13.

40. Lazzaro, *Italian Renaissance Garden*, 142.

41. Orsini mentions *Pantagruel* in a letter of 6 January 1579 to Giovanni Drouet. For a transcription see Bredekamp, *Vicino Orsini*, 274.

42. Bakhtin, *Rabelais*, 325.

43. Ibid., 331.

44. Ibid., 325.

45. Ibid., 281.

46. Ibid.

47. Quoted from Alberti, *Ten Books: The 1755 Leoni Edition*, 193. Alberti himself wrote: "Ne uitupero ne i giardini statue ridiculose, pur che non siano dishoneste." *I dieci libri*,

201. Note that Brunon translates "ridiculose" as "grotesque," following Caye and Choay's French edition of Alberti (Alberti, *L'art d'édifier*, 437), but this—unfortunately—seems less accurate than "comic" or "ridiculous." See Brunon, "Du jardin comme paysage sacral," 297.

48. The phrase is from Bakhtin, *Rabelais*, 64.

49. Ibid., 325.

50. Ibid., 317. Emphasis added.

51. This emphasis on the mundane functions or physical needs and sensations of the body—what Bakhtin describes as the Renaissance "rehabilitation of the flesh"—may also be implicit in the inscription "Abandon all thought you who enter here" (ibid., 18). The haptic, embodied encounter with the building is, in other words, more important than detached, intellectual experience.

52. See Jeanneret, *Perpetual Motion*, 127: "Many of these gardens offer the symbolic spectacle of primeval energies and matter in gestation. What could be better than a garden for such projects? A garden does not have to represent change because, by its very nature, it changes according to the time of day, the season and weather. And art, placed outdoors, is exposed to the action of the wind and rain, altered by sunlight and vegetation. The garden is a privileged genre in the Renaissance because it is the ultimate expression, in both its themes and its metamorphic nature of the principle of the mobile work of art."

53. See, especially, Davis, "Women on Top."

54. Michael Holquist, for example, argues in his prologue to Hélène Iswolsky's translation of Bakhtin's book that the concept of "grotesque realism" is a "point-by-point inversion of the categories used in the thirties to define Socialist Realism." Bakhtin, *Rabelais*, xvii.

55. Bakhtin, *Rabelais*, 25. Eugenio Battisti, in his *L'antirinascimento* proposed a similar argument about the visual culture of the Renaissance in general.

56. The presence of the grotesque in Renaissance gardens has occasionally been noticed, but it has rarely been discussed at any length. See, for example, Zamperini, *Ornament and the Grotesque*, 185: "We also find it [the grotesque] in gardens, and especially in artificially created grottoes, exploiting polychrome pebble mosaics (as in the nyphaeum of Villa Visconti Borromeo Litta at Lainate, and in stuccoes, particularly to fill the pendentives or spandrels of ceilings)." See also Lazzaro's brief but perceptive remarks in "Gendered Nature," 251, and Hanafi, *Monster in the Machine*, 22–24.

57. Connelly, "Introduction," 2.

58. See, for example, Holly, *Panofsky*, 189: "Forever lost in time are the emotions, the motives, and the desires that gave birth to medieval and Renaissance art. Panofsky, composing most of his work in the shadow of war and persecution and the threatened destruction of the values of humanism that he had long cherished, was acutely aware of this inaccessibility."

59. Summers, "Archaeology of the Modern Grotesque," 21.

60. Gay, *Weimar Culture,* 33.

61. According to Zamperini: "We can conclude that the grotesque is antithetical to classical art due to its accessory, anti-naturalistic or improbable character, and it is only by antithesis that it enters into this theoretical framework." Zamperini, *Ornament and the Grotesque*, 15.

62. Connelly, "Introduction," 5.

63. Lazzaro, *Italian Renaissance Garden*, 208.

64. Ibid.

65. See Morel, *Grottes*, 5–42, for a detailed account of generation as a grotto theme.

66. See Dacos, *Domus Aurea*, 128.

67. See Darnall and Weil, "*Il Sacro Bosco*," 53–54. They argue that this inscription is paired with the one under the left Sphinx in the Belvedere, which alerts the visitor to the necessity of initiation (through travel) in order to understand the garden.

68. "During the Middle Ages, Europeans associated natural wonders above all with the margins of the world, most particularly with the plants, animals, and minerals of Ireland, Africa, and Asia. In the renaissance, these wonders began to migrate palpably toward what had been the Mediterranean and European center, and not just in the packs and cargoes of traders, explorers, and collectors. Thus Benvenuto Cellini claimed to have seen a salamander in a blazing fire during his youth in Florence, while the basilisk, once a fearsome Eastern lizard, began to crop up in European settings." Daston and Park, *Wonders*, 173. Note also Ashworth's point about the effect of the discovery of the New World on the tradition of the exotic races. American humans proved to be very similar to European ones, but their customs were marvelous. This reshaped the genre of human monstrosities. Aldrovandi, Schenk, and Liceti, for example, exclude the monstrous races (as well as prodigies and marvels). Ashworth, "Remarkable Humans and Singular Beasts," 135–37.

69. Quoted in Daston and Park, *Wonders*, 175.

70. Ibid., 176–77. Daston and Park here reject their earlier teleological view that there is a historical shift from a religious conception of monsters (as portents) to a naturalistic one (monsters as specimens), which implies an advance in knowledge and which they associate with Jean Céard and Georges Canguilhem. See their "Unnatural Conceptions."

71. Daston and Park, *Wonders*, 176–77.

72. See Ashworth, "Remarkable Humans and Singular Beasts," for an overview of attitudes toward monsters during the period that takes into account the influence of Renaissance exploration.

73. "Half-invented" is Ernst Gombrich's term. On the extraordinary dissemination of the print on both sides of the Atlantic and on its status as an artistic projection rather than a factual account of the animal, see Heuer, "Difference, Repetition, Utopia."

74. Baldinucci, *Bernini*, 103.

75. "Da una grotta sporge in fuori il Tatoù, animale dal Brasile, che emulando la Testugine dell'Europa, si ricopra tutto di scaglie, e di durissime piastre, e da nostri è chiamato Armadiglio, perche di squame è armata, dentro le quali ei schermisce contro colpi di acuto ferro, che penetrare nol può; e gli servono di difesa alla Testa meno armata, ch'egli dentro di quei forti ripari nasconde, è per un forame la manda fuori, quando pensa di godere liberamente del Cielo." Quoted in Huse, "La Fontaine des Fleuves," 13. See also Fehrenbach, *Compendia mundi*.

76. Quoted in Daston and Park, *Wonders*, 177.

77. Ibid.

78. Orsini's letter of 22 December 1573 is reproduced in Bredekamp, *Vicino Orsini*,

258. Paré's treatise has been translated into English by Pallister as *On Monsters and Marvels*. See 3–4 for a succinct list of the "causes."

79. Hanafi, *Monster in the Machine*, 1–15, provides a good survey of the tradition. For a comprehensive and cross-cultural study of monsters, see Mittman and Dendle, *Ashgate Research Companion*.

80. Céard, *La nature et les prodiges*.

81. Paré, *Monsters*, 4.

82. Ibid., 9.

83. Ibid., 73

84. Ibid., 4.

85. Ibid., 6.

86. Paré, *Monsters*, 6. Intriguingly, the accompanying illustration suggests a creature that resembles the animal that Horst Bredekamp identifies as the Ram of the Golden Fleece near the "Hell Mouth" in the Sacro Bosco. See Bredekamp, *Vicino Orsini*, 363. Darnall and Weil claim that this animal is unidentifiable: "The Animal has the hind legs of a horse and the mane of a lion. It is anatomically unlike any known animal or mythological beast and does not have the wings that would identify it as a hippogriff, the only imaginary beast appropriate in this location. Its identity and meaning remain a mystery." "*Il Sacro Bosco*," 53.

87. Paré, *Monsters*, 26. Note that the figure of the hermaphrodite exemplifies the duality of responses to monsters: in the early modern period hermaphrodites are sometimes regarded as marvels (supernaturally complete human beings) and sometimes as monsters (signified by their excess of sexual organs). They have, in other words, a positive and a negative symbolism.

88. Paré, *Monsters*, 8.

89. Ibid., 38. The belief in the extrapictorial agency of images is well attested to by other Renaissance sources and cultural practices. The earliest full-scale depictions of the nude, for example, appeared on the interior lids of late fifteenth-century Florentine *cassoni*, which would be kept in the private bedchambers of married couples to serve as stimulants. Leon Battista Alberti probably had cassoni in mind when he recommended that the master bedroom of a house should be decorated with the most handsome pictures so that they would "have a great influence on the fertility of the mother and the appearance of future offspring." Quoted in Sluijter, *Rembrandt*, 160. Attitudes had changed little by the early seventeenth century when another writer, Giulio Mancini, noted that nudes were appropriate for the bedroom because, in his words, "once seen they serve to arouse one and to make beautiful, healthy and charming children." See Park, "Impressed Images," 263, for a discussion of this passage. Two of the most overtly erotic paintings of the Italian Renaissance— Giorgione's *Dresden Venus* and Titian's Louvre *Venus of Urbino* almost certainly emerged from this context and were intended to perform this function. Clearly, however, the influence of images on procreation could also be malign, as Paré observes.

90. See Paré, *Monsters*, 42–47.

91. Ibid., 66.

92. Ibid., 67–73.

93. Ibid., 67.

94. Ibid., 67–68.

95. The monster was killed by a villager out of fear. Interestingly, when brought before a court of law to explain the murder, the man was absolved on the basis of the defense that he was frightened. Fearful as well as fascinated responses to monsters are well documented throughout the early modern period. Paré, *Monsters*, 71.

96. Ibid., 81–82.

97. Ibid., 105.

98. Ibid., 130–36.

99. Ibid., 107.

100. See Knoppers and Landes, eds., *Monstrous Bodies*, 3.

101. Paré, *On Monsters*, 107 and 125.

102. See my "*Trompe l'Oeil* Garden."

103. The best discussion of the concept of *fantasia* in cinquecento art theory is in Summers, *Michelangelo*, 103ff.

104. See Lee, "*Ut pictura poesis*," for the classic account of Horace's much-quoted dictum.

105. Quoted and translated in Moffitt, "An Exemplary Humanist Hybrid," 316.

106. Quoted and translated in Summers, *Michelangelo*, 135–36.

107. See Gaston, "Love's Sweet Poison," 67, for a discussion.

108. Ibid., 150.

109. See Hall, *A History of Ideas,* 300.

110. Coffin, "Nobility of the Arts," 200. On decorum in Renaissance art generally, see Ames-Lewis and Bednarek, eds., *Decorum in Renaissance Narrative Art.* An earlier example of the exemption of the garden from the formal dictates of decorum as they applied to public and civic spaces is provided by Albert's acceptance of comic statues in the garden (mentioned above).

111. Coffin, "Pirro Ligorio and Decoration," 200.

112. See Pérez-Gómez, *Polyphilo*.

113. Paré, *Monsters*, 3.

114. Williams, *Keywords*, 219.

115. On this point, see Curran, "Afterword," 227–45. The work of Georges Canguilhem and Michel Foucault are crucial to this realignment.

116. Foucault, *Abnormal,* 55–56.

117. See Foucault, *Order of Things*, for the concept of the episteme.

118. As Bakhtin puts it: "The artistic logic of the grotesque image ignores the closed, smooth, and impenetrable surface of the body and retains only its excrescences (sprouts, buds) and orifices, only that which leads beyond the body's limited space or into the body's depths." Bakhtin, *Rabelais*, 317–18.

119. See my article "Monster in the Garden" for these interpretations. See also Dianne Harris's comment: "Classical literature appears frequently in landscape scholarship, but historians have interpreted these works in a somewhat conservative fashion. Just as historians used printed views as testimonial descriptions, so too they have sought garden form and meaning in works such as Giovanni Boccaccio's *Decameron*, Ovid's *Metamorphoses*, and the

Hypnerotomachia Poliphili; but there may be other ways to interpret these works beyond what has become standard." Harris, "Landscape in Context," 24.

120. See, for example, Darnall and Weil, "*Il Sacro Bosco.*"

CHAPTER 3. A MONSTRUARY

1. Elizabeth Grosz, "Intolerable Ambiguity," 57, summarizes Paré's categories slightly differently: anomalies of excess, default, and duplicity.

2. This corresponds closely to Georges Canguilhem's general definition of monstrosity: "The accidental and conditional threat of incompletion or distortion in the formation of form." Canguilhem, "Monstrosity," 188.

3. See Lazzarini, "Wonderful Creatures," 426, for an interesting discussion of Bronzino's "Siamese portrait" in the Uffizi in Florence. See Lazzaro, *Italian Renaissance Garden*, 201, for Cioli's fountain depicting the dwarf in the Boboli Gardens. Pulci's epic poem is *Il Morgante Maggiore* (Florence, 1481).

4. See, for this point, Daston and Park, *Wonders*, 192. In Michel Foucault's view, hybridity is the principal feature of monstrosity from the medieval period to the eighteenth century. Combinations of human and animal characteristics ("the man with the head of an ox, the man with a bird's feet"), or the blending of two species ("the pig with a sheep's head"), are examples. Consequently, according to Foucault, "the monster is the transgression of natural limits, the transgression of classifications, of the table, and of the law as table: this is actually what is involved in monstrosity." Foucault, *Abnormal*, 63.

5. See Paré, *Monsters*, 175, where the passage is reproduced as an appendix.

6. See Lazzarini, "Wonderful Creatures," 431.

7. First published in German in 1553.

8. See Bitbol-Hespériès, "Monsters, Nature, and Generation," 52.

9. Ibid.

10. Oceanus in the Boboli Gardens in Florence, the Fountain of the Giants of the Villa Lante in Bagnaia, the Tiburtine Sibyl of the Villa d'Este, the gigantic personifications of the Apennines in the gardens of the Villa Medici (Demidoff) in Pratolino, the Villa Medici in Castello, and the Villa d'Este in Tivoli, and the Orsini giants in the Sacro Bosco, among many others, are all excessive in scale. Yet this does not necessarily make them monstrous in Paré's sense. Canguilhem has questioned whether enormity necessarily implies monstrosity. He concludes that gigantism is ambiguous. "Enormity tends towards monstrosity," but an unusually large man nonetheless remains a man, despite his enormity and not a monster. Giambologna's *Appennino* in Pratolino may, therefore, be gigantic, but it is not monstrous: "We may say of a rock that it is enormous, but not of a mountain that it is monstrous, except in a mythical universe of discourse in which mountains may possibly give birth to mice." Canguilhem, "Monstrosity," 187. The colossal mode is, however, of clear significance in early modern landscape design. The giants of the garden all raise questions about "abnormal," if not monstrous, scale and its connotations in landscape design, and are discussed in detail in chapter 4. Canguilhem's point recalls Bakhtin's claim

that in grotesque realism "all that is bodily becomes grandiose, exaggerated, immeasurable." Bakhtin, *Rabelais,* 19.

11. Seiterle, "Artemis."

12. A figure of the Ephesian Diana also appeared in the lobby of the casino of Pius IV in the Vatican Gardens. On the relationship between the two, see Fagiolo and Madonna, "La casina di Pio." Niccolò Tribolo was earlier interested in the Ephesian Diana as a subject for a fountain. See his *Allegoria della Natura* in the Musée du Château, Fontainebleau.

13. It is surprising how infrequently specific elements of historical landscape design have been made the subject of dedicated studies. An exception is provided by Elizabeth Hyde's *Cultivated Power.* Hyde's interdisciplinary study of just one element of the garden—the flower—which takes her in multiple directions, some of which are very remote from older concepts of the garden history as a discipline, serves as a model. We need detailed histories like this of the garden fountain, of garden statuary, and so on.

14. Grosz, "Intolerable Ambiguity," 64

15. See Coffin, *Villa d'Este,* 18–19, for the relevant documents.

16. Ibid., 19.

17. Ibid., 19.

18. Ibid., 17, for the (probably) French fountain experts employed to work on the Fountain of the Organ at Tivoli.

19. Ibid., 19.

20. In his *Libro dell'antichità,* Pirro discusses Diana of Ephesus, "whose mysterious veil and dark skin referred to her secrets." See Nielsen, "*Diana Efesia Multimammia,*" 466. Pirro was most likely responsible for the design of the fountain.

21. They have been variously interpreted as breasts, udders, or bull's scrota. Some historians have argued that the protuberances are the testicles of eunuch priests, who offered them to the goddess as a sacrifice. See Pietrograde, "Generative Nature," 190. Note that Garrard, in her critique of the representation of nature as female, does not seem to be aware that in ancient figures of Artemis the "breasts" are actually scrota. See Garrard, *Brunelleschi's Egg,* 282–94.

22. Nielsen endorses Seiterle's identification of the breasts of ancient statues of the goddess as bull's scrota. "*Diana Efesia Multimammia,*" 455.

23. The Renaissance mythographical manual of Vincenzo Cartari provides some evidence. According to Lazzaro, Cartari "described the goddess as carved with breasts, which, he added, signified that the universe takes its nourishment from the earth." Lazzaro, "Gendered Nature," 251.

24. Park, "Nature in Person," 51.

25. Other ancient figures of Artemis could be seen in Rome during the sixteenth century. The Roman copy of a Hellenistic original now in the Museo Capitolino, for example, was in the Rossi (Roscia) collection in Rome during the early sixteenth century. See Bober and Rubinstein, *Renaissance Artists and Antique Sculpture,* 87. For additional figures of Artemis, known to the Renaissance, see Lazzaro, *Italian Renaissance Garden,* 306, n. 85.

26. See Nielsen, "*Diana Efesia Multimammia,*" for other Renaissance images of Artemis.

27. See ibid., 460–64, for Lotto and Vasari.

28. Ibid., 465. See also Giulio's extraordinary drawing *Siren Breast-Feeding Her Young* (Louvre).

29. See Coffin, *Villa d'Este*, 18–19, n. 10. For an illustration, see Ballerini and Medri, eds., *Artifici d'acque*, 280.

30. Lazzaro, *Italian Renaissance Garden*, 144.

31. Quoted in Barisi, Fagiolo, and Madonna, *Villa d'Este*, 86.

32. Lazzaro, "Gendered Nature," 253.

33. See Nielsen, "*Diana Efesia*," 467.

34. Lazzaro, *Italian Renaissance Garden*, 144–45. Note also that Vincenzo Cartari described the goddess as covered with breasts, which, he added, signified that "the universe takes its nourishment from the earth." Lazzaro, "Gendered Nature," 251. Cartari also quotes Macrobius as evidence that the ancients "liked to represent Nature with the traits of Isis-Artemis," examples of which he claims to have seen himself. See Pietrogrande, "Generative Nature," 190. It is worth noting Gaston Bachelard's argument here that "from a psychoanalytic point of view, we must say that all water is a kind of milk." See Bachelard, *Water and Dreams*, 117, and elsewhere for other suggestive remarks.

35. See Nielsen, "*Diana Efesia Multimammia*," 466.

36. Lazzaro, *Italian Renaissance Garden*, 229.

37. Note Nielsen's comment: "Although the grotesque ornament style, so popular in Renaissance interior decoration after the discovery of Nero's Golden House in the 1480s, was not supposed to make use of Ephesian Artemis, she was often included, since her odd countenance fitted so well with the other legless figures mixing with vegetal ornaments. She enriched the visual expression of the endless wonders of *artfiziosa natura*." Nielsen, "*Diana Efesia Multimammia*," 459. On the grotesque versus the classical see, besides Bakhtin himself, Michael Holquist, who writes: "The covering term for the view of the body that emphasizes changes in its nature (eating, evacuation, sex) as in Hieronymous Bosch, rather than a static ideal, as in Greek marbles, is 'grotesque.' The grotesque body is flesh as the site of becoming." "Bakhtin and Rabelais," 15.

38. Bakhtin, *Rabelais*, 26–27.

39. According to Bakhtin: "The grotesque body, as we have often stressed, is a body in the act of becoming. It is never finished, never completed, it is continually built, created, and builds and creates another body. Moreover, the body swallows the world and is itself swallowed by the world. . . . This is why the essential role belongs to those parts of the grotesque body in which it outgrows its own self, transgressing its own body, in which it conceives a new, second body: the bowels and the phallus. These two areas play the leading role in the grotesque image, and it is precisely for this reason that they are predominantly subject to positive exaggeration, to hyperbolization; they can even detach themselves from the body and lead an independent life, for they hide the rest of the body, as something secondary. (The nose can also in a way detach itself from the body.) Next to the bowels and the genital organs is the mouth, through which enters the world to be swallowed up. And next is the anus. All these convexities and orifices have a common characteristic; it is within them that the confines between bodies and between the body and the world are

overcome: there is an interchange and interorientation. This is why the main events in the life of the grotesque body, the acts of the bodily drama, take place in this sphere. Eating, drinking, defecation and other elimination (sweating, blowing of the nose, sneezing), as well as copulation, pregnancy, dismemberment, swallowing up by another body—all these acts are performed on the confines of the body and the outer world, or on the confines of the old and new body. In all these events the beginning and the end of life are closely linked and interwoven." Bakhtin, *Rabelais*, 317–18.

40. Romolo del Tadda, Fontana dei Mostaccini, 1619–1621, Boboli Gardens, Florence. See Pontecorboli, *La Fontana dei Mostri*.

41. For a reproduction, see d'Elia, "Giambologna's Giant," 18.

42. Montaigne, *Complete Works*, 931.

43. Bakhtin, *Rabelais*, 148.

44. Ibid., 150.

45. The pissing boy of the Villa Medici in Pratolino is usually interpreted as little more than a joke. See, for example, Lazzaro's comments: "The pissing boy provided yet another source of water, a witty counterpart to Jupiter at the head of the garden, and together the boy and the laundress present an ironic commentary on the grandiose imagery at the top of the hill, contrasting the water's supernatural origins with its mundane destination." Lazzaro, *Italian Renaissance Garden*, 165.

46. For a discussion of this image, see Simons, "Manliness and the Visual Semiotics of Bodily Fluids," 351. For additional comments on the representation of bodily fluids in garden design, see Lazzaro, "River Gods," 83–86.

47. Poliphilo relates: "No sooner had I set foot on the step to reach the falling water, than the little Priapus lifted his penis and squirted the freezing water in my hot face, so that I fell back instantly on my knees. At this, such a high and feminine laughter echoed around the hollow dome, that as I recovered, I too began to laugh fit to die." Colonna, *Hypnerotomachia*, 84–85.

48. Humfrey, *Lotto*, 139–40.

49. See Battisti, *L'antirinascimento*, 226. See also Hanafi, *Monster in the Machine*, 77. On monstrous lifelikeness, see also: Stoichiță, *Pygmalion Effect*, and Huet, "Living Images."

50. See Marr, "Automata," 110. According to him: "This stemmed principally from the story of Thomas Aquinas's 'oracular head,' supposedly manufactured through the harnessing of astral influences or, far worse, black magic. In his narration of the event in *Trattato dell'arte de la pittura* (1584), the Italian art theorist Giovanni Paolo Lomazzo claimed that Aquinas obliterated the head because 'he thought it the devil.'"

51. See Pietrogrande, "Generative Nature."

52. Ferriolo writes: "[At the Villa d'Este] we find the home of the Great Goddess, recognizable in its multiform individuality. Nature, alternately in the form of Artemis/ Diana, Aphrodite/Venus, Mater Matuta/Sibyl Albunea, and the *nympha loci*, the sleeper in her lair: the Tiburtine landscape. Ovid's verses refer to a tradition of nature that comes from afar, from the ancient Mediterranean world." Quoted and translated in Pietrogrande, "Generative Nature," 194.

53. "Pre-Olympian" is Beneš and Lee's phrase from their "Introduction," 7; "*Diana*

Efesia Multimammia" is the well-chosen title of Nielsen's article. Note that many of the giants of the Renaissance garden are similarly symptomatic of the reemergence of a concept of sacral landscape in the sixteenth century. They are, like the d'Este figure, deities of the landscape and avatars of nature (see Chapter 4).

54. "In the sixteenth and seventeenth centuries, in contrast [to the medieval period], Nature's body was exposed for all to see. But that body was itself opaque and difficult to interpret, like the alien, even grotesque, figure of Diana of Ephesus herself. Where Nature spoke explicitly, voluminously, and directly to medieval writers such as Alan of Lille in dreams and visions, she stood mutely before early modern naturalist inquirers or receded elusively from their grasp." Park, "Nature in Person," 71–72.

55. On the enigma of *La Natura* and her "secrets," see Nielsen, "*Diana Efesia Multimammia*," 466.

56. For a critical account of Foucault's notion of epistemic breaks, see Maclean, "Foucault's Renaissance Episteme."

57. In his comparison of the human body to a machine, Descartes wrote: "External objects . . . are like strangers who, entering some of the caverns containing these fountains . . . unwittingly cause . . . a figure of Neptune to move towards them, threatening them with his trident." See Baltrušaitis, *Anamorphic Art*, 64, for the translation.

58. Canguilhem, "Monstrosity and the Monstrous," 188.

59. Bakhtin, *Rabelais*, 317.

60. See Onians, "I Wonder," 16, and Platt, "*Il Sacro Bosco*," 21, for the latter point.

61. See Theurillat, *Mystères*, 43. Vicino's brother Oratio Orsini captained an Italian ship at the Battle of Lepanto, which, Theurillat argues, accounts for the confusion.

62. For the legend of the Turkish prisoners, see also Zander, "Elementi documenti," 23, n. 2, and Platt, "*Il Sacro Bosco*," 54.

63. Schmidt, *Mouth of Hell*, 32.

64. Schmidt, ibid., 33, notes, interestingly: "The image of falling into a pit—a pit that seems to be in some sense conscious of the role it is playing—is emblematic of damnation."

65. The Bomarzo Hell Mouth has a leonine appearance. Note Anne Bélanger's description of it as "une créature hybride qui rapelle un peu la physionomie du lion." *Bomarzo*, 73.

66. Hunt, *Garden and Grove*, 44.

67. See Schmidt, *Mouth of Hell*, 24–25.

68. Ibid., 14.

69. They also relocate a sacred Christian concept to a secular site dominated by pagan imagery.

70. Well-known examples of the motif in northern art include: *The Hours of Catherine of Cleves* (c. 1440, Morgan Library and Museum, New York), the *Très riches heures* of the duc de Berry (c. 1412–1416, Musée Condé, Chantilly), Pieter Brueghel the Elder's *Dulle Griet* (1563, Museum Mayer van den Bergh, Antwerp), and Hieronymous Bosch's *Garden of Earthly Delights* (c. 1490–1510, Museo del Prado, Madrid). See Ernst Guldan, "Das Monster-Portal," for a discussion of these and other images of the Hell Mouth in art, architecture, and garden design.

71. See Oleson, "A Reproduction of an Etruscan Tomb," 411.

72. See Guldan, "Das Monster-Portal," 247, and Bredekamp, *Vicino Orsini*, 147.

73. See Platt, "*Il Sacro Bosco*," 23 and 42.

74. See Partridge, "The Farnese Circular Courtyard," 288, n. 15.

75. For an earlier Renaissance "face drain," see Maarten van Heemskerck's drawing *Courtyard in the Palazzo della Valle di Cantone* (1532–1537, Kupferstichkabinett, Berlin). For an inventive variation on the theme, see Giulio Romano's design of a silver salver (1542, Chatsworth, Devonshire Collection).

76. Partridge, "The Farnese Circular Courtyard," 261.

77. My emphasis.

78. Noted by Hughes, "The Strangest Garden," 50.

79. Barry, "The Mouth of Truth," 7.

80. Colonna, *Hypnerotomachia*, 27.

81. Bélanger, *Bomarzo*, 251, and Bredekamp, *Vicino Orsini*, 147, both also associate the Hell Mouth with this passage in the *Hypnerotomachia*.

82. See Rabelais, *Gargantua and Pantagruel*, 159.

83. Soderini, *I due trattati*, 276–77. Translated in Coffin, *Gardens and Gardening*, 114.

84. According to Eugenio Battisti: "Un'altra indubbia componente, nonostante il parere discorde di noti orientalisti, è quella esotica, per cui alcuni mostri (come quelli che una scritta dice 'mai vista' proteggenti la Fontana) e la stessa tartaruga ricordano opere (di piccole dimensioni e forse in pietra dura o giada) dell'Estemo Oriente. Anche qui la tradizione locale ci soccorre, parlandoci di un non altrimenti noto Biagio Sinibaldi, orginario della vicina Mugnano, che avrebbe visitato Ceylon, il Giappone, l'Arcipelago orientale, la Cina, l'India. Nulla, infatti, è tanto vicino a Bomarzo quanto gli edifice e le sculture monolitiche dei templi dravidici, come quello di Mahābalipuram (presso Madras). Così il curioso trofeo dell'elefante (che non deriva dal Polifilo, ma poté forse ispirarsi a Pausania), eccezionale in Europa, è comune nell'India dravidica del VII secolo." Battisti, *L'antirinascimento*, 126. Note the (coincidental?) similarity of Sinibaldi's name to that of the legendary traveler Sinbad. George Dennis in *The Cities and Cemeteries of Etruria*, 214, n. 2, suggests that Sinibaldi is himself an invention.

85. "CHI CON CIGLIA INARCATE / ET LABRA STRETTE / NON VA PER QUESTO LOCO / MANCO AMMIRA / LE FAMOSE DEL MONDO / MOLI SETTE." For a transcription of the inscriptions, see Frommel, ed., *Bomarzo*, 333. As Sheeler, *The Garden at Bomarzo*, 42, points out, the lines echo the tenth canto of *Orlando furioso*, which deals with marital fidelity and betrayal.

86. See Bullfinch, *The Age of Fable*, 125. Oedipus's answer was "man."

87. The other sphinx is inscribed with a statement that alludes directly to the *paragone* between art and nature in Renaissance garden design: "TU CH'ENTRI QVA PON MENTE / PARTE A PARTE / ET DIMMI POI SE TANTE / MARAVIGLIE / SIEN FATTE PER INGANNO / O PVR PER ARTE." See Frommel, ed., *Bomarzo*, 333.

88. "SE RODI ALTIER GIA FV DEL SVO COLOSSO / PVR DI QVESTO IL MIO BOSCO ANCHO SI GLORIA / E PER PIV NON POTER FO QVANT IO POSSO." See ibid.

89. Oleson, "A Reproduction of an Etruscan Tomb," 411. These motifs are discussed at greater length in chapter 5 with reference to the pseudo-historical works of Annius of Viterbo.

90. "Una di queste illustrazioni di rettili giganti delle Indie occidentali, in cui Marte, procedendo sulle acque sopra il guscio di une testuggine trainata da quattro leoni, protegge il viaggio di Colombo dalle divinità marine antropofaghe d'America, avrà offerto a Vicino il modello diretto." Bredekamp, *Vicino Orsini,* 122.

91. Ibid., 129. Note that in his review of the German edition of Bredekamp's book, John Bury is not convinced by the interpretation of the Mask of Madness as an Aztec mask. See Bury, Review of *Vicino Orsini.*

92. See Bredekamp, *Vicino Orsini,* 131. The Mask of Madness also marks the boundary of the Sacro Bosco or the Orsini estate, which may account for the prominent inclusion of the family emblem and arms (on the globe). As Coffin points out, it stood at the far end of the artificial lake constructed by Orsini. Coffin, *Gardens and Gardening,* 112. See Bredekamp's comment (*Vicino Orsini,* 131): "Queste maschere erano in verità meno orrifiche di quella del 'boschetto,' ma nella memoria, anche con l'influenza delle grottesche etrusche, esse si possono essere trasformate nel mostro di Bomarzo." I would like to thank Alejandra Rojas for discussing Aztec masks with me.

93. See Wittkower, "Marvels of the East," 160.

94. Topsell, *The History of Four-Footed Beasts,* 3. See also 8–9.

95. Mandeville, *The Travels,* 134.

96. Braham, "The Monstrous Caribbean," 19.

97. Ibid.

98. Ibid., 21.

99. For an illustration, see ibid., 25. Note also Theodore de Bry's popular images of female cannibal feasts, which were widely circulated in the late sixteenth and early seventeenth centuries.

100. Quoted in Ginzburg, "Montaigne," 127.

101. Ibid., 129.

102. Bakhtin, *Rabelais,* 317.

103. Devouring is also an integral element of many of the legends and fables of giants—from classical myths such as that of Polyphemus to popular stories such as Jack and the Beanstalk. The theme is not restricted to obvious images such as the Hell Mouth either, but is present in, for example, the *Appennino,* whose giant body can be entered, and other penetrable anthropomorphic structures.

104. It is precisely these kinds of figures that lead Eugenio Battisti to coin the term "antirinascimento." As he realized, there are simply too many cultural developments and products made during the Renaissance that in fact contest or call into question what have long been established as the "rules" of Renaissance art. The garden is a major site of these motifs.

105. Ariosto, *Orlando furioso,* 409–10.

106. Rose, *Giants, Monsters, and Dragons,* 168.

107. See South, ed., *Mythical and Fabulous,* 156, for the translation.

108. Noted in Rowland, "Harpies," 157.

109. Ibid., 155.

110. The phrase is from Jorge Luis Borges's entry for harpies in his *Book of Imaginary Beings.* See Cohen, *Animals as Disguised Symbols,* for a useful account of harpies and hybrids in art.

111. Lazzaro, "Gendered Nature," 254.

112. Note, again, the difficulty of firmly identifying these figures as harpies. As so often in garden design, the "harpies" are inventive variations on the type.

113. Darnall and Weil, "*Il Sacro Bosco*," 63.

114. Ibid.

115. Note, however, another possible relationship between the harpies and the Hell Mouth, given their proximity: the identification of the diner inside the grotto with Prester John and the consequent implication that his or her food is perpetually at risk of being befouled by the nearby harpies.

116. On garden narratives, see my *Nature as Model.*

117. Paré, *Monsters,* 56.

118. On this, see Finucci, *The Manly Masquerade,* 56.

119. Paré, *Monsters,* 57.

120. Rowland, "Harpies," 158.

121. Cohen, "Andrea del Sarto's Monsters," 42.

122. Quoted and discussed in Miller, "Monstrous Sexuality," 323.

123. See ibid., 322, for a reproduction. Note that the ancient prototype is "the ancient sea-monster Scylla, whose loins often took the form of canine mouths." Ibid., 315.

124. For the female grotesque, see Spackman, "Inter musam et ursam moritur," Russo, "Female Grotesques," and Davis, "Women on Top." See Garrard, *Brunelleschi's Egg,* 275–312, for a discussion of gender, nature, and the grotesque. See also Felton, "Rejecting and Embracing," 122, who argues that in ancient Greece and Rome the excremental discharge from the harpies' bellies may have been understood as menstruation.

125. For this point, see Pizzorusso. "Harpy," 228.

126. Ibid.

127. According to Bakhtin: "Contrary to modern canons, the grotesque body is not separated from the rest of the world. It is not a closed, completed unit; it is unfinished, outgrows itself, transgresses its own limits. The stress is laid on those parts of the body that are open to the outside world, that is, the parts through which the world enters the body or emerges from it, or through which the body itself goes out to meet the world. This means that the emphasis is on the apertures or the convexities, or on various ramifications or off-shoots: the open mouth, the genital organs, the breasts, the phallus, the potbelly, the nose. The body discloses its essence as a principle of growth which exceeds its own limits only in copulation, pregnancy, childbirth, the throes of death, eating, drinking, or defecation. This is the ever unfinished, ever creating body, the link in the chain of genetic development, or more correctly speaking, the links shown at the point where they enter into each other." Bakhtin, *Rabelais,* 26. Note that, as Garrard points out (*Brunelleschi's Egg,* 279), the figure of the harpy is the most common female figure in painted grotteschi during the Renaissance.

128. Note also Pizzorusso's interpretation of the juxtaposition: "The harpy and the

toad are traditionally associated with negative elements and they are sometimes combined to signify avarice or greed. A sorrowful, pleading, or defeated harpy might suggest—as in the emblem of Andrea Alciati (1531)—the principle that 'from honest riches there is nothing to fear.' Such an interpretation, appropriate to the sculpture's location within the sumptuous and undoubtedly coveted palace of the rich merchant family of the Lanfranchi, is, however, problematic due to the unusual appearance of this harpy." Pizzorusso, "Harpy," 228.

129. Leslie, "Spenser, Sidney." Leslie's study remains one of the only serious attempts to systematically compare literary gardens with real ones. Tigner, *Literature and the Renaissance Garden*, has a similar aim, but see Hunt's Review of *Literature and the Renaissance Garden*.

130. I am grateful to one of the anonymous readers for Penn Press for drawing my attention to the importance of the figure of the enchantress in the garden.

131. For this point, see Weil, "Love, Monsters, Movement, and Machines," 170–71.

132. Lazzaro, "Gendered Nature," 253.

133. See ibid., 246–47, for this point.

134. In her discussion of an engraving of Diana of Ephesus from the Raphael workshop and Giulio Romano's version in the Palazzo del Te, Garrard writes: "These examples sustain the dynamic that governed the *grottesche*: conceding visual embodiment to the other as a means to control it. To figure the goddess of nature in a monumental, centralized female image is potentially empowering. Yet she is frozen in typology and cannot act. . . . Thus allegorized, *Natura* is no longer a creative power but a resource, both for human sustenance and the artist's needs." *Brunelleschi's Egg*, 285.

135. Ibid., 296.

136. Lazzaro, "Gendered Nature," 249.

137. Pietrogrande, "Generative Nature," 189.

138. See Lazzarini, "Wonderful Creatures," 429, for the frontispiece.

CHAPTER 4. "RARE AND ENORMOUS BONES OF HUGE ANIMALS"

Epigraph. Rabelais, *Gargantua and Pantagruel*, 159.

1. Alcofrybas (or Alcofribas) Nasier is an anagram of François Rabelais. The cedilla is omitted.

2. Rabelais, *Gargantua and Pantagruel*, 156.

3. Ibid., 158.

4. Filarete, *Treatise on Architecture*, 12.

5. Rabelais, *Gargantua and Pantagruel*, 158.

6. Susan Stewart's comments on the relationship between the gigantic and the environment are relevant here: "Our impulse is to create an environment for the miniature, but such an environment is impossible for the gigantic: instead the gigantic becomes our environment, swallowing us as nature or history swallows us." Stewart, *On Longing*, 89.

7. Ibid., 71.

8. Cole, *Ambitious Form*, 112.

9. See Bush, *Colossal Sculpture*, xxv.

10. See Bober and Rubenstein, *Renaissance Artists*, 159–61 and 216–17, respectively, for the *Dioscuri* and the colossal fragments (of Constantine).

11. Boucher notes the modern neglect of the sixteenth-century colossus and provides a succinct overview of its development in his *Sansovino*, 1: 128–30. Cellini's statement along with other similar sixteenth-century statements appears on p. 128. Note the attitudinal shift implied by the comparison of Cellini's sixteenth-century estimation of colossal statuary and Leon Battista Alberti's fifteenth-century conviction that an *istoria* required more from the artist than a colossus. Bush published her doctoral work in 1976 as *The Colossal Sculpture of the Cinquecento*. See Bush, *Colossal Sculpture*, 13, for Alberti's views.

12. See, for this point, Bush, *Colossal Sculpture*, 294. See also Michelangelo's concept for a mountain carved into the shape of a man overlooking the sea, as reported by Vasari and Condivi. See Bush, *Colossal Sculpture*, 20.

13. This draws attention to the equal interest of the period in the small-scale, or the miniature, specifically in the figure of the dwarf. Valerio Cioli's sculpture of Morgante, which Francesco de' Medici installed in the Boboli Gardens in 1584, provides an example.

14. See d'Elia, "Giambologna's Giant," 1.

15. See Stephens, *Giants in Those Days*, for the idea that giants are symbols of otherness or alterity.

16. The Cyclopes belong to the medieval category of the "monstrous races," derived from Augustine and Pliny. Images of Polyphemus appear in the Oricellari and in the garden of the Villa Aldobrandini in Frascati. See Pallister, "Giants," 307. See Ehrlich, *Landscape and Identity*, 91, for the depiction of Tantalus, Atlas, Hercules, and Polyphemus in the exedra of the Villa Aldobrandini. Note that Francesco Inghirami misidentified Giambologna's Appennino as Polyphemus. See Vezzosi, "Le fortune dell'Appennino," 43.

17. Other early modern Italian sites and structures could be associated with the theme of anthropophagy, such as the figure of Chronos in the garden of the Villa Barbarigo in Valsanzibio (though the idea of Chronos devouring his children, as in Francisco Goya's much later painting, is only implicit), Federico Zuccari's palazzo near Santa Trinità dei Monti in Rome, which incorporates a door and windows represented as cavernous mouths, the fireplace in one of the rooms of the Palazzo Thiene in Vicenza, which closely resembles the mouths of the Villa della Torre in Fumane di Valpolicella, and even, perhaps, the use made of the Bocca della Verità, Rome, on which see Barry, "The Mouth of Truth."

18. It would, of course, be possible to classify the colossi of the garden in a number of different ways. There is, for example, a large group of river gods and goddesses, examples of which can be found in Caprarola, Bagnaia, Tivoli, Castello, Pratolino, and Bomarzo. Most of these are indebted to the Hellenistic figures of the Tiber and the Nile, which in the sixteenth century were installed in the Vatican sculpture court. See Lazzaro, "River Gods," 70–75, for the Tiber and the Nile. The various depictions of the Apennines could also be included in this group of personifications of landscape features. A second group of colossal figures would include representations of the gods and heroes of classical mythology, such as Neptune, Oceanus, Hercules, and Antaeus at Castello, Pan and the head of Enceladus or Tantalus at the Villa Aldobrandini in Frascati, Polyphemus, a number of the colossal

statues in Bomarzo, Giambologna's *Dovizia* and *Giove Olimpico* in the Boboli Gardens, and the figure of Amalthea in Soriano nel Cimino. A third group—of disembodied heads or grotesque faces—would also be necessary. An alternative approach would be to focus on the political significance of the colossus in the sixteenth century, as Bush, *Colossal Sculpture*, does. Neither of these starting points would, however, allow for an exploration of the negative symbolism of the colossus as a *giant*.

19. It is also, of course, indebted to the numerous images of Hercules and Antaeus in Italian art from the late fifteenth century onward. See, for example, Pollaiuolo's small bronze (1470s, Bargello, Florence).

20. The Oricellari Polyphemus and the head of Enceladus (or Tantalus), buried in front of Atlas in the grounds of the Villa Aldobrandini in Frascati, provide two more examples of the representation of mythical giants in gardens.

21. Pliny, *Natural History*, 312. Ghiberti is quoted in Bush, *Colossal Sculpture*, xxvi.

22. De' Servi's colossus was to be three times the size of the *Appennino* ("tre volte di quell di Pratolino"), making it more than a hundred feet tall. See his letter: Archivio di Stato di Firenze, Mediceo del Principato, 1348, fol. 194.

23. See Gauricus, *Sculptura*, 102. For a discussion, see Bush, *Colossal Sculpture*, xxvii.

24. Quoted in Bush, *Colossal Sculpture*, xxvii.

25. Gauricus, *Sculptura*, 102.

26. Bush, *Colossal Sculpture*, xxvii–xxviii.

27. See Bush, *Colossal Sculpture*, xxviii. *Gigante* is used in the same period as a less technical term for large statues. Both Michelangelo's *David* and Sansovino's Neptune and Mars are referred to in the sixteenth century as *giganti*. See Bush, *Colossal Sculpture*, xxx, for the David and see Boucher, *Sansovino* 1: 136–41, for the Mars and the Neptune.

28. Alberti, *On Painting*, 72–73.

29. Quoted in Bush, *Colossal Sculpture*, 7.

30. See, for example, Vasari's account of Fra Bartolommeo's five-*braccia*-high St. Mark, which the artist painted to demonstrate that his style was not "minuta" and that he could adopt the grand manner if necessary. Vasari, *Opere*, 4: 189. Vasari's defense of Bandinelli's much maligned *Hercules and Cacus* was likewise motivated by his estimation of the difficulty of the artist's task. Vasari, *Opere*, 6: 149–51. (See also Vasari's discussion of Michelangelo's *David*, which was all the more impressive for having been "released" from a block that had been started but left uncompleted by other artists. Vasari, *Opere*, 7: 153–56.) See Summers, *Michelangelo*, 177–85, for the value of difficulty.

31. Most of the literature on colossal statuary in the Renaissance, besides Bush, *Colossal Sculpture*, has tended to focus on civic sculptural commissions such as the Florentine *David* and *Hercules* by, respectively, Michelangelo and Bandinelli, or Sansovino's *Giganti* for Venice.

32. The paired river gods in Caprarola, Bagnaia, and Tivoli were influenced by Michelangelo's design for the Capitoline Hill, Rome, which incorporated two ancient representations of the Tiber and the Nile. See Bush, *Colossal Sculpture*, 282.

33. Montaigne, *Complete Works*, 963.

34. Ibid., 964.

35. Keutner, "Note intorno," 19. He is referring to Smith, "Pratolino," and Zangheri, *Pratolino*.

36. Keutner, "Note intorno," 19.

37. See Lazzaro, *Italian Renaissance Garden*, 150, and Keutner, "Note intorno," 21.

38. The Nile is depicted on the Campidoglio in Rome, in the garden of the Villa Lante in Bagnaia, and, in the following century, in Gianlorenzo Bernini's Fontana dei Quatro Fiumi in Rome. The Nile is, in other words, frequently represented in Italy during the period.

39. See Luchinat, "L'Appennino dal modello," 13–14, for a list of sixteenth-century writers who identified the colossus as *Appennino*. (Note that she also acknowledges Keutner's theory.)

40. "La nostra 'bestia,' sulla quale il Gigante sta accovacciato, viene chiamata, da sempre, solo il Mostro." Keutner, "Note intorno," 21.

41. For a study of Pulci's giant, see Jordan, *Pulci's Morgante*.

42. Bakhtin, *Rabelais*, 343.

43. Ibid., 343–44. *The Great Chronicles of Gargantua* is a 1532 chapbook that Rabelais knew and drew upon.

44. Bakhtin, *Rabelais*, 341–42.

45. Vezzosi, "Nota redazionale," 10.

46. "L'Appennino rappresenta una grande macchina idraulica." Pozzana, "Identità dell'Appennino," 109.

47. Stewart, *On Longing*, 70.

48. Ibid., 80.

49. Ibid., 86.

50. See Stephens, *Giants in Those Days*, 31, for a critique of Bakhtin.

51. Berrong, *Rabelais and Bakhtin*, 13–14.

52. Stewart, *On Longing*, 81.

53. Ibid., 84.

54. Mariage, *Le Nôtre*, 44.

55. For an extant example of a garden carriage for children used at Versailles, see the illustration in Snodin and Llewellyn, eds., *Baroque*, 276.

56. Stewart, *On Longing*, 86.

57. See Stephens, *Giants in Those Days*, 157.

58. Calvesi, *Gli incantesimi*, 143. See Coty, "A Dream of Etruria," 46–47, for other examples in the vicinity of Bomarzo.

59. See Stephens, *Giants in Those Days*, 103.

60. See Dotson, "Shapes of Time," 214.

61. Annius and Bomarzo are discussed in greater detail in the next chapter.

62. Translated and quoted in Smith, "Observations," 187. See Brunon, "Pratolino," 729–35, for a detailed study of Renaissance ideas about the world as "vivant et animé" (729).

63. For Pirro, see Gaston, "Ligorio on Rivers and Fountains."

64. Stewart, *On Longing*, 71.

65. Alberti, *Ten Books of Architecture*, 299. See also Broderius, *Germanic Tradition*, 75:

"The bones of prehistoric monsters, mammoths, and even whales are said to be the bones of giants. These tales occur everywhere on Germanic soil. In Oldenburg a man drives through a long cavern. Later he discovers that it is the hollow bone of a giant's leg."

66. Park, "Nature in Person," 51. On the Ephesian Diana, note Park's comments (58–59): "The association made by sixteenth-century Italian humanists between Nature and the ancient goddesses Tellus and Opis underpinned a second visual tradition that depicted Nature as a female figure with many breasts. The history of this particular personification is complicated, but it seems to have its roots in a text from Macrobius's *Saturnalia*: 'All religions worship Isis, who is either the earth or the nature of things under the sun. For this reason, the body of the goddess is entirely covered with breasts, since she sustains with her nourishing moisture [*altu*] the entirety of earth and the nature of things.' On the basis of this description, Renaissance writers and painters began to portray Isis, Terra, and Nature on the model of the many-breasted Diana of Ephesus, statues of which had been brought to light in the early sixteenth century and appeared in numerous accounts of ancient sculpture and topographical guides. By the 1520s, Italian artists were using this figure as a personification of nature in their own paintings and statues, and it quickly spread to Northern Europe as well. Over the course of the sixteenth century, the personification of nature as endowed with many breasts became at least as influential as the image of her naked and lactating, with which it was easily combined."

67. Ripa, cited in ibid., 58.

68. Ibid.

69. Park, "Nature in Person," 71.

70. See Broderius, *Germanic Tradition*, 2.

71. Ibid., 3.

72. In Beccattini, *Il sogno del principe*, 14, the *Appennino* is described as interpreting "the terrifying character of nature on a superhuman scale." There are, of course, many other equally feasible responses. In a Christian reading, for example, Francesco de' Vieri believed that the *Appennino* shows that all who rise up against God are abased. See Vieri, *Discorsi*, 26–29. My discussion in this chapter focuses on the colossal statues of the garden as *giants* (in the popular or folkloric sense), but I would not wish to give the impression that no other interpretation is possible.

73. Stephens, *Giants in Those Days*, 52.

74. Pallister, "Giants," 296.

75. Ovid, *Metamorphoses*, 33.

76. The phrase is Stewart's. See her *On Longing*, 86.

77. Pallister, "Giants," 294.

78. Foucault, *Abnormal*, 55–56.

79. Cohen, *Of Giants*, xvii and 5.

80. Ibid., 21.

81. See Bernheimer, *Wild Men*, for the necessity of the wild-man to societal and individual identity construction. Cohen acknowledges the influence of Bernheimer's work in *Of Giants*, xv.

82. Canguilhem, "Monstrosity," 187–88. Canguilhem's point recalls Bakhtin's claim

that in grotesque realism, "all that is bodily becomes grandiose, exaggerated, immeasurable." Bakhtin, *Rabelais,* 19.

83. Canguilhem, "Monstrosity," 187.

84. Note that the Greco-Roman "gigans" derives from the Sanskrit "gô-jan" meaning "earth and giant." Giants have always, in other words, been closely linked with the landscape. See Pallister, "Giants," 302.

85. On the giants of *Inferno,* see Stoppino, "Error Left Me." See also my comments on Dante's giants and the sublime in the conclusion.

86. According to Brunon, the *Appennino* may be the quintessential "image anthropomorphique du *locus horridus.*" Brunon, "Les mouvements de l'âme," 123.

CHAPTER 5. "PIETRA MORTA, IN PIETRA VIVA"

Epigraph. Tasso, *Liberation of Jerusalem,* 324.

1. To some extent this may reflect the fact that Orsini himself was the principal viewer of his garden. The letters are fully transcribed in Bredekamp, *Vicino Orsini.* See also Frommel, ed., *Fortuna critica,* on the critical fortune and documents of Bomarzo. Theurillat, *Mystères,* also quotes from Orsini's letters, but she gives no sources.

2. For a discussion of this phenomenon, see my *Nature as Model,* 7–32. The two gardens have something in common with Jan van Eyck's *Arnolfini Double Portrait,* Giorgione's *The Tempest,* and Diego Velázquez's *Las Meninas.* In the case of *The Tempest,* in particular, meaning has proved elusive and scholars have been haunted by the premise that a currently undiscovered text would provide the key to its meaning.

3. See Fasolo, "Analisi stilistica," Bruschi, "Problema storico," and Platt, "*Il Sacro Bosco.*" See also Bélanger, *Bomarzo.*

4. See Calvesi, "Il Sacro Bosco," who suggests Bernardo Tasso's *Floridante*; Kretzulesco-Quaranta, *Incantesimo,* for the *Hypnerotomachia Poliphili*; Zander, "Gli elementi," for Tasso's *Gerusalemme liberata*; and Darnall and Weil, "*Il Sacro Bosco,*" for a close reading of the Sacro Bosco in which nearly every step and motif is related to Ariosto's *Orlando furioso.*

5. See Henneberg, "Bomarzo," and Sheeler, *Garden at Bomarzo,* for the idea that the Sacro Bosco is a personal psychomachia, "through which Vicino expresses his involvement with the pleasures of the world and his desire to attain Divine Love." Darnall and Weil, "*Il Sacro Bosco,*" 10.

6. See Bacino, "La valle," and Oleson, "A Reproduction of an Etruscan Tomb." The most interesting recent study is Coty, "A Dream of Etruria." Note, however, that Orsini himself does not mention Etruscan art or civilization in his letters.

7. See Bredekamp, *Vicino Orsini,* for the first four themes. See Jensen, "Lucubratiunculae," for Orsini's Epicureanism.

8. See Dotson, "Shapes of Time," 213–16, and Coty, "A Dream of Etruria," for Annius of Viterbo in relation to the Sacro Bosco. See Bélanger, *Bomarzo,* for Patrizi. Bélanger also argues that the garden has no coherent meaning but, rather, each "reader" produces

idiosyncratic meanings upon encountering the garden, an interpretative position clearly motivated by postmodern theories of reader response.

9. There is equally little agreement about the garden's designer and the artists of the statuary. Should the concept of the garden be attributed to Pirro Ligorio, Jacopo Sangallo, or Orsini himself? Are the colossal sculptures the work of Jacopo del Duca, Bartolommeo Ammannati, Raffaello da Montelupo, Simone Moschino, or Turkish prisoners of war? All of these names have been suggested, but none has achieved consensus.

10. See, for example, Bury, "Review Essay," 223, and Quartermaine, "Vicino Orsini's Garden," 74. Coty, "A Dream of Etruria," 4, n. 4, argues: "The proposed entrance near the *casa pendente* is one of the furthest removed corners of the park from Palazzo Orsini. Operating under the assumption that Vicino Orsini's visitors descended from the palazzo for a sojourn in the *bosco*—instead of trekking across the grounds to reach the palazzo, as is the case at Villa d'Este—the southeastern end of the *bosco* would be the most plausible location for an entry point."

11. Bury first speculated about the presence of an artificial lake at Bomarzo in "Reputation of Bomarzo." Bredekamp includes it in his plan of the site. See *Vicino Orsini*, 392–93.

12. Darnall and Weil, "*Il Sacro Bosco*," 5.

13. Darnall and Weil, "*Il Sacro B*osco," 11.

14. The inscription reads: "CRIST MADRVTIO / PRINCIPI TRIDENTINO / DICATVM." See Frommel, ed., *Bomarzo*, 333.

15. Darnall and Weill, "*Il Sacro Bosco*," 37. See Frommel, *Bomarzo*, 333, for the inscription: "ANIMVS / QVIESCENDO /FIT PRVDENTIOR / ERGO."

16. For two critical accounts of iconology, see Cassidy, ed., *Iconography*, and Holly, *Panofsky*.

17. "Une technique isolée de déchiffrement." Zerner, "L'art," 188.

18. "CEDAN ET MEMPHI E OGNI ALTRA MARAVIGLIA / CH HEBBE GIA L MONDO IN PREGIO AL SACRO BOSCHO CHE SOL SE STESSO ET NVLL ALTRO SOMIGLIA." Transcribed in Frommel, ed., *Bomarzo*, 333.

19. See, for example, Coffin, *Gardens and Gardening*, 106: "Aerial photographs suggest that at some time the area of plowed fields lying between the town and the Sacro Bosco may have been organized as a formal garden." See also Bruschi, "L'abitato di Bomarzo," fig. 5.

20. As Coffin points out: "As none of the sixteenth-century documents mention it, the formal garden is most likely an addition by the Lante family in the seventeenth century or even later." *Gardens and Gardening*, 106.

21. Note also the possibility that the xystus was laid out with geometric compartments, which would imply the more usual juxtaposition of garden and wood.

22. On the idea of the sacred wood in the Renaissance, see the important study by Brunon: "Du jardin comme paysage sacral."

23. See, for example, Coffin, *Gardens and Gardening*, 120–21.

24. For an overview of the relevance of the tradition of the sacred wood in literature, see Bredekamp, *Vicino Orsini*, 98–99. Bredekamp emphasizes the particular importance of Sannazaro.

25. See Calvesi, "Il Sacro Bosco," 373ff., and Henneberg, "Bomarzo," 10.

26. "Per la vicinanza del lor contrario; percio che spesse volte in villa si veggono minacciosi monti, tanne da serpi, oscure caverne, horride balze, strain greppi, dirupati bricchi, rovinati sassi, alberghi d'heremiti, aspre roccie, alpestri diserti, & cose simili, le quali, quantunque senza horror rare volte riguardar si possano; nondimeno piu compiuta rendono la gioia & felicità della villa." Translated in Taegio, *La Villa*, 214–15.

27. "Mais le jardin maniériste ne se contente pas de ce contraste avec le paysage environnant, et intègre la représentation du monde sauvage à l'intérieur de ses murs. Au coeur de Pratolino, dans un site entouré de montagnes boisées, le Colosse de l'*Appennino*, sculpté par Giambologna, incarne cette nature sauvage adossé à une colline artificielle (détruite au cours du XVIIème siècle), le géant est recouvert de roches et presse la terre d'où jaillit un torrent: il propose en somme l'image anthropomorphique du *locus horridus*, face au palais dont il n'est séparé que par un prato, équivalent du *locus amoenus*." Brunon, "Les mouvements de l'âme," 123.

28. According to Calvesi: "Il manoscritto passò nelle mani di Torquato, che rivide l'opera e, ricavati 19 canti, la pubblicò incompiuta. Ma la materia del Floridante è desunta, senza sostanziali variazioni, dall'Amadigi stessa; possiamo quindi ben prenderla in considerazione per i rapporti con il *Sacro Bosco*. Vicino Orsini, del resto, non dovette limitarsi a prendere ispirazione dall'Amadigi per la concezione del suo giardino; ma presumibilmente, in vista dei suoi quasi certi rapporti personali, egli si consultò assiduamente con Bernardo Tasso, che poté anche anticipargli idee e spunti del Floridante." "Il Sacro Bosco," 373.

29. See my *Nature as Model*, 152–55.

30. Soderini, *I due trattati*, 276–77. Translated in Coffin, *Gardens and Gardening*, 114. Note that the treatises, though written in the 1580s or 1590s, were not published until the nineteenth century.

31. Translated in Vasari, *Vasari on Technique*, 55.

32. "Io ho già fatto dare il colore a parechie statue del boschetto e mi fu imparato un secreto, che stemperasse i colori col latte, che così restariano al'acqua et altr'infortunii, e ancora che sia quarto o cinque mesi che habbiano havuto il colore et si conservino assai bene." Transcribed in Bredekamp, *Vicino Orsini*, 267.

33. According to Bush: "The style of the statues fits a date in the 1560s and shows that the sculptor was an artist of considerable talent from the post-Michelangelesque tradition in Florence. The sheer size of the figures and the respect for the material that determined some of their location and configuration point to the Florentine circle, where there was so much enthusiasm for colossal sculpture. Individual figures, such as the fighting giants, the old man and the Sirens reveal an academic classicism reminiscent of Bandinelli." *Colossal Sculpture*, 284.

34. See, among other examples, Michelangelo's madrigal for Vittoria Colonna, which begins: "Si come per levar, donna, si pone / in pietra alpestra e dura /une viva figura, / che la più cresce u' più la pietra scema" ("Just as we put, O Lady, by subtraction, / Into the rough, hard stone / A living figure, grown / Largest wherever rock has grown most small"). Hibbard, *Michelangelo*, 261.

35. For an account of Alberti's distinctions, see Wittkower, *Sculpture*, 80, and Helms, "Materials and Techniques," 18.

36. Buonarotti, *Life, Letters, and Poetry*, 120.

37. Quoted in Scigliano, *Michelangelo's Mountain*, 133.

38. See ibid., 136, for the ancient "doodles" in marble that Michelangelo could have seen, as well as the *fantiscritti* inscribed in the marble (by Michelangelo himself as well as others, such as Giambologna and, later on, Gianlorenzo Bernini).

39. "Tomba etrusca . . . trasformata . . . in sala di banchetto." See Oleson, "A Reproduction of an Etruscan Tomb," 411.

40. See ibid., and Coty, "A Dream of Etruria."

41. Oleson, "A Reproduction of an Etruscan Tomb," 413.

42. See Portoghesi, "Nota," and Lazzaro, *Italian Renaissance Garden*, 118–20, for Pitigliano. Coty argues convincingly that Orsini had no need to travel to Sovana for inspiration: "Why would Vicino turn to a small hill town of the southern Maremma for inspiration and contact with Etruscan Antiquity . . . it would seem perhaps most plausible that Vicino— especially given the illustrious Etruscan history supplied Bomarzo by Annio da Viterbo— looked to his own backyard for elements of Etruscanness with which to flavor his *bosco*. The *campagna bomarzese*, though rarely discussed in literature concerning the Sacro Bosco, is surprisingly rich with Etruscan archaeological finds, effectively encircling the town with a vast web of necropoleis, ruins and remnants that stretches as far as the neighboring cities of Soriano nel Cimino, Vitorchiano and Mugnano." Coty, "A Dream of Antiquity," 61–62.

43. "Pietra viva e bianca, che per lo suono che rende quando si lavora, è in quella città chiamata bronzo." Vasari, *Opere*, 6: 354. Hinds translates the phrase as "soft white stone." Vasari, *Lives*, 3: 275.

44. In his treatise on fortification, *Della fortificazione delle città* (1564), Girolamo Magi (or Maggi) describes walls of "pietra viva." In *Relazione e diario del viaggio di Iacopo Soranzo* (1581), Soranzo describes a bridge made entirely of "pietra viva." Both references are from Battaglia, *Grande dizionario*, 13: 430.

45. Battaglia, *Grande dizionario*, 13: 430.

46. See also the First Day of Boccaccio's *Decameron*: "Da seder levatasi, verso un rivo d'acqua chiarissima, il quale d'una montagnetta discendeva in una valle ombrosa da molti albori fra vive pietre e Verdi erbette, con lento passo se n'andarono." Quoted in Battaglia, *Grande dizionario* 13, 430.

47. Petrarch, *Canzoniere*, poem 129.

48. On Michelangelo, Strozzi, and Vasari, see Barolsky: "Vasari quotes in full Giovan Battista Strozzi's poem on Michelangelo's first Pietà, which uses such a Petrachan conceit. Strozzi says that 'pain, pity, and death are alive in dead marble'—'in vivo marmo morte.' He alludes to Petrarch's *Canzoniere*, where the poet speaks of himself as petrified by his Medusa, himself a dead stone in a living rock: 'pietra morta in pietra viva.' Vasari is saying through Strozzi's Petrarchan poem, which is like Michelangelo's own poetry, that Michelangelo's figures are alive within stone, but this vitality is more than the imitation of nature. Petrarch's Laura is a figure of Christ through whom the poet is reborn. Such rebirth is also intended by the poem quoted purposefully by Vasari. In the description of a sculpture that represents the death of Christ, the phrase 'alive in dead stone' also stands for the rebirth of the soul through the sacrifice—for resurrection." *Why Mona Lisa Smiles*, 37–38.

49. See Darnall and Weil's comments: "Combinations of words and phrases in the inscriptions refer to specific passages in the poetry of Dante, Petrarch, and Ludovico Ariosto. The works of Dante and Petrarch are central to the structure and moral tone of Renaissance literature and art based on this literature . . . Petrarch's search for Divine Love in his Lyric Poems centers on Laura, her death, and his mourning which ultimately leads him to understand true Love. The garden deals with this Petrarchan theme, but uses Ariosto's *Orlando furioso* as a vehicle for its narrative." Darnall and Weil, "*Il Sacro Bosco*," 5. Darnall and Weil's attempts to explain the inscriptions through direct reference to Petrarch's poems are not, however, always convincing. See Coty, "A Dream of Etruria," 20, for Petrarchan sonnets actually written by Orsini.

50. "Il Theatro, il lago, & Il Tempio dedicato alla felice memoria dell'Illustriss. Sig. Giulia farnese già vostra consorte." See Bury, "Reputation of Bomarzo," 108. The best account of the reception of the Sacro Bosco from the sixteenth to the twentieth century is Castelletti, "Bomarzo dopo Bomarzo."

51. In the *Ritratto* Sansovino wrote: "Viterbo . . . is located in a beautiful and spacious territory . . . and there are in it various fortified places among which Bomarzo, owned by Vicino Orsini, is worthy of notice. Below the castle this Lord has built theatres, loggias, rooms and temples in the antique style, dedicating them to the name of Giulia Farnese his late wife, at such great expense that it is an overwhelming experience to see them." Translated in Bury, "Some Early Literary References," 19. In the *Origine*, Sansovino noted: "Giulia Farnese was the former wife of Vicino Orsini, who, loving that most discreet and noble-minded lady, dedicated to her at Bomarzo a most beautiful temple, built by him from its foundations, in which temple it has been arranged for priests to pray to Our Lord continuously for her soul." See Bury, "Some Early Literary References," 20. Note also Annibal Caro's letter to Vicino in which he refers to the "teatri e mausolei" of Vicino's wood. See Bury, "Some Early Literary References," 20.

52. Coty, "A Dream of Etruria," 20, thinks that "Vicino's own writings, however, call into question these romantic interpretations and shed light on his relationship with Giulia, showing him to be less the faithful spouse devoted to the memory of his beloved and more of a serial philanderer." See also p. 22 for Santa Maria della Valle.

53. Translated in Sheeler, *Garden at Bomarzo*, 73. Emphasis added.

54. Translated in Szafranska, "The Philosophy of Nature," 79.

55. The best account of the relationship between sixteenth-century garden grottoes and the theories of the natural historians is Morel, *Grottes*. See especially his section "La formation des pierres: Théories du XVIe siècle," 26–36. See also Brunon, "Pratolino," 471–584.

56. See Vossilla, "Acqua, scultura e roccia," 61.

57. A comment of Jeanneret's is relevant here: "Another effect in Bomarzo's project transports the visitor to an even more primitive stage. Some of the statues are hardly distinguishable, carved right in the rock as if they were just emerging, illustrating the birth of the first living things from the entrails of the earth." Jeanneret, *Perpetual Motion*, 126. Jeanneret illustrates his point with a photograph of the Sleeping Nymph in the Sacro Bosco.

58. Bakhtin, *Rabelais*, 317.

59. Foucault, "Other Spaces," 26.

60. Ibid.

61. According to Coty, "A Dream of Etruria," 92: "Annio's revisionist slant on Old Testament history provides an account of satyrs in ancient Etruria; according to the Friar, Janus/Noah's disobedient son, Ham, was actually Pan, the Greco-Roman satyr god. This tangled genealogical web is further complicated by the writings of Egidio Antonini, a successor of sorts to Annio da Viterbo, who asserted that the Greeks—entirely dependent on the far more ancient and enlightened Etruscan civilization in all aspects of knowledge and culture—modeled their satyr god, Pan, after Janus Bifrons, the double-faced patriarch of the Etruscans. Janus thus becomes the progenitor of the satyr, often found linked to Pan as pastoral deity inhabiting a nebulous, pre-Roman Golden Age often transposed onto idyllic garden landscapes."

62. Ibid.

63. Nagel and Wood, *Anachronic*, 247.

64. Translated and quoted in ibid., *Anachronic*, 247–49.

65. Translated and quoted in ibid., 250.

66. Ibid., 9.

67. Ibid., 11.

68. Ibid., 14.

69. Translated and quoted in ibid., 15.

70. Ibid.

71. Ibid., 13. Note that in their view, this is what distinguishes their categories—substitutional and authorial—from Hans Belting's categories of *Bild* and *Kunst* (many of Nagel and Wood's critics have pointed out the similarities). See Belting, *Likeness and Presence*. In response to two critical reviews, Nagel and Wood argue: "The institution of the artwork thus crystallized around a series of stagings and restagings of the clash between the two theories of origins that we have tried to outline. Art is a sequence of nested reflections on the origins of art. The artwork framed itself, then reframed that framing operation, and then again framed that reframing, and so on, and in this way marked out a provisional place for itself in society as an autopoetic system whose sole function was to generate fictions, or hypotheses about reality. The substitutional and authorial theories of origins, therefore, do not map respectively onto Hans Belting's categories of *Bild* and *Kunst*, as both [Michael] Cole and [Charles] Dempsey suggest. For Belting, *Kunst* adopts some of the rhetorical and semantic mechanisms of *Bild* but eventually, after transportation to a secular and bourgeois sphere, is alienated from *Bild*. In our model, by contrast, *Bild* is a myth invented retrospectively by *Kunst*. Moreover, our model adds a dimension that is not present in either Belting or [Aby] Warburg: the idea of art as a self-staging and self-referential project." Nagel and Wood, "The Authors Reply," 430.

72. See Nagel, *Medieval Modern*.

73. Nagel and Wood, *Anachronic*, 13.

74. Ibid., 364.

75. Ibid., 19.

76. Fehrenbach, Review of *Anachronic Renaissance*.

77. Nagel and Wood, *Anachronic*, 308.

78. Ibid., 308.

79. For a discussion of the painting, see Ames-Lewis, *Intellectual Life*, 194.

80. Miller, *Heavenly Caves*. This remains the only book-length account of grottoes in English.

81. Quoted in ibid., 36.

82. Ibid.

83. Nagel and Wood, *Anachronic*, 11.

84. See Vasari, *Lives*, 4: 108, for the translation. For the original text, see Vasari, *Opere*, 7: 135ff.

85. Nagel and Wood, *Anachronic*, 356.

86. Though note Coffin, who argues that the Tempietto is closely related to Vitruvius's description of an Etruscan temple. Coffin, *Gardens and Gardening*, 116–17.

87. Oleson, "A Reproduction of an Etruscan Tomb," 411, writes: "No-one, however, has yet been able to point out a specific source for any of these Etruscan motifs." In his discussion of the tomb, he claims that Orsini must have had "an architectural model in mind" (415).

88. See Munder, ed., *Forking Paths*, for the monsters of the Sacro Bosco as follies.

89. Oleson, "A Reproduction of an Etruscan Tomb," 413.

90. Ibid.

91. Ibid.

92. Brilliant, "I piedistalli del giardino di Boboli," 2–17.

93. For a discussion of Brilliant's hypothesis and its relevance to "the Venetian sense of the past" in particular, see Brown, *Venice and Antiquity*, 23–24. Brown's comments about invented antiquities and the use of spolia in Venetian art are applicable here too: "Caution is necessary in interpreting these appropriations, for there are important nuances and distinctions. As others have observed, re-used and replicated artifacts have a particularly ambivalent status, being simultaneously past and present with a commingling (and sometimes confusion) of ancient and modern roles." For a broad account of spolia as a transhistorical category, see Brilliant and Kinney, eds., *Reuse Value*.

94. See Bury, "Some Early Literary References," 20. My emphasis.

95. Nagel and Wood, *Anachronic*, 32.

96. See Nagel and Wood's comment: "Ruins represent time, but it proved easier to see this when the ruins were inserted into fictions, for example, into paintings (or later, in the eighteenth century, into fictive landscapes in real space—gardens). The painter of the ruined building in the late fifteenth century was the colleague of the sophisticated forger, for like the forger he fashioned a non-existing artifact in a plausible historical style, and then artificially aged it." Nagel and Wood, *Anachronic*, 303. For a rare study of the motif of the ruin in art, see Hansen, "Representing the Past." I am grateful to Maria for sending me her article, which I rely upon here.

97. Hansen, "Representing the Past," 101.

98. Quoted in ibid.

99. Ibid., 106.

100. Ibid.

101. "Deletto, ma non senza terrore, posciache del tutto pare, che à terra rovini l'edifi-zio." Bocchi, *Le belezze*, 69. See Lazzaro, *Italian Renaissance Garden*, 206, for the translation.

102. My comments are inspired by Hansen's paper "Telling Time: Representations of Ruins in Sixteenth-Century Art," delivered at the Renaissance Society of America annual meeting in New York City in 2014.

103. Ibid.

104. Quoted in Smith, "Observations," 187.

105. Cited in Bakhtin, *Rabelais*, 43. For the original text, see Hugo, *Cromwell*, 14.

106. Coffin, *Gardens and Gardening*, 116–17.

107. The woodcut illustration of the ruined temple in the *Hypnerotomachia Poliphili* is emblematic of this imagined antiquity. See Colonna, *Hypnerotomachia*, 238.

CONCLUSION

Epigraph. Nietzsche, *The Gay Science*, 160.

1. Vinci, *Selections*, 269.

2. Ibid., 269–70.

3. In her introduction to the letter, Irma A. Richter observes: "Leonardo ridicules man's feeling of self-importance by contrasting his puny efforts with the forces of nature which are here personified by a giant." Vinci, *Selections*, 269.

4. Ibid., 271.

5. Colonna, *Hypnerotomachia*, 35.

6. Bakhtin, *Rabelais*, 281.

7. Ibid., 158.

8. But note that Stephens seems to allow for the possibility of a different, more Bakhtinian, reading when he says: "By their very essence they [giants] cannot be cultural protagonists, but are representations of alterity, a cosmic or hominid nature which is hos-tile, threatening, and evil . . . only with Rabelais did they take on their radically modern identity as heroes of culture in 'folklore.'" *Giants in Those Days*, 96–97.

9. Ibid., 31–32.

10. Ibid., 34.

11. "Overly natural" is from Stewart, *On Longing*, 70. The idea is a very ancient one. As Stephens writes: "In primitive mythologies, the figure of the Giant appears to provide an anthropomorphic 'explanation' of the forces of Nature, and primarily those forces con-nected with destruction rather than with creation or reproduction. Like the natural world itself, Giants 'swallowed' or 'devoured' ordinary humans, although unlike Nature, they had no role in the generation of human beings." *Giants in Those Days*, 98.

12. "Depraved" is Vitruvius's term (*Ten Books*, 91). The others are Ruskin's (*Stones of Venice*, 238).

13. Quoted in Hunt, *Garden and Grove*, 44.

14. Bocchi, *Le belezze*, 69. See Lazzaro, *Italian Renaissance Garden*, 206, for the translation.

15. Vinci, *Notebooks of Leonardo da Vinci*, 526.

16. Taegio, *La Villa*, 214–15.

17. The "prehistory" of the sublime in the context of garden design deserves more attention. See, for example, Brunon's comment: "On sent ici une dialectique bien proche de celle du beau et du sublime qui s'épanouira au XVIIIe siècle. Le jardin maniériste aurait-il assimilé avant l'heure l'esthétique du sublime? L'hypothèse mériterait d'être travaillée." Brunon, "Les mouvements de l'âme," 124.

18. For the early dissemination of Longinus's treatise, see Weinberg, "Translations and Commentaries of Longinus."

   19. Eck et al., eds., *Translations of the Sublime*, 3.

   20. Burke, "Philosophical Enquiry."

   21. Besides the essays in Eck et al., eds., *Translations of the Sublime*, see Castillo, *Baroque Horrors*, 44–45, for some comments on "nocturnal horrors" as a Renaissance version of the sublime. Cascardi, "The Genealogy of the Sublime," presents a particularly cogent argument about the origins of the northern European sublime in the southern Mediterranean baroque. See also Jaeger, ed., *Magnificence and the Sublime*, for medieval antecedents of the sublime.

   22. Stewart, *On Longing*, 70.

   23. Cohen, *Of Giants*, 177.

   24. Stoppino, "'Error Left Me,'" 187.

   25. Ibid., 187–88.

   26. On the giant's fragmented body and synecdoche, see Cohen, *Of Giants*, xiii: "When placed inside a human frame of reference, the giant can be known only through synecdoche: a hand that grasps, a lake that fills his footprint, a shoe or glove that dwarfs the human body by its side."

   27. Note in this connection that the same applies to Stewart's point regarding the denial of transcendence to the viewer of the gigantic: one cannot achieve of point of view from which the giant can be viewed. Only the giant itself has this prerogative. The Appennino, whose head could be entered, corresponds rather to Stewart's postindustrial examples: the Eiffel Tower, the Statue of Liberty, and the figure of William Penn on Philadelphia's City Hall.

   28. See Eck et al., eds., *Translations of the Sublime*, 9.

   29. Bélanger has argued that Francesco Patrizi's concept of *meraviglia*, which was derived from Longinus, informed the designs and effects of the Sacro Bosco in Bomarzo.

   30. Note also Sigmund Freud's very similar observation in his essay on the uncanny: "We walk through ourselves, meeting robbers, giants, old men, young men, wives, widows, brothers-in-love, but always meeting ourselves." Freud, *The Uncanny*, 42.

   31. "Je n'ay veu monster ou miracle au monde plus expres que moy-mesme." Translated in Williams, *Monsters and Their Meanings*, 2.

   32. "Leggendo il presente volume, vi ho trovato per entro alcune descrittioni di colli e di valli che rappresentandomi il sito di Bomarzo, me ne hanno fatto venir grandissima voglia." Quoted in Bury, "Reputation of Bomarzo," 108.

   33. Coffin, *Gardens and Gardening*, 121.

Bibliography

Alberti, Leon Battista. *I dieci libri de l'architettura di Leon Battista degli Alberti Fiorentino.* Venice: Vioncenzo Vavgris, 1546.

———. *L'art d'édifier.* Translated by Pierre Caye and Françoise Choay. Paris: Seuil, 2004.

———. *On Painting and On Sculpture.* Translated by Cecil Grayson. London: Phaidon, 1972.

———. *On the Art of Building in Ten Books.* Translated by Joseph Rykwert, Neil Leach, and Robert Tavernor. Cambridge, MA: MIT Press, 1988.

———. *The Ten Books of Architecture: The 1755 Leoni Edition.* New York: Dover, 1986.

Ames-Lewis, Francis. *The Intellectual Life of the Early Renaissance Artist.* New Haven: Yale University Press, 2000.

Ames-Lewis, Francis, and Anka Bednarek, eds. *Decorum in Renaissance Narrative Art.* London: Birkbeck College, 1992.

Anderson, Jaynie. *Giorgione: The Painter of Poetic Brevity.* Paris: Flammarion, 1997.

Ariosto, Ludovico. *Orlando furioso.* Translated by Guido Waldman. Oxford: Oxford University Press, 2008.

Ashworth, William B., Jr. "Remarkable Humans and Singular Beasts." In *The Age of the Marvelous,* edited by Joy Kenseth, 113–44. Hanover, NH: Hood Museum of Art, Dartmouth College, 1991.

Bachelard, Gaston. *Poetics of Space.* Translated by Maria Jolas. Boston: Beacon Press, 1994.

———. *Water and Dreams: An Essay on the Imagination of Matter.* Translated by Edith Farrell. Dallas: Pegasus Foundation—Dallas Institute of Humanities and Culture Publications, 1983.

Bacino, Ezio. "La valle dei mostri." In *Italia, oro e cenere,* 91–97. Florence: Vallechi, 1953.

Bacon, Francis. *The Philosophical Works of Francis Bacon.* Edited by John M. Robertson. London: George Routledge and Sons, 1905.

Bakhtin, Mikhail. *Rabelais and His World.* Translated by Hélène Iswolsky. Bloomington: Indiana University Press, 1984.

Baldinucci, Filippo. *Vita del Cavaliere Giovan Lorenzo Bernini: Scultore, architetto, e pittore.* Edited by Sergio Samek Ludovici. Milan: Edizioni del Milione, 1948.

Ballerini, Isabella Lapi, and Litta Maria Medri, eds., *Artifici d'acque e giardini: La cultura delle grotte e dei ninfei in Italia e in Europa,* Atti del V Convegno Internazionale sui Parchi e Giardini Storiche, Firenze, 16–17 settembre 1998, Palazzo Pitti, Lucca, 18–19 settembre 1998, Villa Buonvisi Bottini. Florence: Centro Di, 1999.

Baltrušaitis, Jurgis. *Anamorphic Art.* Translated by W. J. Strachan. Cambridge: Chadwyck-Healey, 1977.

———. *Réveils et prodiges: Les métamorphoses du gothique.* Paris: Flammarion, 1988.

Barisi, Isabella, Marcello Fagiolo, and Maria Luisa Madonna. *Villa d'Este.* Translated by Richard Bates, Lucinda Byatt, and Anita Weston. Rome: De Luca Editori d'Arte, 2003.

Barocchi, Paola, ed. *Scritti d'arte del cinquecento.* Vol. 1. Milan: Riccardo Ricciardi, 1977.

Barolini, Teodolinda. "The Self in the Labyrinth of Time: *Rerum vulgarium fragmenta.*" In *Petrarch: A Critical Guide to the Complete Works*, edited by Victoria Kirkhma and Armando Maggi, 33–62. Chicago: University of Chicago Press, 2009.

Barolsky, Paul. *Why Mona Lisa Smiles and Other Tales by Vasari.* University Park: Pennsylvania State University Press, 1991.

Barry, Fabio. "The Mouth of Truth and the *Forum Boarium*: Oceanus, Hercules, and Hadrian." *Art Bulletin* 93, no. 1 (March 2011): 7–37.

Barthes, Roland. "The Death of the Author." In *Image, Music, Text*, 142–48. Translated by Stephen Heath. London: Fontana Press, 1977.

Bartoli, Leandro Maria, and Gabriella Contorni. *Gli Orti Oricellari a Firenze: Un giardino, una città.* Florence: Edifir, 1991.

Battaglia, Salvatore. *Grande dizionario della lingua italiana.* Vol. 13. Turin: Unione tipografico-Editrice Torinese, 1986.

Battisti, Eugenio. *L'antirinascimento.* Milan: Feltrinelli, 1962.

Baxandall, Michael. *Painting and Experience in Fifteenth-Century Italy: A Primer in the Social History of Pictorial Style.* Oxford: Oxford University Press, 1972.

Becattini, Massimo, ed. *Il sogno del principe: Il parco Mediceo di Pratolino.* Florence: Edizioni Polistampa, 2006.

Bélanger, Anne. *Bomarzo ou les incertitudes de la lecture: Figure de la* meraviglia *dans un jardin maniériste du XVIe siècle.* Paris: Honoré Champion, 2007.

Belting, Hans. *Likeness and Presence: A History of the Image Before the Era of Art.* Translated by Edmund Jephcott. Chicago: University of Chicago Press, 1994.

Beneš, Mirka. "Italian and French Gardens: A Century of Historical Study (1900–2000)." In *Villas and Gardens in Early Modern Italy and France*, edited by Mirka Beneš and Dianne Harris, 1–16. Cambridge: Cambridge University Press, 2001.

———. "Methodological Changes in the Study of Italian Gardens from the 1970s to the 1990s: A Personal Itinerary." In *Clio in the Italian Garden: Twenty-First-Century Studies in Historical Methods and Theoretical Perspectives*, Dumbarton Oaks Colloquium on the History of Landscape Architecture XXXII, edited by Mirka Beneš and Michael G. Lee, 17–54. Washington, DC: Dumbarton Oaks Research Library and Collection, 2011.

———. "Recent Developments and Perspectives in the Historiography of Italian Gardens." In *Perspectives on Garden Histories*, Dumbarton Oaks Colloquium on the History of Landscape Architecture XXI, edited by Michel Conan, 37–76. Washington, DC: Dumbarton Oaks Research Library and Collection, 1999.

Beneš, Mirka, and Michael G. Lee. "Introduction." In *Clio in the Italian Garden: Twenty-First-Century Studies in Historical Methods and Theoretical Perspectives*, edited by Mirka Beneš and Michael G. Lee, 1–13. Washington, DC: Dumbarton Oaks Research Library and Collection, 2011.

Benjamin, Walter. "The Work of Art in the Age of Mechanical Reproduction." In *Illuminations*, edited by Hannah Arendt, 217–51. Translated by Harry Zohn. New York: Schocken, 1968.

Berger, Robert W., and Thomas F. Hedin. *Diplomatic Tours in the Gardens of Versailles Under Louis XIV*. Philadelphia: University of Pennsylvania Press, 2008.

Bernheimer, Richard. *Wild Men in the Middle Ages: A Study in Art, Sentiment, and Demonology*. New York: Octagon Books, 1970.

Berrong, Richard M. *Rabelais and Bakhtin: Popular Culture in Gargantua and Pantagruel*. Lincoln: University of Nebraska Press, 1986.

Bitbol-Hespériès, Annie. "Monsters, Nature, and Generation from the Renaissance to the Early Modern Period: The Emergence of Medical Thought." In *The Problem of Animal Generation in Early Modern Philosophy*, edited by Justin E. Smith, 47–62. Cambridge: Cambridge University Press, 2006.

Bober, P. P., and R. O. Rubinstein. *Renaissance Artists and Antique Sculpture: A Handbook of Sources*. London: Harvey Miller in conjunction with Oxford University Press, 1986.

Boccaccio, Giovanni. *The Decameron*. 2nd ed. Translated by G. H. McWilliam. London: Penguin Books, 2003.

Bocchi, Francesco. *Le belezze della città di Fiorenza*. Florence, 1591.

Borges, Jorge Luis. "The Analytical Language of John Wilkins." In *Other Inquisitions 1937–52*. Translated by Ruth L. C. Simms, 101=-5. Austin: University of Texas Press, 1964.

Borges, Jorge Luis, with Margarita Guerrero. *Book of Imaginary Beings*. Translated by Norman Thomas di Giovanni. New York: Dutton, 1969.

Boucher, Bruce. *The Sculpture of Jacopo Sansovino*. 2 vols. New Haven: Yale University Press, 1991.

Braham, Persephone. "The Monstrous Caribbean." In *The Ashgate Research Companion to Monsters and the Monstrous*, edited by Asa Simon Mittman and Peter J. Dendle, 17–47. Farnham: Ashgate, 2012.

Bredekamp, Horst. *Vicino Orsini e il Bosco Sacro di Bomarzo: Un principe artista ed anarchico*. Translated by Franco Pignetti. Rome: Edizioni dell'Elefante, 1989.

Brilliant, Richard. "I piedistalli del giardino di Boboli: Spolia in se, spolia in re," *Prospettiva* 31 (1982): 2–17.

Brilliant, Richard, and Dale Kinney, eds., *Reuse Value: Spolia and Appropriation in Art and Architecture from Constantine to Sherrie Levine*. Farnham: Ashgate, 2011.

Broderius, John R. *The Giant in Germanic Tradition*. Chicago: University of Chicago Press, 1932.

Brown, Patricia Fortini. *Venice and Antiquity: The Venetian Sense of the Past*. New Haven: Yale University Press, 1996.

Brunon, Hervé. "Du jardin comme paysage sacral en Italie à la Renaissance." In *Le paysage*

sacré: Le paysage comme exégèse dans l'Europe de la première modernité / Sacred Landscape: Landscape as Exegesis in Early Modern Europe, edited by Denis Ribouillaut and
Michel Weemans, 283–316. Florence: Leo S. Olschi, 2011.

———. "Du songe de Poliphile à la Grande Grotte de Boboli: La dualité dramatique du
paysage." Polia, Revue de l'art des jardins 2 (Autumn 2004): 7–26.

———. "Les mouvements de l'âme: Émotions et poétique du jardin maniériste." In Felipe
II: El rey intimo. Jardin y naturaleza en el siglo XVI, edited by Carmen Añón Feliú,
103–36. Madrid: Sociedad Estatal para la Conmemoración de los Centenarios de Felipe II y Carlos V, 1998.

———. "L'essor artistique et la fabrique culturelle du paysage à la Renaissance." Studiolo:
Revue d'histoire de l'art de l'Académie de France à Rome 4 (2006): 261–90.

———. "Pratolino: Art des jardins et imaginaire de la nature dans l'Italie de la seconde moitié
du XVIe siècle," rev. ed. Ph.D. diss., Université Paris I Panthéon-Sorbonne, 2008.

Bruschi, Arnaldo. "L'abitato di Bomarzo e la Villa Orsini." Quaderni dell'Istituto di Storia
dell'Architettura 7–9 (1955): 3–18.

———. "Il problema storico di Bomarzo." Palladio 13 (1963): 85–114.

———. "Nuovi dati documentari sulle opere Orsiniane di Bomarzo." Quaderni dell'Istituto
di Storia dell'Architettura 55–60 (1963): 13–58.

Bullfinch, Thomas. The Age of Fable: Or the Beauties of Mythology. New York: Heritage
Press, 1942.

Buonarotti, Michelangelo. Life, Letters, and Poetry. Translated by George Bull. Oxford:
Oxford University Press, 1987.

Burke, Edmund. "A Philosophical Enquiry into the Origin of Our Ideas of the Sublime and
the Beautiful; with an Introductory Discourse Concerning Taste." In Works 1: 55–219.
London: Oxford University Press, 1925.

Burshatin, Israel. "Elena Alias Eleno: Genders, Sexualities and 'Race' in the Mirror of Nat-
ural History in Sixteenth-Century Spain." In Gender Reversals and Gender Cultures:
Anthropological and Historical Perspectives, edited by Sabrina Petra Ramet, 105–22.
London: Routledge, 1996.

Bury, J. B. "The Reputation of Bomarzo." Journal of Garden History 3, no. 2 (1983): 108–12.

———. "Review Essay: Bomarzo Revisited." Journal of Garden History 5, no. 2 (1985):
213–23.

———. Review of Vicino Orsini und der heilige Wald von Bomarzo: Ein Fürst als Künstler
und Anarchist, by Horst Bredekamp. Burlington Magazine 128, no. 1002 (Sept. 1986):
679–80.

———. "Some Early Literary References to Italian Gardens." Journal of Garden History 2,
no. 1 (1982): 17–24.

Bush, Virginia. The Colossal Sculpture of the Cinquecento. New York: Garland, 1976.

Callegari, Adolfo. "Il giardino veneto." In Mostra del giardino italiano: Catalogo, 207–10.
Florence: Palazzo Vecchio, Comune di Firenze, 1931.

Calvesi, Maurizio. Gli incantesimi di Bomarzo: Il Sacro Bosco tra arte e letteratura. Milan:
Bompiano, 2009.

————. "Il Sacro Bosco di Bomarzo." In *Scritti di storia dell'arte in onore di Lionello Venturi*, 369–402. Vol. 1. Rome: De Luca, 1956.

Campbell, Paula. "Breaking the Frame: Transgression and Transformation in Giulio Romano's *Sala dei Giganti*." *Artibus et historiae* 18, no. 36 (1997): 87–100.

Canguilhem, Georges. "Monstrosity and the Monstrous." In *The Body: A Reader*, edited by Mariam Fraser and Monica Greco, 187–94. London: Routledge, 2005.

Cascardi, Anthony J. "The Genealogy of the Sublime in the Aesthetics of the Spanish Baroque." In *Reason and Its Others: Italy, Spain, and the New World*, edited by David Castillo and Massimo Lollini, 221–39. Nashville: Vanderbilt University Press, 2006, 221–39.

Cassidy, Brendan, ed. *Iconography at the Crossroads*, Papers from the Colloquium Sponsored by the Index of Christian Art, Princeton University, 23–24 March 1990. Princeton, NJ: Department of Art and Archaeology, Princeton University, 1993.

Castelletti, Claudio. "Bomarzo dopo Bomarzo: Storia, ricezione e fortuna critica del Sacro Bosco dal '500 agli anni Cinquanta del '900." In *Bomarzo: Il Sacro Bosco: Fortuna critica e documenti*, edited by Sabine Frommel and Andrea Alessi, 11–27. Rome: Ginevra Bentivoglio, 2009.

Castillo, David R. *Baroque Horrors: Roots of the Fantastic in the Age of Curiosities*. Ann Arbor: University of Michigan Press, 2010.

Cazzato, Vincenzo. "I giardini del desiderio." In *Il giardino romantico*, edited by Alessandro Vezzosi, 80–88. Florence: Alinea, 1986.

Céard, Jean. *La nature et les prodiges*. Geneva: Droz, 1977.

Cellini, Benvenuto. *The Autobiography of Benvenuto Cellini*. Translated by J. Addington Symonds. New York: Reynolds, 1910.

Certeau, Michel de. "Walking in the City." In *The Certeau Reader*, edited by Graham Ward, 101–18. Oxford: Blackwell, 2000.

Chastel, André. *La grottesque*. Paris: Le Promeneur/Quai Voltaire, 1988.

Coffin, David R. *Gardens and Gardening in Papal Rome*. Princeton, NJ: Princeton University Press, 1991.

————. "Pirro Ligorio and Decoration of the Late Sixteenth Century at Ferrara." *Art Bulletin* 37, no. 3 (Sept. 1955): 167–85.

————. "Pirro Ligorio on the Nobility of the Arts." *Journal of the Warburg and Courtauld Institutes* 27 (1964): 191–210.

————. ed. *The Italian Garden*. Washington, DC: Dumbarton Oaks, 1972.

————. "The 'Lex Hortorum' and Access to Gardens of Latium During the Renaissance." *Journal of Garden History* 2, no. 3 (1982): 201–32.

————. "The Study of the History of the Italian Garden Until the First Dumbarton Oaks Colloquium." In *Perspectives on Garden Histories*, Dumbarton Oaks Colloquium on the History of Landscape Architecture XXI, edited by Michel Conan, 27–35. Washington, DC: Dumbarton Oaks Research Library and Collection, 1999.

————. *The Villa d'Este at Tivoli*. Princeton NJ: Princeton University Press, 1960.

————. *The Villa in the Life of Renaissance Rome*. Princeton, NJ: Princeton University Press, 1979.

Cohen, Jeffrey Jerome. *Of Giants: Sex, Monsters, and the Middle Ages*. Minneapolis: University of Minnesota Press, 1999.

Cohen, Simona. "Andrea del Sarto's Monsters: The Madonna of the Harpies and Human-Animal Hybrids in the Renaissance." *Apollo* 159, no. 509 (July 2004): 38–45.

———. *Animals as Disguised Symbols in Renaissance Art*. Leiden: Brill, 2008.

Cole, Michael W. *Ambitious Form: Giambologna, Ammanati, and Dante in Florence*. Princeton, NJ: Princeton University Press, 2011.

Colonna, Francesco. *Hypnerotomachia Poliphili: The Strife of Love in a Dream*. Translated by Joscelyn Godwin. London: Thames and Hudson, 1999.

Conan, Michel, ed. *Baroque Garden Cultures: Emulation, Sublimation, Subversion*. Washington, DC: Dumbarton Oaks Research Library and Collection, 2005.

———. ed. *Performance and Appropriation: Profane Rituals in Gardens and Landscapes*. Washington, DC: Dumbarton Oaks Research Collection and Library, 2007.

Connelly, Frances S. "Introduction." In *Modern Art and the Grotesque*, edited by Frances S. Connelly, 1–19. Cambridge: Cambridge University Press, 2003.

Coty, Katherine. "A Dream of Etruria: The Sacro Bosco of Bomarzo and the Alternate Antiquity of Alto Lazio." M.A. diss., University of Maryland, 2013.

Crinito, Pietro. *Commentarii De Honesta Disciplina*. Florence: Filippo Giunta, 1504.

Curran, Andrew. "Afterword: Anatomical Readings in the Early Modern Era." In *Monstrous Bodies / Political Monstrosities in Early Modern Europe*, edited by Laura Lunger Knoppers and Joan B. Landes, 227–45. Ithaca, NY: Cornell University Press, 2004.

Curtius, Ernst Robert. *European Literature and the Latin Middle Ages*. Translated by Willard R. Trask. New York: Pantheon Books, 1953.

Dacos, Nicole. *La découverte de la Domus Aurea et la formation des grotesques a la Renaissance*. London: Warburg Institute and Leiden: E. J. Brill, 1969.

Dami, Luigi. *The Italian Garden*. Translated by L. Scopoli. New York: Brentano's, 1925.

Darnall, Margaretta J., and Mark S. Weil. "*Il Sacro Bosco di Bomarzo*: Its 16th-Century Literary and Antiquarian Context." *Journal of Garden History* 4, no. 1 (Jan.–Mar. 1984): 1–81.

Daston, Lorraine, and Katherine Park. "The Hermaphrodite and the Orders of Nature: Sexual Ambiguity in Early Modern France." *Gay and Lesbian Quarterly* 1 (1995): 419–38.

———. "Unnatural Conceptions: The Study of Monsters in Sixteenth- and Seventeenth-Century France and England." *Past and Present* 92 (1981): 20–54.

———. *Wonders and the Order of Nature, 1150–1750*. New York: Zone Books, 1998.

Davis, Natalie Zemon. "Women on Top." In *Society and Culture in Early Modern France*, 124–51. Stanford, CA: Stanford University Press, 1975.

Defert, Daniel. "Foucault, Space and the Architects." In *Documenta X*, edited by Jean François Chevrier, 274–83. Ostfildern-Ruit: Cantz, 1997.

d'Elia, Una Roman. "Giambologna's Giant and the *Cinquecento* Villa Garden as a Landscape of Suffering." In *Studies in the History of Gardens and Designed Landscapes* 31, no. 1 (2011): 1–25.

Dennis, George. *The Cities and Cemeteries of Etruria*. London: J. M. Dent, 1907.

Doni, Antonio Francesco. *Disegno del Doni*. Venice: Gabriel Giolito di Ferrara, 1549.

Dotson, Esther Gordon. "Shapes of Earth and Time in European Gardens." *Art Journal* 42, no. 3 (Autumn 1982): 210–16.

Eck, Caroline van, Stijn Bussels, Martin Delbeke, and Jürgen Pieters, eds. *Translations of the Sublime: The Early Modern Reception and Dissemination of Longinus's Peri Hupsous in Rhetoric, the Visual Arts, Architecture, and the Theatre*. Leiden: Brill, 2012.

Ehrlich, Tracy. *Landscape and Identity in Early Modern Rome: Villa Culture at Frascati in the Borghese Era*. Cambridge: Cambridge University Press, 2002.

Elkins, James. "On the Conceptual Analysis of Gardens." *Journal of Garden History* 13, no. 4 (Winter 1993): 189–98.

Fagiolo, Marcello, and Maria Luisa Madonna. "La casina di Pio IV in Vaticano: Pirro Ligorio e l'architettura come geroglifico." *Storia dell'Arte* 15–16 (1972): 237–81.

———. "The Myths of Ippolito's Garden." In *Villa d'Este*, edited by Isabella Barisi, Marcello Fagiolo, and Maria Luisa Madonna, 83–93. Rome: De Luca, 2003.

Fasolo, Furio. "Analisi Stilistica del Sacro Bosco." *Quaderni dell'Istituto di Storia dell'Architettura* 7–9 (1955): 33–60.

Fehrenbach, Frank. *Compendia mundi: Gianlorenzo Berninis Fontana dei Quattro Fiumi (1648–51) und Nicola Salvis Fontana di Trevi (1732–62)*. Munich: Deutscher Kunstverlag, 2008.

———. Review of *Anachronic Renaissance*, by Alexander Nagel and Christopher S. Wood. *caa.reviews* (8 March 8 2011), doi: 10.3202/caa.reviews.2011.30, http://caareviews.org.

Felton, D. "Rejecting and Embracing the Monstrous in Ancient Greece and Rome." In *The Ashgate Research Companion to Monsters and the Monstrous*, edited by Asa Simon Mitman and Peter J. Dendle, 103–31. Farnham: Ashgate, 2012.

Filarete, Antonio Averlino. *Treatise on Architecture*. 2 vols. Translated by John R. Spencer. New Haven: Yale University Press, 1965.

Findlen, Paula. *Possessing Nature: Museums, Collecting, and Scientific Culture in Early Modern Italy*. Berkeley: University of California Press, 1994.

Finucci, Valeria. *The Manly Masquerade: Masculinity, Paternity, and Castration in the Italian Renaissance*. Durham, NC: Duke University Press, 2003.

Flaubert, Gustave. *Bouvard and Pécuchet*. Translated by T. W. Earp and G. W. Stonier. Norfolk, CT: New Directions Books, 1964.

Foucault, Michel. *Abnormal: Lectures at the Collège de France, 1974–75*. Edited by Velerio Marchetti and Antonella Salomoni. Translated by Graham Burchell. London: Verso, 2003.

———. "Of Other Spaces." Translated by Jay Miskowiec. *Diacritics* 16, no. 1 (1986): 22–27.

———. *The Order of Things*. London: Routledge, 2005.

———. "What Is an Author?" In *Language, Counter-Memory, Practice: Selected Essays and Interviews by Michel Foucault*, edited by Donald F. Bouchard, 113–38. Ithaca, NY: Cornell University Press, 1977.

Francis, Mark, and Randolph T. Hester Jr., eds. *The Meaning of Gardens: Idea, Place, and Action*. Cambridge, MA: MIT Press, 1990.

Frascari, Marco. *Monsters of Architecture: Anthropomorphism in Architectural Theory*. Savage, MD: Rowman and Littlefield, 1991.

Freud, Sigmund. *The Uncanny*. Translated by David McLintock. London: Penguin Books, 2003.

Friedman, John Block. *The Monstrous Races in Medieval Art and Thought*. Cambridge, MA: Harvard University Press, 1981.

Frith, Wendy. "Sexuality and Politics in the Gardens at West Wycombe and Medmenham Abbey." In *Bourgeois and Aristocratic Cultural Encounters in Garden Art, 1550–1850*, edited by Michel Conan, 285=-309. Washington, DC: Dumbarton Oaks, 2002.

Frommel, Sabine, ed. *Bomarzo: Il Sacro Bosco*. Milan: Electa, 2009.

———, ed. *Bomarzo: Il Sacro Bosco. Fortuna critica e documenti*. Rome: Ginevra Bentivoglio, 2009.

Garrard, Mary. *Brunelleschi's Egg: Nature, Art, and Gender in Renaissance Italy*. Berkeley: University of California Press, 2010.

Gaston, R. W. "Ligorio on Rivers and Fountains: Prolegomena to a Study of Naples XII.B.9." In *Pirro Ligorio: Artist and Antiquarian*, edited by R. W. Gaston, 159–208. Florence: Villa I Tatti, Harvard University Center for Italian Renaissance Studies, 1988.

———. "Love's Sweet Poison: A New Reading of Bronzino's London Allegory." In *Sixteenth-Century Italian Art*, edited by Michael W. Cole, 56–87. Oxford: Wiley-Blackwell, 2006.

Gauricus, Pomponius. *De sculptura* (1504). Translated and annotated by André Chastel and Robert Klein. Geneva: Librairie Droz, 1969.

Gay, Peter. *Weimar Culture: The Outsider as Insider*. London: Penguin Books, 1969.

Genocchio, Benjamin. "Heterotopia and Its Limits." *Transition* 41 (1993): 33–41.

Giannetto, Raffaella Fabiani. "Writing the Garden in the Age of Humanism: Petrarch and Boccaccio." *Studies in the History of Gardens and Designed Landscapes* 23, no. 3 (Autumn 2003): 231–57.

———. *Medici Gardens: From Making to Design*. Philadelphia: University of Pennsylvania Press, 2008.

———. "'Grafting the Edelweiss on Cactus Plants': The 1931 Italian Garden Exhibition and Its Legacy.' In *Clio in the Italian Garden: Twenty-First-Century Studies in Historical Methods and Theoretical Perspectives*, edited by Mirka Beneš and Michael G. Lee, 55–77. Washington, DC: Dumbarton Oaks Research Library and Collection, 2011.

Gilbert, Felix. "Bernardo Rucellai and the Orti Oricellari: A Study on the Origin of Modern Political Thought." *Journal of the Warburg and Courtauld Institutes* 12 (1949): 101–31.

Ginzburg, Carlo. "Montaigne, Cannibals, and Grottoes." *History and Anthropology* 6, nos. 2–3 (1993): 125–55.

Greenblatt, Stephen. "Fiction and Friction." In *Reconstructing Individualism: Autonomy, Individuality, and the Self in Western Thought*, edited by Thomas C. Heller, Morton Sosna, and David E. Wellbery, 30–52. Stanford, CA: Stanford University Press, 1986.

Grosz, Elizabeth. "Intolerable Ambiguity: Freaks as/at the Limit." In *Freakery: Cultural*

Spectacles of the Extraordinary Body, edited by Rosemarie Garland Thomson, 55–66. New York: New York University Press, 1996.

Guldan, Ernst. "Das Monster-Portal am Palazzo Zuccari in Rom: Wandlungen eines Motivs vom Mittelalter zum Manierismus." *Zeitschrift für Kunstgeschichte* 32, nos. 3–4 (1969): 229–61.

Hall, James. *A History of Ideas and Images in Italian Art.* London: John Murray, 1983.

Hanafi, Zakiya. *The Monster in the Machine: Magic, Medicine, and the Marvelous in the Time of the Scientific Revolution.* Durham, NC: Duke University Press, 2000.

Hansen, Maria Fabricius. "*Maniera* and the Grotesque." In *Manier und Manierismus*, edited by Wolfgang Braungart, 251–74. Tübingen: Max Niemeyer, 2000.

———. "Representing the Past: The Concept and Study of Antique Architecture in Fifteenth-Century Italy." In *Analecta romana: Instituti danici* 23, edited by Otto Steen Due, Jan Zahle, Steen Bo Frandsen, and Karen Ascani, 83–116. Rome: "L'Erma" di Bretschneider, 1996.

———. "Telling Time: Representations of Ruins in Sixteenth-Century Art." Paper delivered at the Renaissance Society of America, New York City, 2014.

Harris, Dianne. "Landscape in Context." In *Villas and Gardens in Early Modern Italy and France*, edited by Mirka Beneš and Dianne Harris, 16–25. Cambridge: Cambridge University Press, 2001.

Harris, Dianne, and D. Fairchild Ruggles. "Landscape and Vision." In *Sites Unseen: Landscape and Vision*, edited by Dianne Harris and D. Fairchild Ruggles, 5–29. Pittsburgh: University of Pittsburgh Press, 2007.

Helms, G. M. "The Materials and Techniques of Italian Renaissance Sculpture." In *Looking at Italian Renaissance Sculpture*, edited by Sarah Blake McHam, 18–39. Cambridge: Cambridge University Press, 1998.

Henneberg, Josephine von. "Bomarzo: Nuovi dati e un'interpretazione." *Storia dell'arte* 13 (1972): 43–55.

Heuer, Christopher P. "Difference, Repetition, Utopia: Early Modern Print's New Worlds." In *Crossing Cultures: Conflict, Migration and Convergence: The Proceedings of the 32nd International Congress in the History of Art*, edited by Jaynie Anderson, 203–8. Melbourne: Miegunyah Press, 2009.

Hibbard, Howard. *Michelangelo.* Harmondsworth: Penguin, 1978.

Hinds, Stephen. "Landscape with Figures: Aesthetics of Place in the *Metamorphoses* and Its Tradition." In *The Cambridge Companion to Ovid*, edited by Philip R. Hardie, 122–49. Cambridge: Cambridge University Press, 2002.

Holly, Michael Ann. *Panofsky and the Foundations of Art History.* Ithaca, NY: Cornell University Press, 1984.

Holquist, Michael. "Bakhtin and Rabelais: Theory as Praxis." *Boundary 2* 11, nos. 1–2 (Autumn 1982–Winter 1983): 5–19.

Huet, Marie-Helene. "Living Images: Monstrosity and Representation." *Representations* 4 (Autumn 1983): 73–87.

Hughes, Robert. "The Strangest Garden in the West." *Horizon* 18, no. 3 (1976).

Hugo, Victor. *Préface de "Cromwell."* Edited by Edmond Wahl. Oxford: Clarendon Press, 1909.

Humfrey, Peter. *Lorenzo Lotto.* New Haven: Yale University Press, 1997.

Hunt, John Dixon. *The Afterlife of Gardens.* Philadelphia: University of Pennsylvania Press, 2004.

———. "Approaches (New and Old) to Garden History." In *Perspectives on Garden Histories,* edited by Michel Conan, 77–90. Washington, DC: Dumbarton Oaks, 1999.

———. "Experiencing Gardens and Landscapes in the *Hypnerotomachia Poliphili.*" In *The Afterlife of Gardens,* Penn Studies in Landscape Architecture, 57–76. Philadelphia: University of Pennsylvania Press, 2004.

———. *Garden and Grove: The Italian Renaissance Garden in the English Imagination: 1600–1750.* London: J. M. Dent and Sons, 1986.

———. *Greater Perfections: The Practice of Garden Theory.* London: Thames and Hudson, 2000.

———. "Introduction: Making and Writing the Italian Garden." In *The Italian Garden: Art, Design and Culture,* edited by John Dixon Hunt, 1–5. Cambridge: Cambridge University Press, 1996.

———. *Nature over Again: The Garden Art of Ian Hamilton Finlay.* London: Reaktion Books, 2008.

———. "*Paragone* in Paradise: Translating the Garden." *Comparative Criticism* 18 (1996): 55–70.

———. Review of *Literature and the Renaissance Garden from Elizabeth I to Charles II: England's Paradise,* by Amy L. Tigner. In *Renaissance Quarterly* 65, no. 4 (Winter 2012): 1339–40.

Huse, Norbert. "La Fontaine des Fleuves du Bernini." *Revue de l'art* 7 (1970): 7–17.

Hyde, Elizabeth. *Cultivated Power: Flowers, Culture and Politics in the Reign of Louis XIV.* Philadelphia: University of Pennsylvania Press, 2005.

Jaeger, C. Stephen, ed. *Magnificence and the Sublime in Medieval Aesthetics: Art, Architecture, Literature, Music.* New York: Palgrave Macmillan, 2010.

Jay, Martin. "No State of Grace: Violence in the Garden." In *Sites Unseen: Landscape and Vision,* edited by Dianne Harris and D. Fairchild Ruggles, 45–60. Pittsburgh: University of Pittsburg Press, 2007.

———. "Scopic Regimes of Modernity." In *Vision and Visuality,* edited by Hal Foster, 3–23. Seattle: Bay Press, 1988.

Jeanneret, Michel. *Perpetual Motion: Transforming Shapes from Da Vinci to Montaigne.* Translated by Nidra Poller. Baltimore: Johns Hopkins University Press, 2001.

Jellicoe, Geoffrey. *Italian Gardens of the Renaissance.* 4th ed. London: Academy Editions, 1985.

Jensen, Søren Skovgaard. "Lucubratiunculae: Reflections on the Sacro Bosco at Bomarzo." In *Studia Romana in honorem Petri Krarup septuagenarii,* edited by Karen Ascani and Tobias Fischer-Hansen, 204–12. Odense: Odense University Press, 1976.

Johnson, Geraldine A. "Touch, Tactility, and the Reception of Sculpture in Early Modern

Italy." In *A Companion to Art Theory*, edited by Paul Smith and Carolyn Wilde, 61–74. Oxford: Blackwell, 2002.

Johnson, Peter. "Unravelling Foucault's 'Different Spaces.'" *History of the Human Sciences* 19, no. 4 (2006): 75–90.

Jones, Ann Rosalind, and Peter Stallybrass. "Fetishizing Gender: Constructing the Hermaphrodite in Renaissance Europe." In *Bodyguards: The Cultural Politics of Gender*, edited by Julia Epstein and Kristina Traub, 80–111. New York: Routledge, 1991.

Jordan, Constance. *Pulci's Morgante: Poetry and History in Fifteenth-Century Florence*. Cranbury, NJ: Associated University Presses, 1986.

Kelsall, Malcolm. "The Iconography of Stourhead." *Journal of the Warburg and Courtauld Institutes* 46 (1983): 133–43.

Kemp, Martin. *Leonardo da Vinci: The Marvellous Works of Nature and Man*. Oxford: Oxford University Press, 2006.

Kenseth, Joy, ed. *The Age of the Marvelous*. Hanover, NH: Hood Museum of Art, Dartmouth College, 1991.

Keutner, Herbert. "Note intorno all'Appennino del Giambologna." In *L'Appennino del Giambologna: Anatomia e identità del gigante*, 18–27. Florence: Alinea, 1990.

Knoppers, Laura Lunger, and Joan B. Landes, eds. *Monstrous Bodies/Political Monstrosities in Early Modern Europe*. Ithaca, NY: Cornell University Press, 2004.

Kohane, Peter, and Michael Hill. "The Decorum of Doors and Windows from the Fifteenth to the Eighteenth Century." *Architectural Research Quarterly* 10, no. 2 (2006): 141–56.

Kretzulesco-Quaranta, Emanuela. *Incantesimo a Bomarzo*. Florence: Sansoni, 1960.

———. *Les jardins du songe: "Poliphile" et la mystique de la Renaissance*. Rome: Editrice Magma, 1976.

Lasansky, D. Medina. *The Renaissance Perfected: Architecture, Spectacle, and Tourism in Fascist Italy*. University Park: Pennsylvania State University Press, 2004.

Lazzarini, Elena. "Wonderful Creatures: Early Modern Perceptions of Deformed Bodies." *Oxford Art Journal* 34, no. 3 (2011): 415–31.

Lazzaro, Claudia. "Gendered Nature and Its Representation in Sixteenth-Century Garden Sculpture." In *Looking at Italian Renaissance Sculpture*, edited by Sarah McHam, 246–73. Cambridge: Cambridge University Press, 1998.

———. *The Italian Renaissance Garden: From the Conventions of Planting, Design, and Ornament to the Grand Gardens of Sixteenth-Century Italy*. New Haven: Yale University Press, 1990.

———. "Politicizing a National Garden Tradition: The Italianness of the Italian Garden." In *Donatello Among the Blackshirts: History and Modernity in the Visual Culture of Fascist Italy*, edited by Claudia Lazzaro and Roger J. Crum, 157–69. Ithaca, NY: Cornell University Press, 2005.

———. "River Gods: Personifying Nature in Sixteenth-Century Italy." *Renaissance Studies* 25, no. 1 (2011): 70–94.

Lee, Rensselaer. "*Ut pictura poesis*: The Humanistic Theory of Painting." *Art Bulletin* 22, no. 4 (Dec. 1940): 197–229.

Lefebvre, Henri. *The Production of Space*. Translated by Donald Nicholson-Smith. Malden, MA: Blackwell, 1991.

Leslie, Michael. "Spenser, Sidney, and the Renaissance Garden." *English Literary Renaissance* 22, no. 1 (Winter 1992): 3–36.

Llewellyn, Nigel, and Michael Snodin, eds. *International Baroque*. London: V&A Publishing, 2009.

Long, Kathleen P. *Hermaphrodites in Renaissance Europe*. Burlington, VT: Ashgate, 2006.

Luchinat, Cristina Acidini. "I giardini dei Medici: Origini, sviluppi, trasformazioni: L'architettura, il verde, le statue, le fontane." In *Giardini medicei: Giardini di palazzo e di villa nella Firenze del Quattrocento*, edited by Cristina Acidini Luchinat , 46–59. Milan: F. Motta, 1996.

———. "Il modello del giardino fiorentino del Quattrocento nella mostra del 1931." In *Giardini medicei: Giardini di palazzo e di villa nella Firenze del Quattrocento*, edited by Cristina Acidini Luchinat, 138–45. Milan: F. Motta, 1996.

———. "L'Appennino dal modello all'opera compiuta." In *Risveglio di un colosso: Il restauro dell'Appennino del Giambologna*, edited by Cristina Acidini Luchinat, 13–21. Florence: Alinari, 1988.

MacDougall, Elisabeth B. *Fountains, Statues, and Flowers: Studies in Italian Gardens of the Sixteenth and Seventeenth Centuries*. Washington, DC: Dumbarton Oaks Research Library and Collection, 1993.

Maclean, Ian. "Foucault's Renaissance Episteme Reassessed: An Aristotelian Counterblast." *Journal of the History of Ideas* 59, no. 1 (1998): 149–66.

Mandeville, John. *The Travels of Sir John Mandeville*. Translated by C. W. R. D. Moseley. Harmondsworth: Penguin, 1983.

Mandiargues, André Pieyre de. *Les monstres de Bomarzo*. Paris: Éditions Bernard Grasset, 1957.

Mariage, Thierry. *The World of André Le Nôtre*. Translated by Graham Larkin. Philadelphia: University of Pennsylvania Press, 1999.

Marin, Louis. *The Portrait of the King*. Minneapolis: University of Minnesota Press, 1988.

Marr, Alexander. "Automata." In *The Classical Tradition*, edited by Anthony Grafton, Glen W. Most, and Salvatore Settis, 109–10. Cambridge, MA: Harvard University Press, 2011.

Miller, Naomi. *Heavenly Caves: Reflections on the Garden Grotto*. New York: George Brazillier, 1982.

Miller, Sarah Alison. "Monstrous Sexuality: Variations on the *Vagina Dentata*." In *The Ashgate Research Companion to Monsters and the Monstrous*, edited by Asa Simon Mittman and Peter J. Dendle, 311–28. Farnham: Ashgate, 2012.

Mittman, Asa Simon, and Peter J. Dendle, eds. *The Ashgate Research Companion to Monsters and the Monstrous*. Farnham: Ashgate, 2012.

Moffitt, John F. "An Exemplary Humanist Hybrid: Vasari's 'Fraude' with Reference to Bronzino's 'Sphinx.'" *Renaissance Quarterly* 49, no. 2 (Summer 1996): 303–33.

Montaigne, Michel de. *The Complete Works of Montaigne: Essays, Travel Journal, Letters*. Translated by Donald M. Frame. Stanford, CA: Stanford University Press, 1948.

Morel, Philippe. *Les grotesques: Les figures de l'imaginaire dans la peinture italienne de la fin de la Renaissance*. Paris: Flammarion, 2011.

———. *Les grottes maniéristes en Italie au XVIe siècle*. Paris: Éditions Macula, 1998.

Morgan, Luke. "Design." In *A Cultural History of Gardens in the Renaissance*, edited by Elisabeth Hyde, 17–42. London: Bloomsbury, 2013.

———. "The Early Modern *Trompe l'Oeil* Garden." *Garden History* 33, no. 2 (2005): 286–93.

———. "Meaning." In *A Cultural History of Gardens in the Renaissance*, edited by Elisabeth Hyde, 125–37. London: Bloomsbury, 2013.

———. "The Monster in the Garden: The Grotesque, the Gigantic and the Monstrous in Renaissance Landscape Design." *Studies in the History of Gardens and Designed Landscapes* 31, no. 3 (2011): 167–80.

———. *Nature as Model: Salomon de Caus and Early Seventeenth-Century Landscape Design*. Philadelphia: University of Pennsylvania Press, 2007.

Morolli, Gabriele, et al. *Il gigante degli Orti Oricellari*. Rome: Editalia, 1993.

Mostra del giardino italiano: Catalogo. Florence: Palazzo Vecchio, Comune di Firenze, 1931.

Mukerji, Chandra. "Bourgeois Culture and French Gardening in the Sixteenth and Seventeenth Centuries." In *Bourgeois and Aristocratic Cultural Encounters in Garden Art, 1550–1850*, edited by Michel Conan, 173–87. Washington, DC: Dumbarton Oaks Research Library and Collection, 2002.

Munder, Heike, ed. *The Garden of Forking Paths*. Zurich: Migros Museum für Gegenwartskunst and J. R. P. Ringier, 2011.

Nagel, Alexander. *The Controversy of Renaissance Art*. Chicago: University of Chicago Press, 2011.

———. *Medieval Modern: Art Out of Time*. New York: Thames and Hudson, 2012.

Nagel, Alexander, and Christopher S. Wood. *Anachronic Renaissance*. New York: Zone Books, 2010.

———. "The Authors Reply." *Art Bulletin* 87, no. 3 (Sept. 2005): 429–32.

Nielsen, Marjatta. "*Diana Efesia Multimammia*: The Metamorphoses of a Pagan Goddess from the Renaissance to the Age of Neo-Classicism." In *From Artemis to Diana: The Goddess of Man and Beast*, Danish Studies in Archaeology: Acta Hyperborea 12, edited by Tobias Fischer-Hansen and Birte Poulsen, 455–96. Copenhagen: Museum Tusculanum Press, University of Copenhagen, 2009.

Nietzsche, Friedrich. *The Gay Science, With a Prelude in German Rhymes and an Appendix of Songs*, edited by Bernard Williams, translated by Josefine Nauckhoff, poems translated by Adrian del Caro. Cambridge: Cambridge University Press, 2001.

Oleson, John P. "A Reproduction of an Etruscan Tomb in the Parco dei Mostri at Bomarzo." *Art Bulletin* 57, no. 3 (Sept. 1975): 410–17.

Onians, John. "I Wonder: A Short History of Amazement." In *Sight and Insight: Essays on Art and Culture in Honour of E. H. Gombrich at 85*, edited by John Onians, 11–33. London: Phaidon, 1994.

Ovid. *Metamorphoses*. Translated by Mary M. Innes. Harmondsworth: Penguin, 1955.

Pallister, Janis L. "Giants." In *Mythical and Fabulous Creatures: A Source Book and Research Guide*, edited by Malcolm South, 295–324. New York: Greenwood Press, 1987.

Panofsky, Erwin. *Renaissance and Renascences*. London: Paladin, 1970.

Paré, Ambroise. *On Monsters and Marvels*. Translated by Janis L. Pallister. Chicago: University of Chicago Press, 1982.

Park, Katherine. "Impressed Images, Reproducing Wonders." In *Picturing Science, Producing Art*, edited by Caroline A. Jones and Peter Gallison, 254–71. New York: Routledge, 1998.

———. "Nature in Person: Medieval and Renaissance Allegories and Emblems." In *The Moral Authority of Nature*, edited by Lorraine Daston and Fernando Vidal, 50–73. Chicago: University of Chicago Press, 2004.

Partridge, Loren. "The Farnese Circular Courtyard at Caprarola: God, Geopolitics, and Gender." *Art Bulletin* 83, no. 2 (June 2001): 259–93.

Payne, Alina. "*Mescolare, Composti* and Monsters in Italian Architectural Theory of the Renaissance." In *Disarmonia, brutezza e bizzarria nel Rinascimento*, Atti del VII Convegno Internazionale, Chianciano-Pienza, 17–20 luglio 1995, edited by Luisa Secchi Tarugi, 273–94. Florence: Franco Cesati, 1998.

Pérez-Gómez, Alberto. *Polyphilo, or, The Dark Forest Revisited: An Erotic Epiphany of Architecture*. Cambridge, MA: MIT Press, 1992.

Petrarch, Francesco. *Canzoniere, or, Rerum vulgarium fragmenta*. Translated by Mark Musa. Bloomington: Indiana University Press, 1999.

Pietrogrande, Antonella. "The Imaginary of Generative Nature in Italian Mannerist Gardens." In *Clio in the Italian Garden: Twenty-First-Century Studies in Historical Methods and Theoretical Perspectives*, edited by Mirka Beneš and Michael G. Lee, 187–202. Washington, DC: Dumbarton Oaks Research Library and Collection, 2011.

Pizzorusso, Claudio. "Harpy on the Back of a Toad." In *The Medici, Michelangelo, and the Art of Late Renaissance Florence*, edited by Cristina Acidini Luchinat, 228–29. New Haven: Yale University Press, 2002.

Platt, Mary A. "*Il Sacro Bosco*: The Significance of Vicino Orsini's Villa Garden at Bomarzo in the History of Italian Renaissance Garden Design." M.A. thesis, Michigan State University, 1986.

Pliny the Elder. *Natural History: A Selection*. Translated by John F. Healy. London: Penguin Books, 2004.

Pontecorboli, Angelo, and Maddalena Gentile. *La Fontana dei Mostri: Giardino di Boboli*. Florence: Karta, 1982.

Portoghesi, Paolo. "Nota sulla Villa Orsini di Pitigliano." *Quaderni dell'Istituto di Storia dell'Architettura* 7–9 (1955): 74–76.

Pozzana, Mariachiara. "Identità dell'Appennino: La fabbrica, l'acqua, la vegetazione." In *L'Appennino del Giambologna: Anatomia e identità del gigante*, edited by Alessandro Vezzosi, 108–14. Florence: Alinea, 1990.

Praz, Mario. *Il giardino dei sensi: Studi sul manierismo e il barocco*. Milan: Arnoldo Mondadori, 1975.

Pulci, Luigi. *Il Morgante maggiore*. Florence, 1481.

Puppi, Lionello. "The Villa Garden of the Veneto from the Fifteenth to the Eighteenth Century." In *The Italian Garden*, edited by David R. Coffin, 81–114. Washington, DC: Dumbarton Oaks, 1972.

Quartermaine, Luisa. "Vicino Orsini's Garden of Conceits." *Italian Studies* 32 (1977): 68–85.

Rabelais, François. *Gargantua and Pantagruel*. Translated by M. A. Screech. Harmondsworth: Penguin, 2006.

Ricci, Lucia Battaglia. "Gardens in Italian Literature During the Thirteenth and Fourteenth Centuries." In *The Italian Garden: Art, Design and Culture*, edited by John Dixon Hunt, 6–33. Cambridge: Cambridge University Press, 1996.

Rose, Carol. *Giants, Monsters, and Dragons: An Encyclopedia of Folklore, Legend, and Myth*. Santa Barbara, CA: ABC-CLIO, 2000.

Rowland, Beryl. "Harpies." In *Mythical and Fabulous Creatures: A Source Book and Research Guide*, edited by Malcolm South, 155–61. New York: Greenwood Press, 1987.

Ruskin, John. *The Stones of Venice*. London: Collins, 1960.

Russo, Mary. "Female Grotesques: Carnival and Theory." In *Feminist Studies/Critical Studies*, edited by Teresa de Lauretis, 213–19. Bloomington: Indiana University Press, 1986.

Saldanha, Arun. "Heterotopia and Structuralism." *Environment and Planning A* 40 (2008): 2080–96.

Sannazaro, Jacopo. *Arcadia and the Piscatorial Eclogues*. Translated by Ralph Nash. Detroit: Wayne State University Press, 1966.

Schmidt, Gary D. *The Iconography of the Mouth of Hell: Eighth-Century Britain to the Fifteenth Century*. Selinsgrove, PA: Susquehanna University Press and London: Associated University Presses, 1995.

Scigliano, Eric. *Michelangelo's Mountain: The Quest for Perfection in the Marble Quarries of Ferrara*. New York: Free Press, 2005.

Scott, Anne, and Cynthia Kosso, eds. *Fear and Its Representations in the Middle Ages and Renaissance*, Arizona Studies in the Middle Ages and the Renaissance, vol. 6. Turnhout: Brepols, 2002.

Segal, Charles Paul. *Landscape in Ovid's Metamorphoses: A Study in the Transformations of a Literary Symbol*. Wiesbaden: Franz Steiner, 1969.

Seiterle, Gérard. "Artemis: Die grosse Göttin von Ephesos." *Antike Welt* 10 (1979): 3–16.

Seymour, Charles Jr. *Michelangelo's David*. Pittsburgh: University of Pittsburgh Press, 1967.

Sheeler, Jessie. *The Garden at Bomarzo: A Renaissance Riddle*. London: Frances Lincoln, 2007.

Simons, Patricia. "Manliness and the Visual Semiotics of Bodily Fluids in Early Modern Culture." *Journal of Medieval and Early Modern Studies* 39, no. 2 (Spring 2009): 331–74.

Singley, Paulette. "Devouring Architecture." *Assemblage* 32 (Apr. 1997): 108–25.

Sluijter, Eric Jan. *Rembrandt and the Female Nude*. Amsterdam: Amsterdam University Press, 2006.

Smith, Webster. "Observations on the Mona Lisa Landscape." *Art Bulletin* 67, no. 2 (June 1985): 183–99.

————. "Pratolino." *Journal of the Society of Architectural Historians* 20 (1961): 163–64.

Snodin, Michael, and Nigel Llewellyn, eds. *Baroque, 1620–1800: Style in the Age of Magnificence*. London: V&A Publishing, 2009.

Soderini, Giovanni Vittorio. *I due trattati dell'agricoltura*, edited by A. Bacchi della Lega. Bologna: Romagnoli-Dall'Acqua, 1902.

Soja, Edward. *Thirdspace*. Oxford: Blackwell, 1996.

South, Malcolm, ed. *Mythical and Fabulous Creatures: A Source Book and Research Guide*. New York: Greenwood Press, 1987.

Spackman, Barbara. "Inter musam et ursam moritur: Folengo and the Gaping 'Other' Mouth." In *Refiguring Women: Perspectives on Gender and the Italian Renaissance*, edited by Marilyn Migiel and Juliana Schiesari, 19–31. Ithaca, NY: Cornell University Press, 1991.

Stackelberg, Katherine T. von. *The Roman Garden: Space, Sense and Society*. London: Routledge, 2009.

Stephens, Walter. *Giants in Those Days: Folklore, Ancient History, and Nationalism*. Lincoln: University of Nebraska Press, 1989.

Stewart, Susan. *On Longing: Narratives of the Miniature, the Gigantic, the Souvenir, the Collection*. Baltimore: Johns Hopkins University Press, 1984.

Stewering, Roswitha. "The Relationship Between World, Landscape and Polia in the *Hypnerotomachia Poliphili*." *Word and Image* 14, nos. 1–2 (Jan.–June 1998): 2–10.

Stoichiță, Victor. *The Pygmalion Effect: From Ovid to Hitchcock*. Chicago: University of Chicago Press, 2008.

Stoppino, Eleanora. "'Error Left Me and Fear Came in Its Place': The Arrested Sublime of the Giants in Divine Comedy, Canto XXI." In *Magnificence and the Sublime in Medieval Aesthetics: Art, Architecture, Literature, Music*, edited by C. Stephen Jaeger, 179–92. New York: Palgrave Macmillan, 2010.

Strong, Roy. *Art and Power: Renaissance Festivals, 1450–1650*. Woodbridge, Suffolk: Boydell Press, 1984.

————. *The Artist and the Garden*. New Haven: Yale University Press, 2000.

Summers, David. "The Archaeology of the Modern Grotesque." In *Modern Art and the Grotesque*, edited by Frances S. Connelly, 20–46. Cambridge: Cambridge University Press, 2003.

————. *Michelangelo and the Language of Art*. Princeton, NJ: Princeton University Press, 1981.

Szafranska, Malgorzata. "The Philosophy of Nature and the Grotto in the Renaissance Garden." *Journal of Garden History* 9, no. 2 (1989): 76–85.

Taegio, Bartolomeo. *La Villa*. Translated by Thomas E. Beck. Philadelphia: University of Pennsylvania Press, 2011.

Tasso, Torquato. *The Liberation of Jerusalem (Gerusalemme liberata)*. Translated by Max Wickert. Oxford: Oxford University Press, 2009.

Tchikine, Anatole. *"Galera, Navicella, Barcaccia?* Bernini's Fountain in Piazza di Spagna Revisited." *Studies in the History of Gardens and Designed Landscapes* 31, no. 4 (2011): 311–31.

———. "*Giochi d'acqua*: Water Effects in Renaissance and Baroque Italy." *Studies in the History of Gardens and Designed Landscapes* 30, no. 1 (Jan.–Mar. 2010): 57–76.

Teyssot, Georges. "Heterotopias and the History of Spaces." In *Architecture Theory Since 1968*, edited by K. Michael Hays, 296–305. Cambridge, MA: MIT Press, 1998.

Thacker, Christopher. "'Manière de montrer les jardins de Versailles' by Louis XIV and Others." *Garden History* 1, no. 1 (1972): 49–69.

Theurillat, Jacqueline. *Les mystères de Bomarzo et des jardins symboliques de la Renaissance.* Geneva: Les Trois Anneaux, 1976.

Tigner, Amy L. *Literature and the Renaissance Garden from Elizabeth I to Charles II: England's Paradise.* Farnham: Ashgate, 2012.

Topsell, Edward. *The History of Four-Footed Beasts and Serpents and Insects.* Vol. 1. London: Frank Cass, 1967.

Tschumi, Bernard. *Cinégram folie: Le Parc de la Villette.* Princeton, NJ: Princeton Architectural Press, 1987.

Urbach, Henry. "Writing Architectural Heterotopia." *Journal of Architecture* 3, no. 4 (Winter 1998): 347–54.

Varchi, Benedetto. *Lezzioni di M. Benedetto Varchi.* Florence: Filippo Giunti, 1590.

———. *Opere di Benedetto Varchi con le lettere di Gio. Batista Busini.* Vol. 1. Milan: Nicoló Bettoni, 1835.

Vasari, Giorgio. *Le opere di Giorgio Vasari.* 9 vols. Edited by Gaetano Milanesi. Florence: G. C. Sansoni, 1906.

———. *The Lives of the Painters, Sculptors and Architects.* Edited by William Gaunt. 4 vols. Translated by A. B. Hinds. London: Dent, 1963.

———. *Vasari on Technique.* Edited by G. Baldwin Brown. Translated by Louisa S. Maclehose. New York: Dover, 1960.

Vezzosi, Alessandro, ed. *Il giardino d'Europa: Pratolino come modello nella cultura europea.* Milan: Mazzotta, 1986.

———. "Le fortune dell'Appennino e il restauro del mito." In *Risveglio di un colosso: Il restauro dell'Appennino del Giambologna*, edited by Criustina Acidini Luchinat, 38–44. Florence: Alinari, 1988.

———. "Nota redazionale con sintesi dell'intervento di Detlef Heikamp." In *L'Appennino del Giambologna: Anatomia e identità del gigante*, edited by Alessandro Vezzosi, 9–10. Florence: Alinea, 1990.

Vieri, Francesco de. *Discorsi di M. Francesco de Vieri, detto il verino secondo: Delle maravigliose opere di Pratolino & d'amore.* Florence: Giorgio Marescotti, 1587.

Vinci, Leonardo da. *The Notebooks of Leonardo da Vinci*, trans. E MacCurdy, Vol. II. London: Jonathon Cape, 1938.

———. *Selections from the Notebooks of Leonardo da Vinci.* Edited by Irma A. Richter. Oxford: Oxford University Press, 1977.

Visentini, Margherita Azzi. "Il Giardino Giusti di Verona." In *Il giardino come labirinto della storia: Convegno internazionale, Palermo, 14–17 aprile 1984*, edited by Jette Abel and Eliana Mauro, 177–81. Palermo: Centro Studi di Storia e Arte dei Giardini, 1986.

————. "La grotta nel cinquecento Veneto: Il Giardino Giusti di Verona." *Arte veneta: Rivista di storia dell'arte* 39 (1985): 55–64.

————. "Riflessioni intorno alla fortuna critica del giardino storico italiano negli Stati Uniti negli ultima trentacinque anni." In *Giardini storici: A 25 anni dalle Carte di Firenze: Esperienze e prospettive*, vol. 1., edited by Laura Sabrina Pelisetti and Lionella Scazzosi, 31–46. Florence: L. S. Olschi, 2009.

————. "Storia dei giardini: Osservazioni in margine al recente sviluppo di questa disciplina in Italia." In *Storia e storie di giardini: Fortune e storia del giardino italiano e verbanese nel mondo, Atti del Convegno, Verbania, sabato 31 agosto 2002*, edited by Leonardo Parachini and Carlo Alessandro Pisoni, 45–86. Verbania: Alberti Libraio, Comune di Verbania, Magazzeno Storico Verbanese, 2003.

Vitruvius. *Ten Books on Architecture.* Translated by Ingrid D. Rowland. Cambridge: Cambridge University Press, 1999.

Vossilla, Francesco. "Acqua, scultura e roccia: Le statue nella Grotta Grande." In *Bernardo Buontalenti e la Grotta Grande di Boboli*, edited by Sergio Risaliti, 61–77. Florence: Maschietto, 2012.

Weil, Mark S. "Love, Monsters, Movement, and Machines: The Marvelous in Theaters, Festivals, and Gardens." In *The Age of the Marvelous*, edited by Joy Kenseth, 159–78. Hanover, NH: Hood Museum of Art, Dartmouth College, 1991.

Weinberg, Bernard. "Translations and Commentaries of Longinus, 'On the Sublime,' to 1600: A Bibliography." *Modern Philology* 47, no. 3 (Feb. 1950): 145–51.

Williams, Raymond. *Keywords: A Vocabulary of Culture and Society.* London: Fontana, 1976.

Williams, Wes. *Monsters and Their Meanings in Early Modern Culture: Mighty Magic.* Oxford: Oxford University Press, 2011.

Wilson, Edmund. *The Devils and Canon Barham: Ten Essays on Poets, Novelists, and Monsters.* New York: Farrar, Straus and Giroux, 1973.

Wittkower, Rudolf. *Architectural Principles in the Age of Humanism.* 4th ed. London: Academy Editions, 1973.

————. "Marvels of the East: A Study in the History of Monsters." *Journal of the Warburg and Courtauld Institutes* 5 (1942): 159–97.

————. *Sculpture: Processes and Principles.* Harmondsworth: Penguin, 1991.

Wölfflin, Heinrich. *Renaissance and Baroque.* Translated by Kathryn Simon. London: Collins, 1966.

Wright, D. R. Edward. "Some Medici Gardens of the Florentine Renaissance: An Essay in Post-Aesthetic Interpretation." In *The Italian Garden: Art, Design and Culture*, edited by John Dixon Hunt, 34–59. Cambridge: Cambridge University Press, 1996.

Zalum, Margherita. "La storia del giardino italiano: Lineamenti ed evoluzione di una giovane disciplina." In *Bibliografia del giardino e del paesaggio italiano, 1980–2005*, edited by Lucia Tongiorgi Tomasi and Luigi Zangheri, 1–14. Florence: L. S. Olschi, 2008.

Zamperini, Alessandra. *Ornament and the Grotesque: Fantastical Decoration from Antiquity to Art Nouveau.* Translated by Peter Spring. London: Thames and Hudson, 2008.

Zander, Giuseppe. "Gli elementi documenti sul Sacro Bosco." *Quaderni dell'Istituto di Storia dell'Architettura* 7–9 (1955): 19–32.

Zangheri, Luigi. "L'artificio paesaggistico nel Parco di Joseph Frietsch." In *Il giardino d'Europa: Pratolino come modello nella cultura europea,* edited by Alessandro Vezzosi, 119–23. Milan: Mazzotta, 1986.

———. *Pratolino: Il giardino delle meraviglie.* 2 vols. Florence: Edizioni Gonnelli, 1979.

Zerner, Henri. "L'art." In *Faire de l'histoire: Nouveaux problèmes, nouvelles approches, nouveaux objets,* edited by Jacques LeGoff and Pierre Nora, 543–67. Paris: Gallimard, 2011.

Index

abnormality, 9, 33, 52, 75, 80, 113
Aeneas, 105
Aeneid (Virgil), 12
aesthetics, 12, 33, 63, 80, 168
Alberti, Leon Battista, 2, 24–26, 143, 153, 188n89, 199n11; catalogue of architectural defects, 159; on colossal mode, 121, 128; on comic statues, 61; Hell Mouth motif and, 59
Alciati, Andrea, 198n128
Aldrovandi, Ulisse, 106, 108, 141, 167
Alexander the Great, 12, 118
Allegoria della Natura (Tribolo), 86
Alley of the Hundred Fountains, 3–4
Allori, Alessandro, 159
Amalthea (goat-woman), 148, *149*
America (Benzoni), 100
Ammannati, Bartolommeo, 3, 22, 59, 118
Anachronic Renaissance (Nagel and Wood), 152–53
anachronism, 16, 152, 156
androgynes, 68
Annius of Viterbo (Giovanni Nanni), 127, 136, 148–50, 162, 208n61
Antaeus. *See* Hercules and Antaeus images
anthropophagy (cannibalism), 93, 100, 102, 111, 125, 196n99; anthropophagi (man-eaters), 47, 101; of giants, 132
Antiquities (Annius of Viterbo), 127
Antirinascimento, L' (Battisti), 34
Appennino at Castello (Ammannati), 59, *60*, 88
Appennino at Pratolino (Giambologna), 4, *119*, 121, 165, 181n102; ambivalence of, 118; "anti-Renaissance" unreason and, 105; as gigantic but not monstrous, 133, 190n10; *Hypnerotomachia Poliphili* and, 97, 125; landscape as anthropomorphic figure, 116, 140; as mountain and abyss, 12, 127;

Novelli's Polyphemus compared with, 131; as personification of the Apennine mountains, 123–24, 127; popular legends about giants and, 126–27; possible origin as river god, 122–23; reception of, 130, 169, 202n72; the sublime and, 169; in tradition of colossal statuary, 130
Arcadia (Sannazaro), 140, 170
Architect of the Garden, The (Boitard), 44
architecture, 11–12, 15, 28, 64; eroticism and, 78; *mescolanza* (assemblage) and, 53; metamorphosis and, 50, 183n10; modernity as discourse and, 37–38; reconstruction of ancient architecture, 153; "return of reason" in, 21; ruins as architectural defects, 159
Ariosto, Ludovico, 81, 105, 111, 136, 138
Aristotle, 71, 73
armadillo, of Bernini, 69, *70*, 74
"*Ars Hortulorum*" (MacDougall), 18
Ars poetica (Horace), 50, 51, 76
Artemis. *See* Diana (Artemis) of Ephesus
art history, 14, 17–18, 63
Atlas, 4, 12
Augustine, Saint, 47
authorship, 19, 176n1
automata, 91, 93, 111
Aztec imagery, 100, *101*

Bacchus, 57
Bacon, Francis, 31
Bakhtin, Mikhail, 12, 165, 175n49, 189n118; on "becoming" of grotesque body, 87, 148, 192n38, 197n127; on the carnivalesque, 63, 125; definition of grotesque body, 103; on gaping mouth image, 59, 61; on giants in popular culture, 124–26; on "grotesque realism," 19, 61, 62, 125, 126, 186n54; on "town giants," 131
Baldinucci, Filippo, 69

Bandinelli, Baccio, 26, 112, 118, 143, 200n30
Barbaro, Daniele, 52, 68
Baroque Garden Cultures (Conan, ed.),
    179n67
Barry, Fabio, 96
Barthes, Roland, 19
Battisti, Eugenio, 3, 34, 144, 196n104
Baxandall, Michael, 16, 33
Bélanger, Anne, 34, 203n8, 211n30
Belting, Hans, 208n71
Beneš, Mirka, 17, 19, 176n9
Benjamin, Walter, 21
Benzoni, G., 100
Bernheimer, Richard, 133
Bernini, Gianlorenzo, 69, 74, 201n38
Berong, Richard, 125
bestiality, 82
black magic, 74, 193n50
Blemmyae, 47
Boboli Gardens (Florence), 22, 26, 42;
    Fontana dei Mostaccini, 88; Fontana
    dei Mostri, 185n36; Fontane delle Arpie
    (Fountains of the Harpies), 9, 76, 77, 110;
    Fountain of Oceanus, 123, 190n10; Palazzo
    Pitti, 32
Boboli Gardens (Florence), Grotta Grande
    in, 4, 87, 141, 147, 162; apparently
    ruinous state of, 159, 167; Fountain of
    Venus (Giambologna), 65, 66, 155–56;
    substitution principle and, 153, 154, 155, 163
Boccaccio, Giovanni, 127, 189n119
Bocca della Verità [Mouth of Truth] (Santa
    Maria in Cosmedin in Rome), 96, 98, 98
Bocchi, Francesco, 159, 167
bodily fluids and functions, 59, 62, 66, 87;
    garden as living entity, 89, 92; pissing boy
    fountains, 88, 90
Boileau, Nicolas, 168
Bomarzo. *See* Sacro Bosco (Bomarzo)
Bonfadio, Jacopo, 9, 10, 11, 38, 40, 53–54
Borges, Jorge Luis, 35, 38, 42
Bosio, Gherardo, 22
Botticelli, Alessandro, 153, 155, 163
Bourdieu, Pierre, 19
Bouvard and Pécuchet (Flaubert), 43–44
Bracciolini, Poggio, 159
Braham, Persephine, 102
Bredekamp, Horst, 95, 100
Brilliant, Richard, 157, 209n93
Bronzino, Agnolo, 82
Brown, Patricia Fortini, 209n93

Brunon, Hervé, 3, 7, 33, 34; on duality of
    classical and grotesque, 156; on frightening
    landscapes within gardens, 140; on garden
    as "*topos* antagoniste," 38
Buontalenti, Bernardo, 4, 152, 153, 155
Burke, Edmund, 168
Bush, Virginia, 117–18, 121, 199n11, 205n33
Byzantine icon tradition, 151, 155

Cadmus, companions of, 5, 6, 167
Callegari, Adolfo, 17, 20
Callimachus, 53
Calumny of Apelles, The (Botticelli), 153, 155,
    163
Calvesi, Maurizio, 140
Canguilhem, Georges, 79, 93, 133, 190n10
Capece, Scipione, 147
Capello, Bianca, 1–2, 94, 95
carnivals, 46, 62, 63, 96, 98, 125
Caro, Annibal, 111, 158
Cartari, Vincenzo, 191n23, 192n34
Castello. *See* Villa Medici (Castello)
Caus, Salomon de, 135
Céard, Jean, 72
Cellini, Benvenuto, 49, 112, 117, 183n6,
    187n68, 199n11; on difficulty of colossal
    sculpture, 118, 122; on "living rock" (*pietra
    viva*), 145; on size of colossus, 121
centaurs, 74
Certeau, Michel de, 19
Cesariano, Cesare, 47, 52, 68
chimeras, 52, 76, 184n28
Christina of Lorraine, 39
Cinque libri d'architettura (Serlio), 52
Cioli, Valerio, 61, 62, 82, 199n13
Clericho, Lucha (Luc LeClerc), 84
Clio in the Garden (Beneš and Lee, eds.), 17
Coffin, David R., 17, 18, 78; on Fountain of
    Nature, 84; on gardens as man's dominance
    over nature, 19–20, 26; on grotteschi in
    Pirro Ligorio's account, 55, 184n32; on
    Mask of Madness, 196n92; on Tempietto,
    162–63
Cohen, Jeffrey Jerome, 132, 133, 168
Cohen, Simona, 108, 110
Cole, Michael W., 116
Colonna, Francesco, 14, 15, 27, 29–31, 96,
    125, 169
Colossus of Rhodes, 12, 117
Columbus, Christopher, 100, 102
comic statues, 61, 189n110

Commentarii, I (Ghiberti), 121

Conan, Michel, 31–33, 179n67

Condivi, Ascanio, 144

Connelly, Frances S., 63

Conti, Natale, 105

Corinthian capital, invention of, 53, *54*

Coty, Katherine, 144, 146, 148–49, 207n52, 208n61

Counter Reformation, 78, 184n28

Cranach the Elder, Lucas, 21

Cyclops, 47, 69, 118, 125, 130–31, 199n16. *See also* Polyphemus

Cynocephalus (dog-head), 47, 100–101

Dami, Luigi, 20–22, 26

Dante Alighieri, 61, 96, 98, 134, 140, 168, 207n49

Darnall, Margaretta J., 106, 136, 138–39, 207n49

Daston, Lorraine, 68, 69, 187n70

David (Michelangelo), 117, 200n27, 200nn30–31

De architectura (Vitriuvius), 50, 53

Debord, Guy, 126

Decameron (Boccaccio), 189n119

De conceptu et generatione hominis (Rüff), 83–84

Defert, Daniel, 42

deficiency, 93–105

deformity, 75, 79

Dei, Benedetto, 164–66

d'Elia, Una Roman, 118

Della origine et de' fatti delle famiglie illustri d'Italia (Sansovino), 146, 297n50

Deluge, The (Leonardo da Vinci), 165, *166*

De luminus natura et efficentia libri tres (Liceti), 113, *114*

De monstrorum natura (Liceti), 82

De natura divinis characterismis (Gemma), 69

De principiis rerum (Capece), 147

Descartes, René, 93, 194n57

De sculptura (Gaurico), 76

"Des espaces autres" ["Of Other Spaces"] (Foucault), 11, 35–37, 148, 181n91

Des monstres et prodiges [*On Monsters and Marvels*] (Paré), 8, 71, 74, 188n78

De statua (Alberti), 121, 143

Deutsche Mythologie (Grimm), 129–30

devils, 74

Diana (Artemis) of Ephesus, 55, 83, *85*, 86–87, 191n12, 191n20; animated by

water, 91; animistic view of nature and, 93, 161; captive female nature as masculinist creation and, 112, 198n134; grotesque corporeality of, 110; grotesque ornament style and, 192n37; "monstrous" physiological abnormality of, 87–88; multiple breasts of, 26, 86, 92, 129, 192n34, 193n52, 202n66; nipples interpreted as testicles, 84, 191n21; renewed interest in ancient "Great Mother" cults, 91–92; sixteenth-century figures in Rome, 191n25. *See also* Fountain of Nature

difference, 33, 46, 80

Dinocrates, 12, 118, 124, 144

"Di pensier in pensier, di monte in monte" (Petrarch), 147

Distinction, La (Bourdieu), 19

Divine Comedy (Dante), 136, 168

Dolce, Ludovico, 78

Domus Aurea (Rome), 47, 49–50, 55, 117, 182n5

Doni, Anton Francesco, 52

doubling (category of monstrosity), 82, 83

Dragon Devouring the Companions of Cadmus, The (Goltzius), *6*

dragons, 3, *4*, 33, 75

Drouet, Giovanni, 71, 143, 146

Dumbarton Oaks Colloquium on the History of Landscape Architecture, 17–18

Dürer, Albrecht, 21, 69

Duval, Jacques, 9–10

dwarfs/dwarfism, 73, 82, 199n13

Elkins, James, 10–11, 44

Empedocles fresco, Brizio Chapel of Duomo in Orvieto (Signorelli), 66, *67*

Este, Ippolito d', 40–41, 122

Et in Arcadia Ego (Poussin), 44

"Etruscan" motifs. *See* Sacro Bosco (Bomarzo), "Etruscan" elements of

excess, as category of monstrosity, 82–93, *85*, *89–91*

Faerie Queene (Spenser), 111

Fagiolo, Marcello, 34

fantasia (artistic license), 8, 52, 76, 78, 80

Farnese, Alessandro, 96

Farnese, Giulia, 146, 170, 297nn51–52

Fascism, 20–22, 27, 64

fauns, 68

Fehrenbach, Frank, 152–53

Ferriolo, Venturi, 92, 193n52

Filarete, Antonion Averlino, 59, 63, 116

Finlay, Ian Hamilton, 45

fireplaces, 57, 95, *104*

Flaubert, Gustave, 43

Foggini, Giovan Battista, 124

Folengo, Teofilo, 132

"follies," 142, 156, 158, 162

Fontana dei Quattro Fiumi [Piazza Navona, Rome] (Bernini), 69, *70*, 201n38

Fontana Papacqua (Soriano nel Cimino), 148, *149, 150*

Fosforo, Luciano, 86

Foucault, Michel, 8, 33, 133, 174n40; on authorship and discourse, 19; on boat as heterotopia, 39, 40; on heterotopias and time, 148; on "heterotopic space," 11, 19, 34–38; on hybridity, 190n4; on language and heterotopias, 42–44; on monster as challenge to law, 79–80; on play of children, 41–42, 181n100; on shift from animistic to mechanistic worldview, 92

Fountain of Nature (Villa d'Este at Tivoli), *85*, 86–87, 92, 175n49; building of, 78, 84; as example of excessive type, 83; personification of nature as female and grotesque, 108

fountains, 3, 31, 45, *65*, 66

Francis, Mark, 10

Freud, Sigmund, 211n31

Frith, Wendy, 9

Galatea, 55, 130–31

Galle, Philippe, 102

Gambara, Cardinal Gianfrancesco, 160

Gargantua and Pantagruel (Rabelais), 8, 59, 62, 88; giant as ambivalent figure, 118; Hell Mouth and, 97–98, 103; interior of giant as landscape in itself, 115–16; popular traditions about giants and, 124–26

Garrard, Mary D., 112, 113

Gaurico, Pomponio, 76, 121, 141

Gay, Peter, 64

Gay Science, The (Nietzsche), 164

Gemma, Cornelius, 68–69

gender, 9–10, 106, 112

Genocchio, Benjamin, 38

Gentile, Maddalena, 185n36

geometry, 26, 72

Gerusalemme liberata [*The Liberation of Jerusalem*] (Tasso), 81, 111, 135, 140

Gesner, Konrad, 100

Ghiberti, Lorenzo, 121

Giambologna, 1, 3, 66; as most accomplished sculptor of colossi, 118; school of, 76. See also *Appennino* at Pratolino (Giambologna)

Giannetto, Raffaela Fabiani, 178n36, 180n76

giants, 14, 16, 33, 112, 161–62, 170; in art history and folklore traditions, 14–15; bones of prehistoric animals identified with, 169, 211n26; colossal statuary, 117–18; the colossus, 119–24, *120*; disorder associated with, 131–32; as figures of alterity, 130–34, *131*; folkloric legends about actions of, 124–27, 132, 162; gigantomachia (fighting giants), 121, 132, 136, *137*; idenfication with nature, 129; monsters compared with, 132–33; natural environment associated with, 116; as personification of nature, 164–65; the sublime and, 169; vast scale of nature and, 133–34, 165–66. See also *Gargantua and Pantagruel*

Giardino Giusti (Verona), 83, 102, 163; grotesque head, 57, *58*; Hell Mouth in, 156

Giardino italiano, Il (Dami), 20

Ginzburg, Carlo, 102

giochi d'acqua (water games), 3, 45

Goltzius, Hendrik, 5

Gombrich, Ernst, 187n73

Goya, Francisco, 132

Great Chronicles of Gargantua, The (anonymous), 124

griffins, 84

Grimaldi, Giambattista, 31

Grimm, Jacob, 129–30

Grosz, Elizabeth, 84

grotesque realism, 8, 12, 63, 125, 126, 134, 170; bodily fluids and orifices, 61, 66; carnivalesque and, 62; classical aesthetics and, 80; reception and, 19

grotteschi and the grotesque, 8, 15, 51, 76; as antithesis of the classic, 64, 186n61; art-historical hostility toward, 63; "becoming" as typical feature of, 96; criticized as "against nature," 11, 52; defining features of, 54; duality of classical and grotesque, 156; heads, 56–57, *57*, *58*, 59; hieroglyphs compared to, 55; humor as element of, 61; juxtaposed with classical mode, 8–9; keystones, 12, *13*, 56–57, 63, 83, *89*; metamorphosis as central theme of, 50; as mixing of high and low, 9; move toward the gigantic, 11–16, *13*; origin of term, 49, 183n6; ruins associated with, 159–60; of Sodoma, 47, *48*, 49

Guerra, Giovanni, 49, 61, 98

Guldan, Ernst, 95

Hanafi, Zakiya, 34

Hansen, Maria Fabricius, 159, 160, 182n5

harpies, 9, 15, 33, 72, 81, *107*, 141; as cannibals, 105; as female figures, 108, 110, 112, 197n127; generation of, 107–8; as hybrid creatures, 83; negative symbolic meaning of, 105–6; as "outside" nature, 133; as signifiers of disorder and chaos, 112

Harpy Riding a Toad (Tribolo), *109*, 110, 198n128

heads, disembodied, 83, 141

Hell Mouth, 9, 14, 93–94, 102–3, 126, 132; Anglo-Saxon origins of, 94–95; banqueting inside of, 62, 95, 106, 197n115; female sexuality associated with, 108–9; fireplace as, *104*; as fragment of gigantic body, 133; guests figuratively devoured by, 42; as hybrid structure, 59; Italian antecedents of, 96; literary sources of, 96–98; meal and music inside of, 49, *50*; speech desiccated by, 45–46; visual traditions at root of, 167

Henneberg, Josephine von, 140

Hercules and Antaeus, 3, 118, *120*, 133, 179n60, 199n18; as common theme in Italian art, 200n19; as image of gigantomachia, 121, 132

hermaphrodites, 9–10, 70, 174n40, 175n41; category of the excessive and, 82; as monsters and marvels, 73, 188n87

Hermaphroditus, 5, 9

Hester, Randolph T., Jr., 10

Heteropolis (Jencks), 181n91

heterotopias, 11, 16, 181n91; incongruity and, 42; time and, 148; utopias compared with, 35

heterotopic space, 11, 15, 19, 34–38, 42

Hildegard of Bingen, 108–9

Himantipodes, 68

hippogryphs, 74, 188n86

Hippopodes, 68

Historia Animalium (Gesner), 100

Holbein, Hans, 21

Hollanda, Francisco da, 52, 53

Holquist, Michael, 186n54, 192n37

Homer, 2, 130, 132

Horace, 50, 51, 76, 183n10

Hortus Palatinus (Heidelberg), 135

Hugo, Victor, 51, 61, 62, 162

Hunt, John Dixon, 3, 31, 45, 179n68, 182n112

hybrid creatures, 8, 9, 33, 157, 174n30, 190n4; composite animals, 73; as consequence of interspecies sex, 82, 83; as figures of fear, 168; giants as, 132; harpies and other female monsters, 15, 76, *77*, 105–14, *107*, *109*, *114*; in ornament fountains, 88

Hyde, Elizabeth, 191n13

hydras, 76

Hypnerotomachia Poliphili (Colonna), 27–31, *29*, 62, 190n119; *Appennino* at Pratolino compared with, 125, 126; "dark wood" in, 140; as "erotic epiphany of architecture," 78; *Gargantua and Pantagruel* compared with, 115; Hell Mouth precedent in, 96–97; lovesick giant in, 14, 97, 115, 125, 126, 159; pissing boys in, 88, 193n47; substitution model of transmission and, 163

ichthyophages, 68

Iconologia (Ripa), 86, 129

incubi, 74

Inferno (Dante), 61, 134

"Italian garden," 20–21, 63, 178n43; Romantic (English) garden opposed to, 22; as triumph of rationality, 33

Italian Garden, The (Coffin, ed.), 17

Italian Renaissance Garden, The (Lazzaro), 18

Jeanneret, Michel, 207n57

Jellicoe, Sir Geoffrey, 18

Jencks, Charles, 181n91

Joubert, Laurent, 107

Julius II, Pope, 72

Kant, Immanuel, 168

Kelsall, Malcolm, 45

Keutner, Herbert, 122, 123

Ktesias, 100

Lacan, Jacques, 19

landscape design, 16, 17, 40, 64, 111, 168; ambiguities of, 11; animism and, 161–62; anthropophagy and devouring as themes of, 132; bodily emission represented in, 88; English, 20, 21; Euclidean logic of, 72; grotesque realism in, 12; legibility of landscape, 43–46; nature as subject of, 75, 130; polysemy of, 45, 182n112; profane

landscape design (*cont.*)
　imagery in, 25–26; visual appearance of, 31;
　water supply and, 122
Landucci, Luca, 70, 72
language, 42–44
Lasansky, D. Medina, 22
Las Casas, Bartolomé de, 102
Last Judgment (Michelangelo), 78
Lazzaro, Claudia, 18, 22, 23, 174n30,
　175n49, 191n23; on Fountain of Nature
　in Villa d'Este, 86–87; on Giambologna's
　Appennino, 123; on grotto ornamentation,
　59; on hybrid as fusion of art and nature,
　106; on nature as captive and passive female
　protagonist, 112; on pissing boy fountains,
　193n45; on Villa d'Este at Tivoli, 40–41
Lee, Michael G., 17
Lefebvre, Henri, 19, 44
Leonardo da Vinci, 1, 6, 128, 151, 162;
　conflicting emotions about garden grotto,
　167, 169; on giant from Libyan desert,
　164–66
Leslie, Michael, 111, 198n129
Lezione una della generazione de' mostri
　(Varchi), 76
Liceti, Fortunio, 82, 113
Ligorio, Pirro, 15, 49, 54–55, 87, 184n32,
　184nn27–28; analogy between earth and
　living body, 128; antiquarian interests of,
　84; on location of "lascivious things," 78;
　on nature as "wet-nurse," 92, 113
Lives of the Artists (Vasari), 22, 142, 155
locus amoenus ("pleasant place"), 2, 7, 16, 34,
　130, 167; heterotopia contrasted with, 11;
　locus horridus in duality with, 8, 141, 169;
　the sublime and, 168, 170
locus horridus, 7, 8, 16, 141, 168, 169
Lomazzo, Gian Paolo, 47, 53, 121, 141
Longinus, 168, 169, 211n30
Lotto, Lorenzo, 26, 89
Louis XIV, 19, 45
Lualdi, Michelangelo, 69
Luchinat, Cristina Acidini, 21
Lusini, Enrico, 22–24, 29

MacDougall, Elisabeth, 18
Macrobius, 192n34, 202n66
Madonna (the Virgin), depiction of, 151, 155
Madonna, Maria Luisa, 34
Madruzzo, Cardinal Cristoforo, 127, 136, 149,
　162, 169

Malespini, Clelio, 1–2
Mancini, Giulio, 188n89
Mannerism, 102, 182n5
Marcis, Marie le, 9–10, 46, 174n40; category
　of the excessive and, 82
Mariage, Thierry, 126
Marin, Louis, 19
Marmo osiriano, 149–51, 157
Martini, Francesco di Giorgio, 24
marvels, 68, 79
Marxism, 176n9
masks, 57, 59, 96
Meaning of Gardens, The (Francis and
　Hester), 10
Medici, Cosimo I de', 100, 155
Medici, Grand Duke Ferdinand de', 39
Medici, Francesco I de', 1
Medici, Giovan Carlo de', *131*
Medici, Piero de',1
Medici, Don Virginio de', 39
medicine, 9, 71, 74, 80, 81
Medici sculpture garden (Piazza di San
　Marco, Florence), 1
Medusa, 96, 97, 112, 145, 206n48
Megasthenes, 47
meraviglia (marvelousness, wonderment), 75,
　136, 211n30
mescolanza (assemblage, mixture), 54, 55, 167,
　170
Metamorphoses (Ovid), 3–8, 50, 55, 80,
　189n119; amorality and cruelty of nature
　in, 166; garden as material reenactment
　of, 161, 167; landscape descriptions in,
　153; nature as destructive force in, 129;
　Polyphemus legend in, 130–32; Renaissance
　architecture and, 183n10; as source of
　Giambologna's giant, 12; on Vatican's *Index
　of Prohibited Books*, 78
Michelangelo, 52–53, 76, 78, 117, 118, 124;
　subtractive sculptural technique of, 143,
　145; unrealized project to carve from
　Carrara mountains, 144; works installed in
　Grotta Grande at Boboli, 147, 155
Miller, Naomi, 153
modernism, 152, 181n91
monsters, 7, 16, 33, 51, 66, 168, 170; catalogues
　of types of, 68–69; causes of generation
　of, 72–74; early modern domains of, 46;
　giants compared with, 132–33; at margins
　of the world, 68, 187n68; marine, 72, 74–
　75, 95; in medical/scientific discourse, 8–11;

monster as failed *mescolanza*, 53; Monster of Ravenna, 70, *71*, 72, 188n86; multiple meanings of, 34; as portent of catastrophe or sin, 11, 69, 72, 187n70; thought to exist in the Americas, 102, 103

Montaigne, Michel de, 44, 45, 59, 88, 102, 103; on jets of water in gardens, 122; on the monster within, 170

Monte Oliveto (Siena) cloister fresco (Sodoma), 47, *48*, 49, 68, 100, 103

Morel, Philippe, 47

Morgante, 82, 124, 199n13

Moses (Old Testament patriarch), 148, *150*

Mostra del giardino italiano (Ojetti), 18, 20, 177n15; "Giardino fiorentino del Cinquecento" (Lusini), 22–24, *23*, 29; purpose of, 21; rejection of Romantic (English) garden, 22; triumphalist model of Italian garden in, 63

Mukerji, Chandra, 178n43

Müller, Wilhelm, 130

mural painting, 50

Muses, the, 56

Mussolini, Benito, 21

mystery plays, medieval, 96

Nagel, Alexander, 150–53, 155, 156, 158, 208n71

nationalism, 21

natural history, 69

Natural History (Pliny), 75, 86

nature, 7, 26, 68, 75, 176n9; agency and power of, 113; amorality and cruelty of, 34, 129, 130, 166; destructive potential of, 14; as female figure with many breasts, 26, 86, 92, 129, 192n34, 193n52, 202n66; female nature opposed to male culture, 112; fertility of, 89, 129; frightening scale of, 15, 130; garden as "third nature" (*terza natura*), 9, 10, 11, 38, 40, 126, 134, 141; geometric shapes and, 24, 26; as Great Mother goddess, 91–92, 113, 127; inventiveness and variety of, 8, 76, 80; man's dominance over and dependence upon, 19, 21, 33, 112–13; medieval and humanist conceptions of, 92, 194n54; monsters as jests of, 69, 72; normativity of, 80; outlandish forms produced by, 52; playfulness (ludic propensity) of, 75, 80; river gods as personification of, 126; as wet nurse, 92, 113, 129

nature–art relation, 106, 133; art triumphant over nature, 19, 20, 25; conflict, 6, 22, 178n43; mingling of art and nature, 26–27, 53–54

neoclassicism, 63, 66

Neoplatonism, 110, 143, 145

Neptune (god), 55–56, 87, 199n18

Nietzsche, Friedrich, 164, 170

Nile River, 106, 122–23, 199n18, 201n38

Novelli, Antonio, 1, 125, 130–33

nymphs, gigantified, 119

Odyssey (Homer), 130

"Of Gardens" (Bacon), 31

Ojetti, Ugo, 20–22, 32, 63, 112

Oleson, John P., 99, 144, 156, 209n87

On Hermaphrodites (Duval), 9–10

Order of Things, The (Foucault), 35, 36, 42

Orlando furioso (Ariosto), 81, 106, 107, 111, 136, 138–39, 207n49

Orsini, Pierfrancesco "Vicino," 12, 15, 42, 59, 71, 127, 194n61; family of, 156; garden allusions in correspondence of, 135, 143, 203n1; Hell Mouth motif and, 98; at Medici court, 100; as prisoner of war, 95; Sacro Bosco as memorial to wife, 146–47, 170, 207n51; social circle of, 160

Orti Oricellari [Rucellai Gardens] (Florence), 2, 33, 94; dissection of conjoined twins in, 1, 3, 69, 80; Polyphemus statue (Novelli), 55, 105, 118, 125, 130–33, *131*

Ovid, 3–9, 33, 130, 183n10

painting, 64, 76, 151

Palazzo del Te (Mantua), 121, 198n134

Palazzo Pucci (Florence), 88, 109

Palazzo Vecchio (Florence), 20, 22

Palazzo/Villa Farnese (Caprarola), 24, *25*, 56, 88; Artemis fountain, 84, 86; drain cover as face, 96, *97*; keystones (*mascheroni*), 56, *89*

palisade, 23

Palladio, Andrea, 145

Pallister, Janis L., 132

Pandae, 47

Panofsky, Erwin, 17, 18, 139, 186n58

Pantagruel, 12, 59, 61

Paré, Ambroise, 8, 15, 71, 175n41, 188n78; categories of monsters described by, 82, 83; on causes of generation of monsters, 72–74; on distinction between monsters and marvels, 79; on harpies, 107–8, 133, 141; on monsters and mythological beasts, 74–75

Park, Katherine, 68, 69, 86, 187n70; on
 humanist conception of Nature, 92; on
 nature viewed in Renaissance allegories, 129
Partridge, Loren, 96
Patrizi, Francesco, 136, 211n30
Paul III, Pope, 96
Paul IV, Pope, 78
Pavoni, 39, 40
Payne, Alina, 53, 183n10
Pegasus, 55
Perez-Gomez, Alberto, 78–79
Performance and Appropriation (Conan, ed.),
 180n70
Peri hupsous [*On the Sublime*] (Longinus), 168
"period eye," 16, 25, 33, 141, 169
Perseus (Cellini), 117
Petrarch, Francesco, 2, 145, 146, 206n48,
 207n49
Pierino da Vinci, 88, 89, 109
Pietà (Michelangelo), 145, 206n48
Pietrogrande, Antonella, 91–92, 113
pissing boys, 88, *90*, 193n45
Pius IV, Pope, 191n12
Pizzorusso, Claudio, 110
Plato, 128
Pliny the Elder, 9, 12, 64, 86, 153, 175n58; on
 colossal statuary, 117, 121; monstrous races
 described by, 47, 71; on sirens (mermaids),
 75
poetry, 76, 113, 145, 206n48, 207n49
Polo, Marco, 102
Polyphemus, 55, 105, 130–33, *131*, 196n103,
 199n16; as anthropophagus (man-eater),
 118; nature signified by, 165. *See also*
 Cyclops
Porphyrios, Demetri, 181n91
Poussin, Nicolas, 44
Pratolino. *See* Villa Medici (Pratolino)
Prester John, 106, 197n115
Prigioni [*Prisoners*] (Michelangelo), 147, 155
Proof of the Wool (Romano), 88
Pulci, Luigi, 82, 124, 132
Puppi, Lionello, 17, 176n9
Putto Urinating Through a Grotesque Mask
 (Pierino da Vinci), 88, *90*

Quattro libri dell'architettura, I (Palladio), 145

Rabelais, François, 8, 12, 51, 59, 124;
 "grotesque realism" and, 62; Hell Mouth
 motif and, 97–98

Rape of the Sabines (Giambologna), 117
Raphael, 86, 152, 159
reception, 19, 27–34, 82, 139, 169
Renaissance garden, 3, 17, 18, 76, 113;
 academic study of, 19; as Arcadian refuge,
 2; change and, 186n52; chiaroscuro lighting
 in, 21–22; classical aesthetics and, 80; as
 collaboration of nature and art, 133; colossi
 (giants) of, 14–16, 117–19, 126, 199n18;
 contradictoriness of, 9, 33; dragons in, 5; as
 heterotopic space, 35–38; heterotopology
 of, 38–43; landscape as living body, 128,
 148, 162; as liminal space, 34; "monstrous"
 figures in, 8; Ovid as principal source for
 design of, 3–7, *4*, *6*, *7*, 55; "participatory
 grotesque" of, 126; reception history of,
 27–34, 179nn67–68; sensual experience of,
 31; time and, 148–60
representation, 47, 73; of domination of
 nature, 27; of gardens through history, 22,
 32; of monstrosity, 8, 16, 69, 70
Rerum vulgarium fragmenta (Petrarch), 145
Rhodiginus, Coelius, 74
Ripa, Cesare, 86, 129
Ritratto delle più nobili et famose città d'Italia
 (Sansovino), 146, 207n51
river gods, 88, 116, 121; colossal mode of,
 122; local tributaries personified by, 116,
 200n32; personification of nature, 126, 165
Romano, Gaspare, 86
Romano, Giulio, 78, 86, 88, 121, 198n134
"Romantic" (English) garden, 20–22
Rome, 21, 26, 140
Rometta (Alley of the Hundred Fountains),
 40
Rucellai Gardens. *See* Orti Oricellari
 [Rucellai Gardens] (Florence)
Rucellai, Palla, 1
Rüff, Jakob, 83
ruins, 28, 153; Etruscan, 144, 156, *157*;
 grotesque associated with, 159–60;
 Melancholy/Romantic frame of mind and,
 44; negative perceptions of, 159; simulated,
 16; time and, 142, 160, 209n96
Ruskin, John, 11–12, 63

sacred groves, 140
Sacro Bosco (Bomarzo), 5, 12, 14, 16, 34, 170–
 71, 185n36; animistic view of nature and,
 161–62; Casa Pendente, 136, *138*; difficulties
 of interpretation and, 135–36; disembodied

heads in, 83; *Dragon Mauled by Lion and Dog*, 3, *4*, 141; duality of classical and grotesque in, 156; entrance location, 136, 138, 204n10; Fighting Giants (Orlando and Woodsman), 136, *137*, 139, 141, 167; giant representations at, 119; Harpy sculpture, *107*; as heterotopic space, 46; inscription on travel and marvelous things, 68, 111; "living" rock sculptures, 16, 142–48, 161; Mask of Madness, 100, *101*, 141, 143, 196nn91–92; "masks" at, 57; Orsini's designs for, 71; as park of monsters, 76; Pegasus in, 55; principle of substitution at, 150; as psychomachia, 135, 203n5; seemingly incompatible juxtapositions in, 42; Tempietto, 156, *158*, 162–63, 209n86; visual culture of Americas in, 100, *101*, 105, 111; Wilson's reaction to, 11, 38; as wood rather than garden, 139–40

Sacro Bosco (Bomarzo), "Etruscan" elements of, 99, 136, 161, 203n6, 206n42; as anachronistic monument, 16, 162; faux or "reproduction" tomb, 142, 144–45, 149, 156–58, *157*, 160, 209n87

Sacro Bosco (Bomarzo), Hell Mouth in, 9, 45–46, 49, *50*, 57, *94*, 141; Bakhtin's definition of the grotesque and, 103; body fluids as grotesque dimension and, 59; deficiency of, 15; duplicated at other sites, 156; as Etruscan tomb, 144; Fountain of Nature compared to, 93; gigantic devouring appetite of, 134; harpies and, 106, 108, 197n115; *Hypnerotomachia Poliphili* and, 97; identity of artist, 93–94; playful opposition and, 42; rock carved to make, 142; symbolic death in mouth of monster, 61; traditions recalled by, 98–99

Sadler, John, 82
Salamacis, 5
Saminiati, Giovanni, 59
Sannazaro, Jacopo, 140, 170
Sansovino, Francesco, 127, 170
Santa Maria Formosa (Venice), grotesque keystone, 12, *13*, 57, 63
Santa Maria Maggiore (Bergamo), 26
Satan, 94
Saturnalia (Macrobius), 202n66
Saturn Devouring His Children (Goya), 132
satyrs, 57, 68, 74, 76, 156, 208n61
Scamozzi, Vincenzo, 59
scatological figures, 8, 61

Schmidt, Gary D., 94, 95
Sciopodes, 68
Sciritae, 47
sculpture, 64
Segal, Charles Paul, 5
Seiterle, Gérard, 83, 84
Serlio, Sebastiano, 52
Servi, Costantino de,' 121, 200n22
sexuality, 66, 75, 89; context for display of images, 78; deviant eroticism, 131; extrapictorial agency of images and, 73, 188n89; female sexuality as threat, 108, 112; interspecies copulation, 82, 83
Seymour, Charles, Jr., 12
Shearman, John, 112
Sicke Woman's Private Looking-Glasse, The (Sadler), 82
Signorelli, Luca, 66
Sinibaldi, Biagio, 99
sirens (mermaids), 74, 75, 83, 102; as female figures, 108, 112; gigantified, 119; Ulysses' resistance to, 111
Smith, Webster, 122
Soderini, Giovanvettorio, 99, 142
Sodoma, Il, 47, 49, 68, 100, 103
Soja, Edward, 37
"Some Medici Gardens of the Florentine Renaissance" (Wright), 32
Soriano nel Cimino, 42, 108, 144, 148, 162
Soviet Union, 63
spectatorship, 33, 83
Spenser, Edmund, 111
sphinxes, 33, 83, 84, 187n67; as female figures, 108, 112; inscriptions in Sacro Bosco and, 99, 195n87
Spinazzi, Innocenzio, 76
spolia in re (reuse of virtual objects/reproductions), 157, 160
spolia in se (reuse of material objects), 157
Starobinski, Jean, 37
Stephens, Walter, 125, 130, 133, 165–66, 210n8, 210n11
Stewart, Susan, 116, 125, 126, 128, 198n6; on the gigantic, 134; sublime and, 168
Stoppino, Eleanora, 168, 169
Stourhead, garden at, 45
Strozzi, Giovan Battista, 145, 206n48
sublime, the, 168–69, 211n17; proto-sublime, 16, 161; pseudo-sublime (interrupted sublime), 134, 168, 169
Summers, David, 64

supernumerary, the (category of monstrosity), 82

Swift, Jonathan, 132

Taegio, Bartolomeo, 9, 54, 140, 141, 167
Tasso, Bernardo, 140
Tasso, Torquato, 81, 111, 135, 140
Tchikine, Anatole, 3
Tempesta, Antonio, 159
teratology, 11, 68, 70, 80, 81
Teyssot, Georges, 42
Theocritus, 2
Theseus, 121
Thetis, 12
Tiburtine Sibyl, 40, 190n10
Timaeus (Plato), 128
Tolomei, Claudio, 26, 31, 53, 111
Topsell, Edward, 100
Trattato di architettura, ingegneria e arte militare (Martini), 24
Travel Journal (Montaigne), 122
Travels of Sir John Mandeville, 100–102
Trevi Fountain (Rome), gardens near, 26, 53
Tribolo, Niccolò, 3, 22, 23, 86, 110; design for Villa Medici (Castello), 44–45; on sense of touch, 30; Vasari's "Life" of, 27
Tritons, 74, 75
trompe l'oeil, 75
Tschumi, Bernard, 45

Uffizi, ceiling decorations of East Wing, 159, *160*
Urbach, Henry, 181n91
Utens, Giusto, 22, 23, 178n36
"Utopie et littérature" (Foucault radio broadcast), 36, 41–42, 181n100

Valadier, Giuseppe, 84
Varchi, Benedetto, 1, 8, 30, 76, 80, 82, 143
Vasari, Giorgio, 22, 27, 29–30, 46, 112, 181n100; on artistic technique, 142–43; on colossal statuary, 122; on genius of Michelangelo, 155; grotteschi defined by, 52; on house facade as face, 59; on "living rock" (*pietra viva*), 145; notion of artistic genius, 151; on Tribolo's design for Villa Medici (Castello), 44–45
Venard, Claude, 84
Venus, *65*, 66, 87, 156
Venus and Cupid (Lotto), 89, *91*
Vergerio, Pier Paolo, 159

Versailles, 19, 45, 126
Vertumnus, 56
Vezzosi, Alessandro, 125
Vieri, Francesco de,' 202n72
Villa, La (Taegio), 140, 167–68
Villa Aldobrandini (Frascati), 18, 55, 57, 199n18; disembodied heads in, 83; Hell Mouth grotto, 102, *103*, 156; Water Theatre, 4
Villa della Torre (Fumane di Valpolicella), 57, 83, 95, 102, *104*, 199n17
Villa d'Este (Tivoli), 19, 49, 54, 55, 111, 161; Fountain of Proserpina, 56; Fountain of the Dragons, 5, *7*, 75, 95, 167; Fountain of the Organ (Fountain of the Deluge), 84, 87; Goddess of Nature, 15, 127, 175n49; Oval Fountain (Fountain of Tivoli), 40, 55; river gods depicted in, 116, *117*; Rometta (Alley of the Hundred Fountains), 3–4, 40, *41*, 55, *56*, *57*, 116; Tiburtine Sibyl, 40, 190n10. *See also* Fountain of Nature
Villa Farnese (Caprarola), 24, *25*
Villa in the Life (Coffin), 179n67
Villa Lante (Bagnaia), 123, 140, 160, 161, 201n38
Villa Madama (Rome), 86
Villa Medici (Castello), 3, 22, 34, 40, 177n33; colossal statuary in, *120*, 121; Hercules and Antaeus (Ammannati), *120*, 121, 167; menagerie (Grotto of the Animals), 42, *43*, 49; political power in design of, 46; sensual response emphasized in, 30, 179n60; tree house, 181n100; Tribolo's design for, 44–45; Typhon monster, 34; Utens lunettes, 22, 23, *24*; Vasari's discussion of, 27, 29. *See also Appennino* at Castello (Ammannati)
Villa Medici (Pratolino), 3, 5, 12, 14, 32, 34, *119*; Galatea in grotto of, 55; pissing boys and river gods in, 88, 193n45; Rabelaisian scatological humor in, 61–62; woods (boschi, boschetti) incorporated in, 161. *See also Appeninno* at Pratolino (Giambologna)
Villa Medici (Rome), 56
Virgil, 2, 12, 140
Vitruvius, 15, 50–51, 53, 153, 163, 175n58, 209n86
Vliete, Gillis van den, 78, 84, 85
Volterra, Daniele da, 78
voyeurism, 66

Warburg, Aby, 64
water chains, 59
Weil, Mark S., 106, 136, 138–39, 207n49
Williams, Raymond, 79
Wilson, Edmund, 11, 38, 167
witches/witchcraft, 74, 110
Wittkower, Rudolf, 25
Wölfflin, Heinrich, 18

Wood, Christopher S., 150–53, 155, 156, 158,
    208n71
Wright, D. R. Edward, 32–33, 178n43, 180n74
Wunderkammer, 75, 102

Zamperini, Alessandra, 64, 186n61
Zangheri, Luigi, 122
Zuccari, Federico, 199n17

Acknowledgments

This research was supported under the Australian Research Council's Discovery Projects funding scheme (project number DP120103652). I am most grateful to the ARC, as well as to the Graham Foundation for Advanced Studies in the Fine Arts, the Garden and Landscape Studies Program at Dumbarton Oaks, and the Faculty of Art, Design and Architecture at Monash University for funding my research. I would also like to thank the Society of Architectural Historians and the Renaissance Society of America for awarding me, respectively, a Senior Fellowship and a Kress Fellowship during the course of this project.

Many people were kind enough to discuss my work with me, both formally and informally. My month at the Dumbarton Oaks Research Library and Collection in Washington, DC, toward the end of this book's composition was especially valuable. At Dumbarton Oaks, it is a pleasure to thank John Beardsley, Stephen Bending, Daniel Bluestone, Sarah Cantor, Rachel Koroloff, Alejandra Rojas, and Anatole Tchikine. Raffaella Fabiani Giannetto and Denis Ribouillaut also made valuable suggestions, for which I am grateful. I would like to acknowledge my graduate students at Monash University— especially Stephen Forbes and Simone Schmidt—who have assisted me in numerous ways. At Monash, I am also grateful to Ruth Bain, Kathie Barwick, Peter Howard, Anne Marsh, Callum Morton, Kathie Temin, and Kit Wise for their advice and support.

I owe Maria Fabricius Hansen my thanks for sending me her important paper on ruins, Attila Györ and Kristof Fatsar for the photograph of the Orti Oricellari, and Jerome Singerman at the University of Pennsylvania Press for his enthusiasm for this book. I am equally grateful to one of the anonymous readers for the Press, whose comments on an earlier version of the manuscript have had a significant influence on my thinking. Noreen O'Connor-Abel at the Press skillfully steered this book toward publication.

It is a particular pleasure to acknowledge John Dixon Hunt, the editor of Penn Studies in Landscape Architecture, for his long-term support of my work. I am most grateful to him.

My friends and family, both in Australia and abroad, have contributed to this project in numerous ways. Among the former, I would especially like to mention Kelly D. Cook, Jennifer Ferng, Stephen Garrett, Christopher P. Heuer, Justin Mallia, Alana O'Brien, Sarah Scott, Alexandra Young, and Dion Young. I would also like to acknowledge my grandfather Michael Morgan, who will not see the book in print but with whom I would have greatly enjoyed discussing it. Anthony Morgan, Patricia Morgan, and James Morgan have also been most supportive. I suspect that my children, Amelia, Hannah, and Christopher, remain skeptical, but they have always good-naturedly accepted my frequent absences from Australia, for which I thank them. Last, but by no means least, I am grateful to Anita La Pietra for her unflagging interest in and support of my work.